Rembrandt
May 1949

FLORIDA'S FLAGLER

HENRY M. FLAGLER

Florida's Flagler

by

SIDNEY WALTER MARTIN

PROFESSOR OF HISTORY

THE UNIVERSITY OF GEORGIA

The University of Georgia Press

ATHENS

TO

CLARE PHILIPS MARTIN

CONTENTS

PREFACE

HENRY M. FLAGLER died in 1913 and since that time many fantastic tales about him and his career have accumulated. It was this wide variety of stories that first attracted me; no two of them were ever exactly alike. An aged employee of Flagler's railroad once declared that his boss came to America on a cattle boat from Scotland; another person said he was born in Florida, while still another contended his birthplace was in Ohio. Many people with whom I talked had the idea that he made his money in the Florida east coast venture, very few being aware that he had been associated with John D. Rockefeller in the Standard Oil Company. His private life was steeped in even more hearsay. Some of the old-timers along the Florida east coast were reluctant to talk about it, while others were ready to pour forth with all they knew. But, as in the case of the other phases of his life, few of the stories jibed. After a preliminary investigation, it was very evident that Henry M. Flagler could be the subject of an intriguing study. This book is a result of the research which followed my first interests in the millionaire.

I have attempted to cut my way through a mass of material and arrive at a just conclusion concerning Flagler. No rumor was accepted unless it was authenticated. Nevertheless my findings herein will not please everyone. At a recent historical meeting in Miami where I read a paper on Flagler, one lady in the audience shook her head in disapproval at nearly half of the statements I made about the millionaire, explaining later that I was entirely too sympathetic and easy on the man. Upon returning home, I received many letters from Florida, some conveying the same feeling which the lady in Miami had expressed; while on the other hand, some implied that I was

Preface

unfair because of the many harsh things I had said about Florida's benefactor.

Although Floridians differ as to their opinion of Henry M. Flagler, none can deny that he was the greatest developer the state ever had. Though virtually all of his millions were made in the North, he found his way to the South, as so many others had done, and gave the better part of his life and his fortune to the development of the southernmost American state. The wand of the millionaire was first waved over St. Augustine, and the ancient city roused from its state of lethargy. Other towns received the same treatment and many new ones were born. The whole area from Jacksonville to Key West was injected with new life. Flagler gave Florida a future, something for which she had been waiting for many years. The state had its past; she gloried in her history and her Spanish, British and American heritage, but neglected to take advantage of the natural conditions which had been given her. Ponce de Leon's visit to Florida in 1513 was hardly more significant than Flagler's first trip there late in the nineteenth century.

Judging from his accomplishments, the years Flagler spent in Florida were far more beneficial to his fellow man than those he spent engaged in the Standard Oil Company. It was apparent that he was more determined on making money than anything else as long as he was actively associated with John D. Rockefeller, whereas after he began his developments in Florida he was satisfied to be a money spender. During his early years he was very close to Rockefeller both as a friend and as a business associate. Much of Flagler's contribution to the Standard Oil Company found expression in Rockefeller; therefore it is difficult to separate many of Flagler's activities from those of his associate. After 1885 the two men saw less and less of each other. Flagler had planted stakes in Florida by this time.

Many persons have made contributions to this study. I am especially indebted to William R. Kenan, Jr., of New York,

Preface

Flagler's brother-in-law; Harry Harkness Flagler, also of New York, the millionaire's only son; and Mrs. Clarissa Anderson Dimick, of Delray Beach, Florida, close friend of the family, for putting at my disposal certain information in the form of records, letters, and newspapers. Professors E. Merton Coulter, University of Georgia; Allan Nevins, Columbia University; and Robert S. Cotterill, Florida State University, have given critical and constructive criticism, for which I am grateful. Special acknowledgment also is made to Julien C. Yonge, University of Florida; Mrs. Jessie D. Wynn, West Palm Beach; and the late Mrs. Katherine S. Lawson, St. Augustine, for helping locate much of the material on Flagler. Among the many others whom I wish to thank for assistance in this undertaking are: Mrs. Jean Adams, E. D. Anthony, Joseph Borman, Mrs. Lillian Bradstreet, Louis Clarke, George Conway, Mrs. Ida Cross, Dorothy Dodd, Mrs. Bell Enos, Clyde E. Feuchter, Carl Fremd, Paul H. Giddens, Harris Gillespie, Mrs. Anna Hadley, Nina Hawkins, Fred M. Hopkins, J. D. Ingraham, Mrs. Alberta Johnson, Mrs. Virginia Jordan, C. J. King, Scott Loftin, Harvey Lopez, Amy McMillan, James P. Martin, Horace Montgomery, Joanne Newman, James M. Owens, Ruby Pierce, Theodore Pomar, Theodore Pratt, Mrs. Isabel Rath, the late Sims W. Rowley, Donna L. Root, Mrs. Ruth Tebeau, J. Chal Vinson, and Agnew Welsh.

Financial assistance for the study was received through the office of George H. Boyd, Director of Research at the University of Georgia, from funds made available jointly by the Carnegie Foundation and the University; and also through the office of William M. Crane, University of Georgia Alumni Secretary, from the M. G. Michael Memorial Fund. This generosity is appreciated.

Lastly, to my friends and associates who gave encouragement all along the way, I shall ever be indebted.

October 1, 1948   S. W. M.

Heritage and Youth

H E WAS a lad of fourteen years—tall, erect, and handsome. His eyes were gray, and his hair was light brown,
blending perfectly with his ruddy complexion. There was a
shy but determined look on his face. He was dressed in coarse
homespun clothes and in his hand he held a fat country carpetbag which contained all of his possessions. Hidden in his safest
pocket was a little money to be used for the necessities of
travel. It was October, 1844, when Henry Morrison Flagler
bade farewell to his pious mother and father in western New
York and began his journey to the edge of the Western Reserve in northern Ohio. It was a long distance for a boy to
travel alone, but there was not much this ambitious youth
could find to do around his home; so he finally persuaded his
parents to let him find employment in more promising surroundings.

Republic, Ohio, was his destination.[1] For several months he
had sought parental permission to join his half brother, Daniel
M. Harkness, who resided at that place. The fact that he would
not be entirely unknown in Ohio made his departure a little
more bearable for his mother. Flagler was anxious to test his
mettle in the game of life without too much protection from
his elders. His father, Isaac Flagler, a poorly paid preacher-
farmer, ministered to a small Presbyterian congregation nine
miles fom Medina, New York. The elder Flagler had served
several other churches in western New York and northern

[1] *New York Tribune*, December 23, 1906.

1

Ohio, and the boy had become tired of moving from one poor congregation to another. It was always the same story: hard work and little remuneration. He was tired of poverty and often dreamed of the day when he might have some of the luxuries which money could buy. Despite the wishes of his father that he remain on the farm, young Flagler gave very little consideration to doing so. The farm had no attraction for him, and besides he was too ambitious to live in such circumstances.[2]

The frugal home which Flagler was leaving became established from a long line of Flaglers. He traced his ancestry to an immigrant who came to America in the early part of the eighteenth century from Franconia in the German Palatinate. The Wars of Louis XIV, which devastated that region, caused a great number of people to lose their property and flee to England, among them being one Zacharra Flegler (as the name was then spelled). Zacharra Flegler spent several years in Walworth, England, with other Palatines working as a carpenter.[3] Their stay in England was only temporary because they hoped eventually to find new homes in America. They saved what money possible and, with some governmental aid from England, crossed the Atlantic in several groups.

Flegler, with his wife, two small sons, and a baby daughter, left England for America in January, 1710. This particular company of Palatines, which was led by the Reverend John Tribbeko, filled ten small ships, and the horrors of the six-month trip across the ocean were indescribable. Many of the voyagers died, one of the victims being the wife of Zacharra Flegler. The company finally reached New York in June, 1710, and proceeded up the Hudson River where they established settlements on both banks of the river in Columbia and Ulster counties. Only the river separated the newly created towns which were called East Camp and West Camp. Of the

---

[2] Edwin Lefèvre, "Flagler in Florida," *Everybody's Magazine* (February, 1910), 181.

[3] Flagler Family Records, File I, Flagler Collection.

2

Palatines who settled at this particular point, the majority built homes and became permanently located. However, the more adventurous spirits sought other homes. Most of this minority group drifted into Dutchess County to the territory owned by Henry Beekman, a German who sold them land on favorable terms. Zacharra Flegler was one of this group who was attracted to Dutchess County, but not until he had courted and married a second time. The wedding took place in August, 1710, less than six months after the death of the first Mrs. Zacharra Flegler. This second wife also died shortly and, in May, 1711, he married for the third time. Flegler died in March, 1720, having established firmly the roots of what was destined to become a prominent New York family. All of the American Flaglers are descended from one or the other of the three sons of Zacharra Flegler—Philip Solomon, Simon, and Zachariah.[4]

Zachariah Flegler was the youngest son, having been born in 1719 to Zacharra's third wife. He lived most of his lifetime in the town of Clinton, Dutchess County, probably in the portion of it which was set off in 1821 as the town of Pleasant Valley. Zachariah Flegler was married three times and to his different wives were born sixteen children, most of whom grew up and settled in Dutchess County. Solomon Flegler, the eighth child, was born on May 8, 1760. He subsequently became the grandfather of Henry M. Flagler, the capitalist.

Solomon made at least one contribution to the family. He changed the spelling of the name Flegler to Flagler, and the revision was readily accepted by all of the relatives. He, too, lived in Dutchess County all of his life with the gradually increasing Flagler clan. Though not quite as prolific as his father, Solomon and his wife, Ester Ostron, had eleven children, the fifth of whom, Isaac Flagler, who was born on April 22, 1789, became the father of the oil magnate and railroad builder.[5]

Isaac Flagler spent his early life in his home surroundings

[4] *Ibid.*
[5] *Ibid.*, also in collected data, Kenan Collection.

at Pleasant Valley. His formal education was scant, but he was a widely read man. He heeded the call to preach and was ordained as a Presbyterian minister in 1810. He married his childhood sweetheart, Jane B. Ward, October 7, 1813. Isaac, an able minister and a good farmer, continued to live in Dutchess County until after his wife's death on October 1, 1820. There were no children from the marriage, and since there were no responsibilities which tied him to his Dutchess County home, he decided to leave his birthplace and go to some other section of the state and start over. He accepted a call to Milton, New York, and began his ministry there in 1821. He soon became attracted to one of his parishioners, Ruth Deyo Smith, and was married to her on May 10, 1824. They spent three very happy years together, and one child, named Ann Caroline but called Carrie, resulted from the union. Mrs. Flagler died on September 25, 1827, and for the second time in his life Isaac Flagler was left a widower and this time with the responsibilities of a very young daughter. Within a few months, however, he met a young widow, Elizabeth Caldwell Harkness, who attracted him from the start. Their acquaintance led to a short courtship, and they were married in the fall of 1828.[6]

Elizabeth Flagler was a good Christian woman and made the preacher an excellent wife. She, too, had been married twice before. Her first husband was Hugh Morrison of Washington County, New York, and her second was David Harkness, a physician, of Bellevue, Ohio. The Harkness family was large and prominent, and was to play an important part in the life of Henry Flagler. After the death of her second husband, in 1825, Elizabeth Harkness went with her only child, a young son, Daniel M. Harkness, to Salem, New York, where she made her home with relatives. It was while she was living here that she met Isaac Flagler, who at that time was serving a pastorate in Seneca County, New York. They started life to-

[6] W. W. Williams, *History of the Firelands*, 416.

4

gether with a ready-made family, consisting of young Dan
Harkness and little Carrie Flagler. From all indications, they
were extremely happy. Shortly after their marriage, they
moved to Hopewell, New York, a little town not far from
Canandaigua. It was in Hopewell that Henry Morrison Flagler
was born on January 2, 1830.[7] At that time Carrie was five
years old, and Dan was eight. A new baby in the family was
a novelty for them both. The rural congregation at Hopewell

(1) First wife m. DAVID HARKNESS m. (2) Elizabeth Caldwell Morrison
name | (widow of Hugh Mor-
unknown | rison) second wife

Stephen V. Harkness
only son

Daniel M. Harkness
only son

Isaac Flagler m.————

Henry M. Flagler
only son

Parentage of Henry M. Flagler

rejoiced with the parents, and many gifts, including things to
eat, were brought to the minister's home when the baby arrived. The child was named for Henry Flagler, an uncle, and
Hugh Morrison, Mrs. Flagler's first husband.

Baby Henry's father was proud of the new son, and very
early made plans to interest the boy in remaining on the farm
and following in his footsteps as a minister. But as soon as
young Flagler began to grow older he showed other inclina-
tions. Henry and his half brother, Daniel Harkness, grew to
like each other and became very companionable, despite the
several years difference in their ages. As Dan reached his early

[7] Flagler Family Records, File II, Flagler Collection.

5

teens he became restless at home, and often talked with his mother about returning to his birthplace in northern Ohio. There were Harkness relatives in both Bellevue and Republic. His mother had no particular objection other than the fact that her son was too young to be so far from parental influence. After much discussion she persuaded him to defer his plans until he was a little older.

Finally in 1837 the opportunity for which young Harkness had been wishing arrived. Isaac Flagler was called to the ministry of a rural church not far from Toledo, Ohio, and he accepted.[8] Dan was fifteen years old, and instead of going to Toledo with the family he was allowed to proceed to Bellevue where he was given a job with a relative in the firm of Chapman and Harkness. Several years later he went to Republic, Ohio, where he was employed as a salesman in the store of L. G. Harkness and Company.[9] The boy liked his work in Republic and never went back to live with his mother and stepfather.[10]

The Flaglers' sojourn in Ohio was a short one. The preacher decided to return to New York within two years after he left; so he accepted a call as pastor of a rural church nine miles from Medina. Carrie and Henry enrolled in the country school, but the latter followed very closely the success of his half brother in Republic. Occasionally a letter came from Dan telling how well he was doing, and it was not long before Mrs. Flagler realized that young Henry wanted to follow the other son and make his way alone. The pinch of poverty at home spurred him on in his determination. He became restless and dissatisfied and neglected his work in school. However, he did finish the eighth grade before dropping out. He tried working at several odd jobs, but he did not seem particularly suited for any of them. For a time he worked as a deck hand on one of

[8] *Western Reserve Historical Society Publication* (October, 1920), 26.
[9] W. W. Williams, *History of the Firelands*, 416.
[10] *New York Times*, May 21, 1913.

6

the Erie Canal boats running out of Medina; but that, too, was far from what he liked. He would not be denied a chance in life.

It is not unusual for a lad of fourteen to be unable to find himself in life. He was too young. But Henry Flagler was anxious to satisfy a desire which he had had since he was old enough to realize the economic situation in which he and his family were living—a desire to make money. His immature mind had long pondered the thought. He was a confident lad and was not concerned over failure. He knew he could succeed when given the opportunity, but that opportunity would never present itself as long as he remained under his father's roof. In some respects the boy hated to leave home; he was genuinely fond of his younger sister, as well as his parents. He knew very little about northern Ohio. But Dan Harkness had written him that he would like it, and that there were opportunities in which he would be interested. Mrs. Flagler had at one time lived in Bellevue and Milan, Ohio, but she knew very little about Republic. At any rate, however, she realized that her older son would take a brotherly interest in the boy.

He received his last-minute instructions as he stood at the gate of the fence encircling his father's modest home. It was a chilly fall day, and signs of a cold winter were beginning to appear. He assured his parents that he was thoroughly familiar with the route he was to take. He was to walk the nine miles to Medina, but he did not mind that [11] as there was no other means of getting there and he had walked many times before. He gave his parents a fond farewell, then turned slowly and started down the little path leading from the house. Of all his qualities his ambition and energy were most outstanding. Despite a little tinge of sadness over leaving his parents, his heart must certainly have pounded rapturously on that Oc-

[11] Samuel E. Moffett, "Henry Morrison Flagler," *The Cosmopolitan* (August, 1902), 417.

7

tober day when he tramped onto a dirt road and into an adventurous future. Whether this day or the day sixty-eight years later when he completed his life's greatest achievement gave him the biggest thrill was never known.

TWO

Early Career

ALTHOUGH Medina, New York, was an interesting little canal town, Henry M. Flagler lingered there just long enough to make plans for his journey on to Buffalo, some forty or fifty miles down the Erie Canal. There were all kinds of boats plying the route from Medina to Buffalo, ranging from the larger and more luxurious type to the smaller freight boats. Within a few hours the boy found a small boat headed for Buffalo which needed an extra crew member to help handle the large amount of freight it was carrying. It was not difficult for Flagler to talk the skipper into allowing him to make the trip free of charge in return for his services while on board. Arriving in Buffalo late at night, the boy was required to help unload the boat as part of his payment of the fare. It was early morning before the task was finished and he was tired, hungry, and sleepy. As Buffalo was an enterprising lake town, where the docks were always busy with shipping activities, Flagler easily got a boat for the next part of his journey. His fare on the lake boat took almost all the money he had, but he had saved it for that purpose. Early on the morning of his second day away from home, the boat pulled slowly away from the dock at Buffalo with young Flagler on board. The northern shore of Ohio lay in the distance. Sandusky was his next stop.[1]

The journey across the lake, which took three days and nights, was not as pleasant as he had expected. During the first

[1] *New York Times,* May 21, 1913.

day the weather was extremely rough. The little boat was tossed and tumbled about by the waves, and most of the passengers, including Flagler, got terribly seasick. He was as miserable as he had ever been and wished many times during those three days that he had never left home. To the discomforts of seasickness were added those of homesickness. He declared to himself that, if he ever saw shore again, he would head in the nearest direction towards home—on land. As the weather got better, however, his spirits rose, and he was actually able to eat a little of the now four-day-old lunch which his mother had prepared and put in his carpetbag when he left home. Finally, the little vessel reached Sandusky. He was very weak from lack of nourishing food, and still a bit dizzy and groggy from the rough trip. As he left the boat, he staggered along the wharf, fearful that someone might see him and believe that he was drunk. Then, and throughout his life, he detested liquor. After eating a hot breakfast he felt much better. The dizzy sickness left him, and he regained his strength quickly.[2] Since he did not feel quite as lonely as he had during the boat trip, he took the time to walk around Sandusky for a portion of the day and enjoy land once more. Sandusky, which had been settled in 1817, was a thriving town with a population of about 3,000. The ice, fish, and lumber trade had grown with the town. Sandusky Bay, on which the town was situated, was an important place on Lake Erie, offering excellent shipping facilities. Four large harbors were indicative of the volume of commerce the town attracted from the lake.[3]

Henry Flagler was not attracted to Sandusky, but he spent a day and night there before starting the last lap of his journey. It is not known exactly how he travelled the thirty-odd miles from Sandusky to Republic, but in all probability he walked most of the way. At any rate, the trip took him several days. He stopped for a day or so with friends of his

[2] *New York Tribune*, December 23, 1906.
[3] H. L. Pieke, *History of Erie County, Ohio*, I, 67.

mother in Bellevue, which was about halfway between Sandusky and Republic. He liked Bellevue and this short visit
may have influenced him to return there later to live. Nevertheless he pushed on to Republic, a town of a little less than
a thousand persons, where he was met by Dan Harkness, who,
more than anyone else, was responsible for his coming to Ohio.
It was well that he had someone in Republic whom he knew,
for he arrived with only a French coin, a nickel, and four
pennies in his pocket, his entire fortune in 1844.[4]

The newcomer to Republic began work the very next day
with L. G. Harkness and Company. The founder of the company, Lamon G. Harkness, an uncle of Dan Harkness, was a
prominent physician and a native of Salem, New York. After
taking his medical degree at Union College in New York, he
moved westward to northern Ohio in 1823. He first practiced
in Lynne and then for a short time lived in Republic, but he
finally settled in Bellevue in 1833, where he made a reputation
of being a good doctor but a much better business man. Soon
after settling in Bellevue, Harkness was married to Julia Follett, a native Ohioan. They established a distinguished home,
into which seven children were born; namely: Isabella, Follett,
Mary, Lamon, Julia, Tryphene, and Louisa.[5] Mary Harkness,
the third child, later became the wife of Henry M. Flagler.

After moving to Bellevue, Lamon Harkness still kept in
close touch with his business at Republic, but relied considerably on Dan for its management. Dan's father, David Harkness, was a brother of Lamon. After David Harkness's death,
Dan's mother married Isaac Flagler.[6] Dan, who was an exceptionally good business man, gave young Henry a sound background in the business world.

Henry Flagler worked hard for his half brother. He was

[4] Flagler kept the French coin the rest of his life as a good luck piece, and
also as an imitation of the character in the Bible who had but one talent.
New York Tribune, December 23, 1906.
[5] W. W. Williams, *History of the Firelands*, 415.
[6] Flagler Family Records, File II, Flagler Collection.

anxious to make an impression not only on Dan but also on Lamon Harkness, who visited the store frequently from nearby Bellevue. He never asked for time off and labored uncomplainingly for six days in a week. He earned the sum of five dollars per month, plus room and board. Henry and Dan lived in a room in the rear of the store, which was not too comfortable. There was a large wood-burning stove in the store where the boys cooked most of their meals, a feature of bachelor life to which Henry never became accustomed. On cold nights the boys would abandon their unheated sleeping quarters and seek a warmer place under a counter near the stove. Sometimes their thin blankets would have to be supplemented with coarse brown wrapping paper from the table in the front of the store. There were perhaps easier jobs he could have found, but young Flagler believed that there might be a future with the Harknesses. However, he was not satisfied. Even at the age of fifteen, he was ambitious to advance and never seemed thoroughly contented. Speaking later about his first job, he said that he had wanted to do things, not especially to become rich, but that he "might be useful and take a part in the work of the world." [7]

At first his advancement was very slow, or so it seemed to him. Ten months after he was first employed by L. G. Harkness and Company his pay was increased to seven dollars a month. It is safe to say that Flagler saved a good portion of each monthly pay envelope. He was never a spendthrift, and often when other boys insisted that he accompany them for an evening or a Sunday of fun, he remained behind because of the expense which the outing involved. Dan Harkness watched with interest the boy's ambition and ability. Through methods of his own Flagler boosted the business of L. G. Harkness and Company, and the community soon took notice of his untiring efforts and his keen mind.

In near-by Rome (the name was later changed to Fostoria)

[7] *New York Tribune*, December 23, 1906.

another young man was making a name for himself in the field of salesmanship.[8] He was Charley Foster, who at that time was working for his father in a general store. He and Flagler, who became fast friends, were said to be the best salesmen in Seneca County. Occasionally the boys visited each other, and the elder Foster tried several times to get Flagler to come to Rome and take a job with him. The boy thought seriously of going, but his employer there would have been an extremely hard taskmaster. Foster took young apprentices into his store to learn the art and trade of merchandising, and would not let them "gamble, mingle with women, nor marry, nor could they frequent taverns. They were to learn to read and cipher and to know the 'rule of three.'" It was not that Flagler wanted to indulge in vices prohibited by Foster, but he did want a little more freedom than he could have found in this village of less than three hundred persons. Consequently, he decided to remain with his kinsman in Republic. It was a wise decision, perhaps one that meant the difference between ultimate success and failure. The futures of young Flagler and young Foster turned out differently. Both later made great fortunes, but Foster entered politics and became governor of Ohio; later he was appointed Secretary of the Treasury in the Benjamin Harrison administration. Business and politics are unlike, however, and he died a poor man.[9] Flagler saw how Foster's money was so easily lost, and it is needless to say that he profited by his friend's example. He resolved never to become deeply involved in politics.

The boy learned many things during his three-year stay at the general store in Republic. Besides salesmanship, he had much training in the exercise of thrift, ingenuity, and good judgment. Both Dan Harkness and Lamon Harkness were pleased with their discovery of such a person as Henry Flagler. Perhaps, at times, he thought the tangible compensations for

[8] C. W. Butterfield, *History of Seneca County, Ohio,* 181.
[9] C. S. Van Tassil, *Book of Ohio,* II, 754.

selling candles, weighing coffee, measuring calico, and crank-
ing molasses faucets were not enough, but on reflection he
realized that his experiences behind the counter gave him the
foundation for a business education. While there he acquired
a sense of commercial values and learned the rudiments of
good and profitable business.[10] Many were the lessons the boy
learned, one being to inquire closely into the merits of what
is offered for sale. There were some things in stock that he had
to sell which he knew were not worth the price. For example,
in the cellar of the store there was a keg filled with brandy
from a larger vessel. There were three classes of people in
the country around Republic, living in separate communities
—English, German, and natives. The price of brandy was
different for each of the three groups. Out of that same keg
Flagler was instructed to sell one kind of brandy to the English at four dollars a gallon, another kind to the Germans at
one dollar and fifty cents a gallon, and still another kind to the
native inhabitants for what he could get.[11]

In the meantime, while Flagler was gaining a reputation as
a teen-age business man, his half brother, Dan Harkness, was
continuing to grow in the estimation of his Uncle Lamon. In
1845, Dan, a young man in his early twenties, was asked to
come to Bellevue and join the partnership of F. A. Chapman
and L. G. Harkness, dealers in general merchandise. The
partnership was re-organized and young Harkness became a
member of the new firm, which took the name of Chapman,
Harkness and Company.[12] For the next few years Flagler
continued in Republic, taking Dan's place as manager of the
store there. The reputation which he won soon after his arrival continued to flourish. Given the chance, he proved to his
employers that he was a mature business man though only in
his late teens.

[10] "He Made Florida," *Literary Digest*, XLVI (May 31, 1913), 1241.
[11] *New York Tribune*, December 23, 1906.
[12] W. W. Williams, *History of the Firelands*, 416.

In 1849, after five years in Republic, nineteen-year-old Henry Flagler was given a job in Bellevue with Chapman, Harkness and Company.[13] This was a deserved promotion. His salary was increased to nearly $400 a year. Bellevue, which offered many more opportunities than Republic, was the place in which he laid the foundations for the great fortune which he later made. The town was situated about twelve or fifteen miles northwest of Republic. It was about the same size as Republic, but was a much faster growing place. About half of Bellevue was in Huron County and half in Sandusky County. It had a very slow growth before 1840, but in 1839 the Mad River Railroad was completed to the village from Sandusky, an outlet to Lake Erie, and people began to move in. F. A. Chapman, T. F. Amsden, and L. G. Harkness bought all the land in Bellevue on the Huron County side, and began to encourage outsiders to settle there. These men sold their land at fancy prices to the newcomers, and subsequently became the most wealthy and influential citizens of the community. There were nearly a thousand citizens there when the town was incorporated in 1851. In 1852 a branch line of the Toledo, Norwalk, and Cleveland Railroad was built to Bellevue, greatly increasing the commercial advantages of the town.[14]

Young Flagler was happy to be with Dan Harkness again and to accept the challenge which the business opportunities in Bellevue offered him. He roomed with Dan and often accompanied him to the home of Lamon Harkness. Dan and Isabella, oldest daughter in the Lamon Harkness home, were involved in a gradually deepening courtship, which, despite their being first cousins, culminated in their marriage on August 23, 1849.[15] The entire Harkness family liked young

---

[13] *Western Reserve Historical Society Publication* (October, 1920), 26.

[14] W. W. Williams, *History of Huron County, Ohio*, I, 184.

[15] Isabella died on July 5, 1864, at the age of thirty-five. Daniel M. Harkness was remarried on June 22, 1897, to Edith Hale, who survived him. See Flagler Family Records, File II, Flagler Collection.

Henry. After all, he was part of the Harkness clan, though no blood relation. The fact that his mother had at one time been married to David Harkness, Lamon's brother, made him feel like one of the group. There were two younger Harkness sisters, Mary, fifteen, and Julia, only nine, who enjoyed keeping Henry company while Dan courted Isabella. He made quite an impression on the two girls, and his visits became very regular. After Dan and Isabella were married, Henry Flagler continued to visit in the evenings with Mary and Julia. It was perhaps at first through sheer habit, but as time passed something kept drawing him back to the Harkness home. He followed the path of least resistance, and did not try to discipline himself. The attention he gave the Harkness girls did not interrupt his work; instead, it seemed to stimulate him. Mary thought at first that he visited there to gain the good will of her father, but he already had that. Flagler was just slow about getting to the point and declaring his intentions. Everyone in Bellevue knew that Henry Flagler was in love before he realized it himself.

Before long Julia Harkness began to get in his way. She wanted to play children's games, but he preferred to be entertained by Miss Mary, a lovely young woman with considerable charm and talent. In due time Flagler knew that his actions towards Mary were prompted by love. Henry's visits to the Harkness home became more frequent and more formal. Julia was withdrawn from the picture by the thoughtful parents, and every encouragement was given the young man of Mary's choice. After a short engagement they were married on November 9, 1853.[16] The only unhappy member of the family was thirteen-year-old Julia. In her childish way, she, too, claimed Henry, who was always fond of her. Her chance came later when she became interested in a newcomer to Bellevue, young Barney York, who showed nearly as much business ability as Henry Flagler. Julia and Barney York were

[16] Flagler Family Records, File II, Flagler Collection.

married on January 8, 1863,[17] thus bringing the third son-in-law into the Lamon Harkness family. All three were prominent businessmen in Bellevue; their father-in-law had set a good example for them.

Perhaps the most successful of all the Harkness clan was

LAMON G. HARKNESS m. Julia Follett
brother of David
Harkness

Isabella Harkness m. Daniel M. Harkness

Mary Harkness m. Henry Morrison Flagler

Julia Harkness m. Barney H. York

Louisa Harkness m. Gerrit S. Wheaton

Lamon G. Harkness
died when six years old

Tryphene Harkness
died at the age of twenty

Follett Harkness
died in infancy

Family of Flagler's wife

one Stephen V. Harkness. Henry Flagler had heard much about him because he was the only son of David Harkness by his first wife. Dan and Stephen were half brothers; Henry and Dan were half brothers; yet Stephen and Henry were no kin at all. Until about 1850 Henry had never seen Stephen and

[17] They had three children: Georgia Harkness York, born March 18, 1865; Robert Hamlin York, born October 29, 1866; and Roy Follett York, born February 4, 1871. See *Ibid.*

even Dan had been with him very little. Stephen was born in Seneca County, New York, on November 18, 1818, and spent most of his early years in that state with his mother's people. He worked hard as a boy, having been an apprentice in the trade of harness making at the age of fifteen. He applied himself to the task with determination to become its master and make of it a stepping stone to the success he was already determined to achieve. At the age of twenty-one he moved to Bellevue to be with his uncle Lamon Harkness. He ran a general store for a number of years in connection with an eating establishment. In the early 1850's he settled in Monroeville, a small town not far away. His stay there was of short duration, as the urge to find greener pastures got the better of him. He tried several northern Ohio towns, but finally went back to Monroeville, where he became established in business as a grain dealer and distillery operator. He soon had good business connections in Bellevue and Cleveland.[18]

In Bellevue, Flagler watched Stephen closely and noted with interest the progress he continued to make in Monroeville. No doubt, he was admired by the younger man for his ability to get ahead. There was mutual admiration between them because Stephen Harkness observed the progress young Flagler made, too. Flagler had opportunity to prove his ability because Chapman, Harkness and Company expanded into the distillery and liquor field. They also began to deal in grain. Ohio, which at that time was in the center of the grain belt, was particularly suited for the raising of corn. Its production laid the foundation for other related crops and industries. The grain business was new to Flagler, but he perceived its place in the business world and learned it. When Chapman, Harkness and Company doubled their volume of business through Flagler's efforts, they began paying him a commission as well as a salary.

[18] J. H. Kennedy, "Stephen Vanderburg Harkness," *Magazine of Western History,* IX (November, 1888), 188–189.

Early Career

By 1852, Flagler had saved several thousand dollars from commissions he had made shipping grain, and was so highly thought of by his business associates that he was invited to join the firm. Chapman, who had saved enough upon which to retire, decided that it might be well if he withdrew. Lamon Harkness was ready to retire but was persuaded by the two younger men to remain on with them. Henry Flagler bought the Chapman interest, and the firm was renamed Harkness and Company.[19] It is not known exactly how much Flagler paid for the third interest in the business. He perhaps had saved enough for that, but if he had not done so, either Daniel or Lamon Harkness would have lent him the money. They were anxious for him to become associated in the business, because neither underrated his ability.

From Bellevue, Harkness and Company shipped large quantities of wheat during the 1850's to Cleveland for market. One commission merchant in Cleveland, John D. Rockefeller, handled most of the shipments, and in the course of time Flagler came to know his agent there.[20] Little did either of the men realize that some day they would become associated in a business known around the world for its great concentration of wealth. Rockefeller's dealings with Flagler made it possible for the two men to know each other fairly well. They had much in common, one characteristic being their great desire to get ahead in life.

The distillery business in the 1850's was eminently respectable, and it was one which Harkness and Company found very profitable. Most companies dealing in grain found it easy to establish a distillery in connection with their other interests because the manufacture of liquor gave them an outlet for considerable grain. Flagler had scruples about dealing in liquor; his strict Puritan training would not have permitted anything else, but the paramount thing in his life was making

[19] W. W. Williams, *History of the Firelands*, 414.
[20] "Sketch of Henry M. Flagler," *The Outlook*, CIV (May 31, 1913), 231.

money.[21] Since the liquor business was profitable, Flagler tucked his convictions in his pocket and hurried on in the making of a small fortune.

While Dan Harkness and Henry Flagler were increasing their earthly holdings in Bellevue shipping grain and making liquor, Stephen V. Harkness was doing the same in nearby Monroeville. They worked separately as two organizations but cooperated to their mutual benefit. In fact Monroeville claimed Flagler as a resident. Though he never moved there from Bellevue, he spent much time there with Stephen learning more about the distillery business. In addition to wines and liquors, Stephen dealt in grain, livestock, and banking. He was accustomed to big money deals, and always traded on a larger scale than did the two liquor makers in Bellevue. After Flagler had spent several years in the business, those scruples which he had had from the beginning began to worry him, and he sold out, but not before making a sizeable fortune. Dan Harkness, who took over Flagler's liquor interest, did not sell the Bellevue distillery, which was a part of Harkness and Company, until 1868.[22] Stephen Harkness held on to his Monroeville distillery, too. If he had any scruples concerning the making of whiskey, they were never detected. His big money haul in this business came with the first comprehensive Internal Revenue Act on July 1, 1862.[23] Among other things, this law included a tax upon malt and distilled liquors. Prior to the passing of the law, Senator John Sherman, prominent Ohio politician, warned Harkness of its significance and what its results might be. Sherman, who was on the Senate finance committee, had inside information. He foresaw the tax of two dollars on each gallon of spirits. Harkness immediately set forth to accumulate an abundant stock before the law went

---

[21] "He Made Florida," *loc. cit.*, 1242.
[22] W. W. Williams, *History of the Firelands*, 400.
[23] T. E. Burton, *John Sherman*, 123.

into effect. He used all of his reserve to buy up supplies of whiskey, so that he could sell it at the high prices exacted by the tax. The local bank in Monroeville, which he owned, felt the strain of Harkness's determination to buy up everything in whiskey that he could find, and its funds became almost exhausted. Farmers who had funds on deposit became alarmed when they heard of the Harkness scheme, especially those who had difficulty in cashing their corn receipts. Business in the town was tied up for days, but Harkness was never at a loss to keep the people fooled. He employed Hiram Latham to stand on the street and assure the anxious farmers that "old Steve Harkness" was all right, and that his intentions were sound and good. Latham did not get very far in trying to persuade the farmers that Harkness was not building his own fortune at their expense. The tension was fierce. One story was told of a man who entered the bank and demanded the cash for a couple of loads of corn. Harkness, who appeared on the scene just in time, talked to the irritated farmer about the prospect for rain, while the cashier disappeared through the back door to borrow the sum of money from a nearby druggist in order to meet the demand.

He was also shipping grain constantly at this time in order to raise further capital. Harkness, who was blunt and frank at all times, in the midst of the excitement became irked at John D. Rockefeller, in Cleveland, who acted as commission merchant for him as well as for his acquaintances in Bellevue. It seems that Rockefeller, whom he knew well, had delayed in payment for a shipment of grain. His tardiness prompted Harkness to dispatch the following pointed message: "Why in the hell don't you remit for the last car of corn I shipped you? Unless I get it soon I will bust."

Harkness's frantic efforts proved lucrative, because the law was passed, as he had been advised. He was stocked from cellar to ceiling with all sorts of whiskey and wines. He sold out his stock at the advanced price without having to pay the tax and made over $300,000 clear profit.[24] Not every liquor dealer could have succeeded so well. Steve Harkness had impressed the best businessmen in northern Ohio. In 1866 he sold his property in Monroeville and moved to Cleveland, where he continued in various business interests for a number of years.[25]

[24] T. W. Latham, "Revelations of an Old Account Book," *Firelands Pioneer*, XXII (January, 1921), 135.

[25] At his death his estate was estimated to be worth $30,000,000. See *Ibid.*, 138; also Kennedy, "Stephen Vanderburg Harkness," *loc. cit.*

THREE

Success and Failure

THE years in Bellevue were happy ones for Mary and Henry Flagler. From 1853 until 1862 they lived there among their friends and relatives and became a part of an expanding community. In the meantime Henry Flagler was growing in his business experience, just as the town was developing about him. It was a trying period in American history. The argument between the North and South over the extension of slavery was rapidly reaching a breaking point. Flagler, a keen student of national affairs, watched with much interest the situation in Kansas following the passage of the Kansas-Nebraska Act in 1854. Being a Republican he probably disagreed strongly with the decision in the Dred Scott Case in 1857, and no doubt he cheered Lincoln's rapid rise to prominence just prior to the election of 1860. He was aware of the significance of the Republican victory in 1860, and was not surprised when the Southern states began to secede from the Union soon after the election.

The Civil War followed with four years of bitter struggle. Flagler remained calm. His thinking was not as confused as that of the nation as a whole. He shared the views of most fellow Ohioans on the slavery issue, but he was not a radical by any means. To him, war meant waste and destruction. It was not a profitable business in an economic sense. He favored very strongly a compromise with the South, and saw no reason why some workable plan could not be adopted. When Lincoln issued his call for volunteers in 1861, Dan

Harkness was one of the first to offer his services to the Union army, but Flagler did not feel urged to do so.[1] There was no moral obligation on his part to become engaged in the hostilities. After all, John D. Rockefeller, Philip Armour, and John Wannamaker did not enlist.[2] Like them, Flagler probably made financial arrangement for several other persons to join the Union forces. He no doubt preferred it to doing military service himself.

This period in American history was one of profit and gain for Flagler. The war increased the volume of his grain business many times. With Dan Harkness in the army his work in Bellevue was made very heavy, but as long as he could count substantial gains each month he did not mind. He routed grain purchased by the United States government to the federal troops, a transaction which meant great financial returns for him.[3] While his fortune was growing in Bellevue, his family, to which he gave much attention, was also increasing. He was fond of children, and was exceedingly happy when his first child, Jenny Louise Flagler, arrived on March 18, 1855.[4] His home life became more interesting, the baby becoming the center of his attention. A second child was born on June 18, 1858, and was named Carrie for his half sister. Little Carrie was never well, and died when only three years old. The youngest child, Harry Harkness Flagler, was born a number of years later.[5] Flagler's wife was never a robust woman; therefore many of the home responsibilities were thrown upon him. From childhood her health had to be safeguarded, and her husband derived great pleasure from making her comfortable and economically secure. They usually spent their evenings at home, and very seldom did either seek entertain-

---

[1] W. W. Williams, *History of the Firelands*, 417.
[2] Allan Nevins, *John D. Rockefeller*, I, 140.
[3] *New York Tribune*, December 23, 1906.
[4] Flagler Family Records, File II, Flagler Collection.
[5] Carrie Flagler died on December 7, 1861. Harry Harkness Flagler was born in Cleveland, December 2, 1870. *Ibid.*

ment in other places. Despite Mary Flagler's infirmities, they lived a fairly normal life. She was naturally happy and cheerful, and the rest of the family were influenced by the way she acted.[6]

The Flaglers associated with the best people in Bellevue. Most of their friends were members of the Congregational Church, in which the Flaglers also held membership since there was no Presbyterian Church in the community.[7] Both Mary and Henry Flagler were religiously inclined and participated as frequently as her health would permit in all activities of the church. Their closest associates were Isabella and Dan Harkness; Isabella had always been Mary's favorite sister, and the relations of Dan and Henry were very warm. In fact, the four seemed like one family, since Isabella and Mary were sisters, Dan and Henry were half brothers, and Isabella and Dan were first cousins. Mary's parents were frequent visitors at the modest home of the Flaglers, and in 1855 Henry's parents retired and moved to Bellevue to spend their last years. With them came Carrie Flagler, the half sister who had always been a favorite with young Flagler.[8] Another couple who liked the company of the Flaglers was Julia and Barney York. Julia York was the younger sister of Mary Flagler, and, though young York was a newcomer to Bellevue, he immediately won his way into the affections of the entire family. He, too, was associated with his father-in-law in business. L. G. Harkness prided himself upon his business associates, his three sons-in-law, Dan Harkness, Henry Flagler, and Barney York. The three young men remained fast friends all of their lives.

The Bellevue years brought sorrows and joys alike to the Harkness and Flagler clans. Isabella and Dan Harkness had five children; all but one, however, died in early infancy.[9]

[6] Harry Harkness Flagler to the author, October 25, 1945.
[7] Harriett T. Upton, *History of the Western Reserve*, I, 441.
[8] Harry Harkness Flagler to the author, November 26, 1945.
[9] Flagler Family Records, File II, Flagler Collection.

When Dan went into the Union army in 1861 he left a despondent wife, who never fully recovered from the loss of her babies. Mary and Henry Flagler lost their second baby during their residence in Bellevue, and Mary had one or two serious illnesses which kept her husband disturbed for a long time. Henry's mother died in 1861 and his father's health was bad until his death a number of years later. There were happier times, however; so life was anything but drab. Dan, Henry, and Barney always had a good time when they got together. Instead of relaxing at a game of tennis or a few holes of golf as the young men of a later day perhaps would have done, those of the fifties and sixties found much sport in playing tenpins. Henry and Dan were frequently found at the tenpin alley at lunch time, but after an hour or so they were back at their desks at the office of Harkness and Company.[10] Business always came first.

By 1862, Henry Flagler had accumulated $50,000. Although he was happily settled in Bellevue, he was becoming restless and dissatisfied. He could not help feeling that he might get ahead faster if he went to some other place. After he reached the top in Bellevue, his interest in the grain business seemed to wane. There was more money to be made if he stuck with it, but the business had lost its charm; consequently, he decided to push on to something more speculative and more adventurous, perhaps something that might make him a bigger fortune in a shorter time. No one tried to persuade him against the course he set out to follow. His family and friends knew him too well. Henry Flagler was a man of much determination. In 1860 salt had been discovered in abundance around Saginaw, Michigan, and the first salt made in that section was put on the market in May of that year. Earlier the Michigan legislature had passed an act paying ten cents a bushel for salt produced in the state. The law also

[10] Thomas W. Latham, "Revelations of an Old Account Book," *Firelands Pioneer*, XXII (January, 1921), 133.

26

made salt-producing property tax exempt, a decided inducement.[11] Excitement ran high, and many capitalists, or would-be
salt producers, moved in hoping to make a fortune. The little
town of Saginaw felt the effects of the boom. People went
wild. The get-rich-quick feeling spread rapidly; and Flagler
was not the only person to get caught in the wave of enthusiasm.

Encouraged by the act giving a bounty on each bushel of
salt, a group of Michigan businessmen organized the East
Saginaw Salt Manufacturing Company, with a capital stock of
$50,000, consisting of 2,000 shares of $25 each. The whole
amount was subscribed in two days, and the work on the first
well was completed in 1860. The company at once proceeded
to the erection of works for the manufacture of salt, consisting of two kettle blocks after the manner of those which
were in use in other salt-producing areas. Production the first
year was 10,722 barrels of salt consisting of five bushels each.
In the second year, July 1, 1861, to July 1, 1862, the production of this company alone was 32,250 barrels.[12]

Flagler's father-in-law, L. G. Harkness, was the first person from Bellevue to be attracted by the salt strike. He already
had extensive interests in the lumber business in Michigan.
As soon as the boom commenced, he immediately realized the
possibility in producing salt, and bought a large block of
shares in the East Saginaw Manufacturing Company. For the
first two years Harkness was pleased with the profits he made
from the venture. His enthusiasm no doubt influenced the
son-in-law's thinking, because it was at this time, in 1862, that
Henry M. Flagler yielded to the temptation of casting his
fortune with this new and uncertain industry. He pulled
stakes in Bellevue and moved his family to Saginaw in the
hope of becoming a wealthy man in record time. His brother-
in-law, Barney York, was persuaded to go to Saginaw also.

[11] Charles R. Tuttle, *History of Michigan,* 580.
[12] James C. Mills, *History of Saginaw County, Michigan,* I, 430.

York did not have as much money to put in the business as Flagler did, but borrowed an equal amount from his father-in-law. Flagler sank his savings of $50,000 into a new firm named the Flagler and York Salt Company. Many other speculators had the same idea as Flagler and York, and several new salt-producing companies were formed in Saginaw in 1862 and 1863.

Flagler, who entered his new work with all the energy that characterized his previous business ventures, received encouragement from everyone who knew him. He made an impressive beginning. From the start he liked Saginaw, and was happy to be a part of so progressive a community. Mary Flagler continued in poor health, but the presence of her sister, Julia York, kept her from becoming despondent among so many strangers. The Flaglers took an active interest in the community, especially in religious activities. For several generations the Flaglers had been Presbyterians, but in Saginaw, as in Bellevue, the Presbyterian Church had recently become united with the Congregational Church due to the rapid growth of the latter group. Naturally the Flaglers affiliated with this group, and before many months Flagler was made superintendent of the Sunday School, a position for which he was well qualified. Until his departure from Saginaw in 1865 he continued his work, not only in the Sunday School, but also in the church as a member of the board of trustees.[13]

For about two years Flagler and York made money in the salt business; however, the process was not as easy as they had expected. There was much to be learned in producing salt. Those manufacturers who had had previous experience had the advantage over those who began without experience. The many processes of manufacture were never completely mastered by the get-rich-quick fellows. Sad to say, many did not discover, until they had invested their money, that skill was required to make good salt. Henry M. Flagler was one who soon learned this fact. One thing which drove Flagler

[13] *Ibid.,* 336.

out of salt production was the keen competition in Michigan and Ohio which cut down drastically on the desired profits. Perhaps the thing that finally forced him out of the business was the collapse of salt prices at the close of the Civil War. After several years of overproduction the salt market went to pieces, and Flagler was left with nothing.[14] By late 1865 Flagler had not only lost the $50,000 that he had sunk in the venture, but in addition was $50,000 in debt. It was his first and last financial failure, one that he never forgot, and one which he profited by many times later when the urge to try something new arose. It made him cautious about speculating on anything until he had thoroughly investigated its merits and possibilities.[15] Flagler's financial failure came the same year the Civil War ended. Although the nation was crippled and bruised from four years of bitter fighting, it had made remarkable progress during the first sixty years of the nineteenth century, and the four years of Civil War marked only a temporary halt in its advancement. So it was with Flagler: his reverses of the sixties were of a temporary nature. After the war the American nation started through a slow process of recuperation; Flagler's comeback was much quicker.

Emerging from the financial debacle with much determination, Flagler looked about for a new start in the business world. He went to Bellevue and talked the matter over with his father-in-law and Dan Harkness, who were still engaged in the grain business. From them he borrowed $50,000 at ten per cent interest and paid off his debts in Saginaw. He was not bitter over his failure; however, he was a little disgusted with himself. His greatest desire was still to make money. In fact, this desire became more persistent than ever, for he had a sizeable debt hanging over his head; his back was against the wall.[16]

Flagler was thirty-five years old when he left Saginaw. No

[14] *Ibid.*, 436.
[15] "He Made Florida," *Literary Digest*, XLVI (May 31, 1913), 1241.
[16] *New York Tribune*, December 23, 1906.

doubt it was a temptation for him to go back to Bellevue and enter his father-in-law's business. The Harknesses encouraged him to do it. Mary Flagler had little to say about it because she relied wholly on Henry's judgment. The easiest thing would have been to take up in Bellevue where he had left off in 1862, but the enterprising Flagler chose Cleveland as the place where he would try to remake his fortune.[17] Cleveland in 1865 was one of the leading towns in Ohio and offered many opportunities. It was a city of about 45,000 people at this time, strategically located on Lake Erie. Its founder, General Moses Cleaveland, an agent and director of the first Connecticut Land Company, came there in the 1790's. When Flagler arrived, the city had transportation facilities that were almost unrivaled. Situated on Lake Erie, Cleveland had access to the other Great Lakes and the Erie Canal. It was served by five railroads: the Cleveland, Columbus and Cincinnati; the Cleveland and Pittsburgh; the Lake Shore Railroad, which connected with the Erie and the New York Central; the Cleveland and Toledo; and the Cleveland and Mahoning. The Atlantic and Great Western was added a few years later. In 1860 there were no more than 30,600 miles of railroad in the United States, but that was great progress over the 2,818 miles in 1840.[18] Flagler was fortunate to have chosen Cleveland as his home, and Cleveland was fortunate to have another citizen so enterprising as Flagler.

His family accompanied him to Cleveland, refusing to remain in Bellevue until he was well settled. Mary Flagler went against the wishes of her family, but she chose to be near her husband. They rented a modest home and with only a few hundred dollars, which his father-in-law forwarded him, Flagler set himself up in the grain business. His knowledge of the business was good; and, since he had made money in it before, he had hopes of doing so again. It was a slow start for

[17] *Savannah* (Georgia) *Morning News*, May 21, 1913.
[18] Allan Nevins, *John D. Rockefeller*, I, 115.

Flagler, who was impatient and anxious to begin to pay back his debts. He got very little business at first; so on the side he became associated with a concern which made barrels, a venture that proved a failure, too. In another effort to make money quickly, he tried to market a specially-built horseshoe which was a creation of his own mind, but this scheme fell through. For the first time in his career, he was about to become discouraged and ready to quit. Everything seemed to be against him, and Bellevue, with all that the Harknesses had to offer there, seemed more inviting than ever before. He remarked to a friend one day that if he ever paid off his debts and was $10,000 ahead, he would retire from business.[19] But this loss of enthusiasm and desire to make a fortune did not last long.

In 1866 Maurice B. Clark, grain commission merchant in Cleveland, heard that young Flagler was having a hard time getting started and offered him a job with his firm, Clark and Sanford. Clark was a likable young Englishman who was about the same age as Flagler. Before the formation of Clark and Sanford he had been associated with Otis, Brownell and Company, probably the oldest grain dealers in Cleveland. For a while he was associated with John D. Rockefeller in the same kind of business, and it was at this time that both Clark and Rockefeller became acquainted with Flagler. In 1865 the partnership was dissolved, with Rockefeller following the oil interests and Clark remaining in the grain business. Clark was looking for an experienced dealer in grain, and when Flagler arrived on the scene, financially exhausted, his search was over. Flagler cheerfully took the job Clark offered him, but did not invest any money in the partnership. He enjoyed his association with Clark and ably filled the place left by Rockefeller. This marked a turning point in his life. Clark gave him considerable authority in the business;

[19] Edwin Lefèvre, "Flagler and Florida," *Everybody's Magazine*, XXII (February, 1940), 182.

he had freedom to act as if he were an investor in the partnership. He met with success from the start and Clark and Sanford liked his work. Within a few months the firm began to show a noticeable increase in its volume of business. Flagler's commission increased each month, and he began to think in terms of large sums again. By 1867, he owed less than $30,000 on the $50,000 he had borrowed two years before from the Harknesses.

The Flaglers moved into a larger home on Euclid Avenue. There were nine rooms in the two-story structure, some of which were often occupied by relatives. Flagler's mother had died a number of years earlier; so his father spent some time with them before his death in July, 1876.[20] In 1870 his father-in-law, L. G. Harkness, came to live with them after his retirement from his business in Bellevue. In that same year, Mary Flagler gave birth to their third child, a son, Harry Harkness Flagler.[21] The father had long anticipated the boy's arrival and started early making plans for his future.

Flagler's friends in Cleveland were all influential men, some of them exceedingly wealthy. Stephen V. Harkness, who moved to Cleveland in 1866 after selling his liquor business in Monroeville, was an intimate associate of the Flaglers. His fortune, one of the largest in the city, continued to increase through his efforts in the real estate business.[22] Mary Flagler, Stephen's first cousin, was his favorite kinsman. Her physical infirmities grew worse with the years, and Stephen shared her husband's growing concern over her condition. Stephen was a regular visitor in the home and enjoyed the Flagler hospitality of many a winter evening.

Flagler's business again brought him in contact with John D. Rockefeller, whom he had known since the days he had worked as a grain dealer in Bellevue. Their acquaintance soon

[20] Both Flagler's mother and father were buried in Bellevue. Flagler Family Records, File II, Flagler Collection.

[21] Conversation with Harry Harkness Flagler.

[22] *Cleveland Leader*, December 27, 1867.

grew into friendship. The early years of the two men were quite different. Rockefeller, who was born in Richford, New York, July 8, 1839, was nine years younger than Flagler.[23] His father engaged in the business of peddling medicine throughout western New York. The elder Rockefeller also had many other pursuits in life, some of which he never followed too closely, but neither he nor his family was ever poverty stricken. They always had plenty to eat and wear, and usually saved a little on the side. The Rockefeller family was large, and one brother, William Avery, Jr., born in 1841, was also among Flagler's acquaintances. William A. Rockefeller, Jr., later became associated with his brother in the Standard Oil Company.

John D.'s mother perhaps had more influence over the child than did the father, because of the latter's frequent absence from home. Eliza Rockefeller was stern with her children in their guidance and discipline. The boy grew to be more like his mother than any of the other children, a resemblance which pleased her, for he had been named for her father, John Davison. The boy became more serious minded and conscientious as he grew older. He was considered more outstanding than William. Young William was more like his father and was always carefree and restless. He gave evidence of becoming a good salesman, which he later proved to be. He had an attractive personality and was a good mixer with people.

As a boy, John D. Rockefeller was thorough in everything he did. This instinct was deeply embedded. The story is told about how cautiously he played checkers. He would ponder a move at great length, and never let anyone hurry him in making the decision. When urged on by his opponent to move more rapidly, he always let it be known that he was playing the game to win, and not to lose; therefore, to him time was of minor consequence in the game. Certainly that

[23] Allan Nevins, *John D. Rockefeller*, I, 22.

instinct, so early seen in his character, stayed with him throughout his life.

In 1850 the Rockefellers moved to Owego, New York, which was not far distant from their previous home. There were financial reverses from time to time in the family, but John and William were given the advantages of what educational training they could get in the village. Not only did the children attend school, but they all were required to attend Sunday school and church on Sunday. Religion was a passion with Eliza Rockefeller but her husband merely respected it. They were members of the Baptist Church, and John D. Rockefeller always leaned strongly in its favor. They were taught to contribute regularly to their church, a habit which young John never forgot. This training perhaps had a great deal to do with his later program of philanthropy.

In 1853 the elder Rockefeller sought greener pastures, and turned his attention westward as so many people were doing. As his business of selling medicine flourished in frontier places where trained physicians were few in number, he moved out on the fringe of the Western Reserve, and settled in Cleveland, Ohio.

As a lad of fourteen, young John, accompanied by his younger brother William, entered the Cleveland schools that fall. Among his many associates in Cleveland was Mark Hanna, son of a prosperous grocer Leonard Hanna, with whom he became very intimate. Hanna was to become a leading politician in Ohio, and then in national politics. It was quite by accident that another one of Rockefeller's boyhood chums was Tom Platt, who later became a chief figure in New York politics. At first his chief interest in girls centered around Lucy Spelman, whom he respected and admired for her scholastic attainments; however, Rockefeller later married Lucy's younger sister, Laura Spelman.

John D. Rockefeller graduated from high school in 1855, but he did not go to college. His mother hoped that he could go to Western Reserve or possibly Oberlin, but his father felt that practical experience would be of more value to him in later life. For three months he attended a commercial college in Cleveland, after which he began to look for employment. Business was bad in Cleveland in 1855, and getting a job was no easy matter. Finally he was given employment by Hewitt and Tuttle, commission merchants and produce shippers. This was the beginning of his steady rise to the top. The sixteen-year-old lad did well, and the way soon opened for further opportunities. In 1858 he and Maurice Clark organized the Clark and Rockefeller Company grain commissioners, each having invested $2,000 in the business. Rockefeller was happy to be independent, and to know that his advancement depended entirely on himself. The firm prospered during the war, and Clark and Rockefeller came out of the war period well-to-do businessmen.[24] Their next venture was in the oil business, but Clark retired shortly and resumed the selling of grain. At this point Samuel Andrews joined Rockefeller in the steadily expanding oil industry. Like Clark, Andrews was an Englishman, and had come to Cleveland in 1857. He was an energetic young man with a special liking for chemistry. He fitted into the petroleum picture perfectly. He first found employment in a lard-oil refinery where he gained much knowledge about oil, tallows, and candle-making. He made many practical experiments which added to the knowledge of petroleum and its uses.[25] Andrews was bound to go far in his field. All he needed was financial backing and some energetic partners. He soon got both.

[24] *Ibid.,* 28 ff.
[25] *New York Herald,* November 29, 1908.

FOUR

Flagler Strikes Black Gold

DURING the time that Henry M. Flagler was dealing in grain and salt, the petroleum industry in America was making rapid strides. The natural resources of this country were virtually untouched before 1800, but soon after that time considerable attention was centered on petroleum. In the states of Pennsylvania, Ohio, Kentucky, and what was later West Virginia traces of petroleum were discovered on the surface of springs and streams. Some time later it was found by speculators drilling for salt. Salt producers detested the dark green, evil-smelling substance which was mixed with the water. Oil and salt do not mix. Some of the salt wells which were actually abandoned because of the abundance of crude petroleum were later turned into productive oil wells.[1]

As more and more crude oil appeared, speculators began to wonder if some real value might not be derived from it. In Burkesville, Kentucky, where oil was found in abundance, it was first used for medicinal purposes. "American Medicinal Oil," which was used as a liniment or rubbing oil, was bottled and sold not only in the area where it was found but in the East and even in Europe. The fluid was also used as fuel for lamps in shops and factories, and later in homes. It was found to give a good light, and before long, streets were clearly lighted by it.[2] More and more uses were made of petroleum, and consequently the demand began to increase.

[1] Paul H. Giddens, *The Birth of the Oil Industry*, 3, 4.
[2] Allan Nevins, *John D. Rockefeller*, I, 149.

Flagler Strikes Black Gold

In western Pennsylvania where petroleum was found in great abundance the substance was called "Seneca Oil," being named perhaps for the Seneca Indians who inhabited that region.[3] It was in this section where most of the oil was discovered prior to 1845. The exact location was on a little stream known as Oil Creek which emptied into the Allegheny River. In this area boom towns like Titusville and Oil City sprang up.

Chemists were busy during the forties and fifties working with petroleum. Its value was partially known, but its real worth had not been fully discovered. Tallow candles, beeswax, and whale oil had been used for lighting purposes, but their place in the American home was soon to be at an end. Because of the decline of whale fisheries, the price for whale oil was exceedingly high by 1850. Lard oil was found only in small quantities; in fact, there was an increasing shortage of oil not only in the United States but all over the world. In the face of this shortage there was increasing demand for more oil. Many new machines were in use which required oil, factories had grown up in various sections, railroads had been constructed with much rapidity, and steamboats were plying more and more of our rivers. All these facilities were making demands on the small supply of oil in America.[4]

Prior to 1860 there were many advances in the field of petroleum. Samuel M. Kier, who owned some salt wells in western Pennsylvania, near Pittsburgh, in the late 1840's, was one of the earlier leaders. Like many other salt men he grew tired of the smelly green substance which came in such abundance from his salt well. It was such a nuisance that he sought some way of using it; in 1849 he conceived the idea of selling it as medicine. His wife, who was a consumptive, had used several bottles of this oil which had been sent from Kentucky. Kier compared the bottled medicine with the sub-

---

[3] P. H. Giddens, *The Birth of the Oil Industry*, 7.
[4] *Ibid.*, 18–19.

37

stance he was getting from his salt wells. As it seemed to be identical, he had his wife use the local product rather than the Kentucky oil which her doctor had prescribed. Since it had the same results, Kier opened a business in nearby Pittsburgh where the curative spirit was bottled and sold. These eight-ounce bottles of "Kier's Petroleum," which were selling widely by 1850, were used chiefly as a liniment, but were also recommended for a number of other things including consumption, bronchitis, liver complaints, and cholera morbus. Kier also distilled small quantities of petroleum to use as an illuminant; however, none of his experiments sought to use the substance for its own quality; he worked only on the by-products of petroleum. There is little doubt that Samuel M. Kier was the first man to test the possibility of refining it. He hit upon this process in 1849 after consultation with a chemist in Philadelphia.[5]

Another person to become actively engaged in the development of raw petroleum was George H. Bissell, a graduate of Dartmouth, who, at the time, was practicing law in New York. Just by chance, he happened to make a visit to Hanover, New Hampshire, in the fall of 1853, and while there, saw a small bottle of petroleum in the office of Doctor Dixi Crosby of the Dartmouth Medical School. Francis Beattie Brewer, a graduate of the Dartmouth Medical School, and at that time practicing physician in Titusville, Pennsylvania, had brought the sample to his professor at Hanover for inspection and study. Bissell got interested in the petroleum after talking with Professor Crosby about its possibilities.[6]

Bissell was an enterprising young man, who was determined to find out more about this strange substance. He arranged for Professor Crosby's son, Albert H. Crosby, to visit Titusville and bring back further evidence of petroleum in that

[5] Ida M. Tarbell, *History of the Standard Oil Company*, I, 5.
[6] Frank A. Taylor, "George H. Bissell," *Dictionary of American Biography*, II, 301–302.

section. Young Crosby made the investigation and returned with a favorable report. In the fall of 1854 Bissell and his law partner bought about 105 acres of oil lands in the Titusville area, and on December 30, 1854, they organized the Pennsylvania Rock Oil Company, the first of its kind in America.[7]

The newly organized oil company sent a small quantity of surface petroleum to a noted Yale chemist, Benjamin Silliman, Jr., for an analysis. Silliman's father, Benjamin Silliman, Sr., also a noted Yale professor, had made a chemical analysis of some petroleum secured from the springs at Cuba, New York, as early as 1833. Young Silliman had no doubt been interested in the strange oily substance since the time of his father's experiment. At any rate, he made the tests, and in the spring of 1855, his report was ready for delivery. His interests were apparently mercenary, for he refused to deliver the report to Bissell until a bill of $426.08 was paid him. After a short time, however, the first important scientific analysis of petroleum was delivered. The report was significant in that it was a prime factor in the beginning of the oil industry.[8]

The report listed petroleum as a promising commodity. It emphasized the usefulness of oil as an illuminant and as a lubricant. The findings stated further that many valuable products could be manufactured from it, and mentioned many uses for the refined substance. Silliman also explained how the oil was to be refined. For some time general attention was focused on the report and many of the activities dealing with petroleum were more vigorously undertaken. Bissell himself thought strongly of drilling extensively for oil on the land he bought near Titusville, but because of the depression of 1857 his plans never materialized.

Before Bissell could get financial backing and make preparation to drill for oil, the feat was accomplished by Edwin L. Drake, a thirty-eight-year-old jack-of-all-trades. He went to

[7] I. M. Tarbell, *History of the Standard Oil Company*, I, 7.
[8] P. H. Giddens, *The Birth of the Oil Industry*, 40.

Titusville in 1857 with the financial support of James M.
Townshend, Eastern banker, and after studying the situation
became enthusiastic over the possibilities. He had no practical
experience in drilling, but he hired several men and began
work. The task was long and tedious. In August, 1859, oil
was struck and Drake became a famous man. He had tapped
the subterranean supply of petroleum in a section that had
already become known for its surface oil. The opening of
this well meant that petroleum could now be secured in large
quantities, and there was no more doubt about the supply's
being exhausted. With the value of petroleum already well
known, the United States stood on the threshold of an era
marked by a rich new industry. Few men knew much about
oil and the refining process, but there were many who were
anxious to learn. The second well was drilled by William
Barnsdall, a Titusville tanner, in 1860, and in five months the
owner had sold over $16,000 worth of oil.[9] Many new wells
were opened along Oil Creek and the Allegheny River in
western Pennsylvania during the early sixties, and soon an
even greater expansion of the industry was under way. Fortune hunters poured forth in streams.

The oil regions of western Pennsylvania became the center
of bustle and activity. Both oil men and persons connected
indirectly with the industry made money fast. The manufacturers of wooden tanks for oil receptacles made fortunes;
teamsters who drove the wagons carrying the barrels of oil
out of the oil regions became rich; traffic on the Allegheny
River grew so rapidly that it could hardly take care of the
accelerated activity. By 1863 a railroad was extended into
Titusville, and by 1865 Oil City was supplied with rail service.[10]

Other places rapidly felt the impact of the boom. In 1865

[9] I. M. Tarbell, *History of the Standard Oil Company*, I, 9.
[10] *Ibid.*, 14, 15.

Pithole, Pennsylvania, was engulfed in the tide of prosperity. In ten months there the field was producing over 10,000 barrels of petroleum a day. The Civil War had just ended and many soldiers were anxious to get a chance to find some of the "black gold." Persistent rumors about its value had reached the Union soldiers as the war was drawing to a close and hundreds of them joined other enthusiasts in Pithole. Within a year the place had grown from a village to a town of 6,000 inhabitants. The region suffered and profited simultaneously. Pine shanties and oil derricks silhouetted the skies. Among the newcomers were whiskey sellers, horse traders, and dead beats. Everyone was there for one purpose—to get rich quick. Not everyone who rushed into the oil regions retired with a fortune. Many hardships awaited the newcomers—fluctuation of prices, speculation, and discrimination by the railroads gradually helped to bring order and sobriety to the boom towns.[11]

Prosperity soon spilled across the neighboring borders of New York and Ohio, especially into Cleveland, Ohio, where people became oil conscious. Because of Cleveland's good transportation facilities, oil was soon being shipped there for refinement, and then on to other places for sale. By 1865 Cleveland had about thirty refineries, and more were being built. Located on the southern shore of Lake Erie, and connected with other important points by rail, Cleveland was destined to go far as an outstanding petroleum center. By 1864, pipe lines were used to send oil out of the oil regions to nearby refining and marketing points. Samuel Van Syckel laid the first successful line, which carried about eighty barrels of oil per hour. This was a great improvement in the transporting of oil. The teamsters, who had carried large portions of the petroleum to the refineries before 1864, were definitely through. They resented the coming of the pipe

[11] *Ibid.*, 24 *ff.*

41

lines, but there was nothing that they could do. Railroads and pipe lines became the chief mediums of transportation for unrefined oil.[12]

During the sixties the fabulous story of oil was being discussed throughout New York, Ohio, and Pennsylvania, and the news seeped into other sections of the country as well. Henry M. Flagler, working hard first at his grain business and later in his salt venture, did not have much time to think about oil and its possibilities. It no doubt aroused his curiosity, as it did that of John D. Rockefeller and other get-rich-quick seekers. The first connection John D. Rockefeller had with oil was in 1862, the year in which Flagler went to Saginaw to invest in a salt mine. That year Rockefeller and his partner in the grain business, Maurice B. Clark, backed Samuel Andrews in starting a refinery in Cleveland. This move was a gamble for Rockefeller because he knew very little about Samuel Andrews or the oil game. His first loan was $4,000. Andrews proved that he had ability. He was a genius in mechanics and soon devised a new process for refining oil. As a result Rockefeller and Clark poured more capital into the Englishman's refinery.[13] In 1865 Rockefeller invested more heavily in the oil business. Since business differences had come between him and Clark, he pulled out of the partnership which dealt in grain. Oddly enough, by this time Maurice Clark was a full-fledged partner with Andrews in the oil business; Rockefeller gave his half in the grain business, plus $72,500 in cash, for Clark's share in the refining company.[14] The $72,500 in itself was a small fortune, but the new oil firm of Rockefeller and Andrews was the largest of its kind in Cleveland, and certainly one of the largest in the United States. Both men were extremely capable. Andrews knew the mechanics of the re-

[12] Gilbert H. Montague, *The Rise and Progress of the Standard Oil Company*, 6, 7.

[13] Ida M. Tarbell, "The Rise of the Standard Oil Company," in *McClure's Magazine*, XX (December, 1902), 116.

[14] Allan Nevins, *John D. Rockefeller*, I, 192.

fining business, and Rockefeller had a flair for buying and selling. Together they worked well.

While twenty-five-year-old John D. Rockefeller was teaming up with Samuel Andrews in the refining business in Cleveland, Henry M. Flagler was moving to the same town, with hopes of remaking a fortune after the Saginaw debacle. It was a great era for American business. Speculation, expansion, and competition, the order of the day, were to last until the Panic of 1873. Many great fortunes were in the making, for there was no limit to the amount of money a man might acquire. Rockefeller was caught in the rising tide of prosperity, and it was not long before Flagler was to share this success with him. By January, 1866, Rockefeller and Andrews had a business worth $1,200,000, which led the field of refineries in Cleveland. Second came Hussey, McBride and Company and then the Pioneer Oil Works, both with much smaller capital. Rockefeller and Andrews hired thirty-seven workers and had a capacity of 505 barrels a day. This was more than twice the output of any of their competitors in Cleveland.[15]

In 1866 Rockefeller had a good chance to renew his acquaintance with Flagler. They both had offices in the Sexton Building in Cleveland, and they often talked of the days when Flagler shipped grain from Bellevue to Rockefeller in Cleveland. Their associations became more intimate, and they enjoyed the company of each other. They frequently walked home together, sharing with each other the day's happenings in their respective offices. Grain did not have much of an attraction for Rockefeller, although Flagler thought well of the business because he was in the process of making money from it. Flagler, who was thirty-six, was not a handsome man, but was distinguished and erect. He had black hair and a closely cropped mustache. His eyes were dark, and he possessed a magnetic personality. His passion for wealth was equal to that

[15] *Cleveland Leader*, January 3–25, 1866.

43

of Rockefeller. In business both men were determined and untiring in their efforts. Neither would be denied success.[16]

Rockefeller and Andrews soon began to think of expansion. Early in 1866 William Rockefeller was taken into partnership to handle the sales and was sent to New York to establish an office there. Andrews superintended the refinery while John D. Rockefeller directed the organization. In the second year of their business it is believed they sold more than $2,000,000 worth of oil. There was still room for expansion, however, because with more capital there could be a much larger output. Rockefeller had great faith in the future of his industry, and believed it would make money as long as it was given attention. By 1866 rapid development was being made in the field of petroleum. The invention of a more efficient refining-still, the use of torpedoes in drilling, replacement of the clumsy flat car with its wooden tubs by the tank-car, and regular use of pipe lines to transport petroleum from the wells to the railroads helped refiners to turn out their product at a greatly accelerated rate. But not all of the refiners could afford these economies. Small concerns either had to increase their capital to about $500,000 or else combine with some larger unit. Rockefeller, who was among the first to realize the situation, began to look about to find more capital. The man whom Rockefeller wanted was Henry M. Flagler, but Flagler did not have the capital which Rockefeller needed to feed to the growing business. In fact, Flagler still owed several thousand dollars in 1866; however, within a year he had paid back all his debts.

Rockefeller could not dismiss the possibility of using Flagler. After trying unsuccessfully to persuade John Gardiner of Norwalk, Ohio, to join him in the firm, he approached Flagler on the matter. Flagler told him about Stephen V. Harkness, his wife's first cousin, who had made a fortune in the liquor business, and who had a flair for speculation and

[16] Matthew Josephson, *The Robber Barons*, 111, 112.

uncertainty. Rockefeller immediately went to see Harkness, and within an hour Harkness agreed to put $100,000 in the business with the understanding that Henry M. Flagler should have complete control of the investment.[17] As far as Rockefeller was concerned it was a perfect arrangement because he was thoroughly familiar with Flagler's ability as a businessman, and had talked with him about joining the firm. Flagler was doing well in the grain business, but at his cousin's insistence, was delighted to enter the oil company with Rockefeller. It meant that not only Harkness but also Rockefeller had complete faith in him. With Flagler in the business, Rockefeller tapped the Harkness treasury chest several times later and he never failed to get what he wanted.[18]

In 1867 the partnership of Rockefeller, Andrews and Flagler was formed, which marked the beginning of a petroleum oligarchy which lasted for several years. Stephen Harkness remained a silent partner in the new firm throughout, leaving all interests in the hands of his kinsman. Flagler worked well with Rockefeller in the organizing and handling of the business. William Rockefeller, who had been sent to New York, did very little of the partnership's planning. Samuel Andrews remained busy at his job of superintending the refinery.[19]

On March 4 and 5, 1867, the new firm advertised its product in the *Cleveland Leader,* and announced its offices in Cleveland at the Case Building, and in New York at 181 Pearl Street. The *Leader* commented on the new partnership as follows:

> Our readers will notice by the advertisement in another column, that the old and reliable firm of Rockefeller and

[17] Thomas W. Latham, "Revelations of an Old Account Book," in *Firelands Pioneer*, XXII (January, 1921), 136.
[18] *Firelands Pioneer*, XIII (June, 1916), 137, 138.
[19] G. H. Montague, "The Rise and Supremacy of the Standard Oil Company," *The Quarterly Journal of Economics*, XVI (February, 1902), 267.

Andrews has undergone a change, and now appears under the new title of Rockefeller, Andrews, and Flagler.

This firm is one of the oldest in the refining business and their trade already a mammoth one, is still further enlarged by the recent change; so that with their New York House, their establishment is one of the largest in the United States. Among the many oil refining enterprises, this seems to be one of the most successful; its heavy capital and consummate management, having kept it clear of the many shoals upon which oil refining houses have so often stranded.[20]

For the next ten or fifteen years Flagler was Rockefeller's strongest and closest associate. In his "Random Reminiscences" Rockefeller frankly discusses his warm friendship with Flagler. As Flagler once remarked, it was a "friendship founded on business rather than a business founded on friendship." [21] For years the two men worked together in the same office, their desks being only a few feet apart. They always walked home together in the evening, and back to the office in the morning. If there was ever any time off from the office, they usually got together and did their planning for days to come.[22] Rockefeller knew he could team with Flagler to make a great organization. His observations had not deceived him. Though Flagler was nine years older than Rockefeller, there seemed to be perfect understanding between them. Flagler's imagination and bold temperament lighted the way.[23] He lived on Euclid Avenue where he was a neighbor of Rockefeller. Euclid Avenue was perhaps one of the most beautiful streets in any American city. What was once a muddy trail and later a road had by the late sixties become a fashionable avenue. Most of Cleveland's wealthy citizens lived on this street. There were spacious homes, beautiful lawns, and well-kept

[20] *Cleveland Leader*, March 5, 1867.
[21] John D. Rockefeller, "Random Reminiscences of Men and Events," *World's Work*, XVII (November, 1908), 10881.
[22] John K. Winkler, *John D., A Portrait in Oils*, 74.
[23] John D. Rockefeller, "Random Reminiscences of Men and Events," *loc. cit.*, 10882.

flower beds. In view of the waters of Lake Erie, there lived the railroad builder Amasa Stone, the banker Stillman Witt, the politician Henry B. Payne, and industrialists John D. Rockefeller, Samuel Andrews, and Henry M. Flagler. Rockefeller's home was perhaps one of the most pretentious of the lot. It was a brick structure of two stories surrounded by yards as beautiful as could be found. In 1880 Samuel Andrews built a new home on Euclid Avenue that outshone all his neighbors. He had a flair for doing the unreasonable and his new home was no exception. It was a five-story brick structure with thirty-three rooms. It required a hundred servants to keep it and the grounds. It was soon abandoned because of lack of help to run it.[24]

Flagler took an active part in the business life of the city, but engaged in none of the social activities.[25] His religious activities which he always enjoyed were limited because of his wife's increasingly poor health. It was said that for the last seventeen years of his wife's life, 1864 to 1881, Flagler spent only two evenings away from home. He found diversion from business in reading aloud to his wife. His children also claimed much of his time. Occasionally he would take a portion of an afternoon from his office to carry the two little Flaglers on a picnic in the country. He was an ardent member of the Cleveland Board of Trade, and the Manufacturers Association of Cleveland, but neither took much time away from his family or his business. Two years after the Civil War was over he urged the Board of Trade to donate money for the destitute people of the South, especially Georgia, where the horrors of war were so forcibly seen. At the insistence of J. J. Jones of Harrison County, Georgia, Flagler contributed $110.00 to the cause, his sum being equalled by four other Cleveland citizens.[26] On December 2,

[24] Ella G. Wilson, *Famous Old Euclid Avenue*, 2–15.
[25] *Cleveland Leader*, 1865–1880.
[26] *Ibid.*, May 7, 1867.

1867, he was elected one of the seventy-three delegates from Cleveland to attend the National Manufacturers Convention, to be held in the same city. He felt that such activities were a part of his business.[27]

The new firm of Rockefeller, Andrews and Flagler was a thriving business from the start. Its growth was never in doubt. Among Flagler's duties was the one of drawing up the contracts. This he always did well despite the fact he had no legal training. The intent and purpose of the contract was always stated accurately and clearly. Rockefeller, a fair judge of men, always insisted that Flagler had more common sense than almost anyone else.[28] Another of his activities included the construction of new refineries. He always insisted on putting up sound structures. He would not allow a flimsy shack to be built. As John D. Rockefeller later stated,

> Everyone was so afraid that the oil would disappear and that the money expended in building would be a loss that the meanest and cheapest buildings were erected for use as refineries. This was the sort of thing Mr. Flagler objected to. While he had to admit that it was possible the oil supply might fail and that the risks of the trade were great, he always believed that if we went into the oil business at all, we should do the work as well as we knew how; that we should have the very best facilities; that everything should be solid and substantial; and that nothing should be left undone to produce the finest results.[29]

The new firm expanded its business widely. William Rockefeller opened up European markets and sold a large amount of oil abroad. Flagler and Rockefeller were elated over the increase in the volume of business. Rockefeller later

[27] *Ibid.*, December 3, 1867.
[28] J. K. Winkler, *John D., A Portrait in Oils,* 85.
[29] J. D. Rockefeller, "Random Reminiscences of Men and Events," *loc. cit.,* 10881.

spoke of the fun they had as young men watching their business enlarge.[30] When Flagler went into the business they were refining about 500 barrels each day. Two years later they were shipping 1500 barrels of refined oil and 3,000 barrels of crude oil each day.[31]

The partnership did not fail to make use of the by-products of petroleum. For instance, no market had yet developed for gasoline, and while most refiners were trying to find a place to dispose of it, Rockefeller and Flagler used it as fuel. Flagler had added to the partnership energy, aggressiveness and drive, along with the combination of qualities already contributed by Rockefeller. Together they formed a smoothly functioning unit. Flagler's most important contribution to the business was perhaps in the field of freight-rate negotiations. He took over that task as soon as he joined Rockefeller, realizing that transportation continued to be one of the biggest obstacles the refiners had to hurdle. Any refiner who had the advantage in the transportation business usually had the advantage in the petroleum industry; so he put himself to the task of out-maneuvering the other refiners. Pipe lines were used and so was water transportation, but not as extensively then as railroads, because the railroads had early learned what profits might result from the petroleum industry.

In the late sixties there were three different railroad systems serving as an outlet from the oil regions. The Atlantic and Great Western, which in 1868 was absorbed by Jay Gould into his Erie System, shuttled into the oil regions at Titusville and Franklin. The second railroad, the Lake Shore and Michigan Southern, which later became a part of the New York Central, tapped the regions at Oil City. The Pennsylvania was the third road reaching into the petroleum-producing area. It controlled the Allegheny Valley Railroad,

[30] Allan Nevins, *John D. Rockefeller*, I, 275.
[31] Matthew Josephson, *The Robber Barons*, 112.

terminating at Franklin, and the Philadelphia and Erie which served Franklin and Titusville. All three of these railroad systems made great profits from oil traffic, and competition among them was spirited.[32]

Jay Gould's Erie System was possibly the first railroad to favor Rockefeller, Andrews and Flagler with special rates and rebates, because Gould wanted to divert all of the crude oil shipments to the Cleveland market.[33] Gould also favored two other Cleveland refineries at this time. As chief negotiator, Flagler also began to bargain very early with the Lake Shore. This was one of the few roads which brought crude petroleum from the oil regions to Cleveland where it was refined. From Cleveland the refined product could easily be routed on to New York by the Lake Shore–New York Central route. J. H. Devereux became vice-president and general manager of the Lake Shore in 1868, and Flagler very soon found favor with the Civil War general. Both Flagler and Devereux were just beginning in their respective fields, and each was determined to make good. Flagler approached Devereux on the proposition that Lake Shore give him a rate of thirty-five cents a barrel on crude oil from the oil regions to Cleveland and $1.30 on refined oil from Cleveland to New York. In return for this consideration, Rockefeller, Andrews and Flagler would guarantee to ship sixty carloads each day, and in addition would assume any risk due to fire. It is not known exactly what the refund or rebate amounted to, but it was probably not less than fifteen cents on each barrel of oil shipped. At any rate, the agreement was made which put

[32] Allan Nevins, *John D. Rockefeller*, I, 254, 255.

[33] C. M. Destler, "The Standard Oil, Child of the Erie Ring, 1868–1872. Six Contracts and a Letter," *Mississippi Valley Historical Review*, XXXIII (June, 1946), 93. Professor Destler differs with Professor Nevins on this point concerning the first rebate received by the firm of Rockefeller, Andrews and Flagler. Destler maintains that this early connection between the Erie System and Rockefeller, Andrews and Flagler was very significant, and helped materially in the later development of the Standard Oil Company. *Ibid.*, 96.

the partnership in a fair position to out-distance its competitors.[34] Flagler was jubilant over the agreement, because he had won a great victory.

Flagler was, without doubt, one of the pioneers in the practice of rebates; however, he later maintained that Thomas Scott, of the Pennsylvania Railroad, was the instigator of the practice.[35] Much concerning these early rebates was held in secrecy; however, it was pretty generally known that many of the refiners were being favored by them. Because of Flagler's efforts, his firm began to receive greater concessions from the Lake Shore. One railroad was played against the other by the shrewd Flagler and his associates until they became the favored refiners in Cleveland, as far as railroad rates were concerned. As their volume of shipping increased, their rebates grew. When other refiners complained, as they often did, and petitioned for equal treatment, their request was usually denied. The railroads always told them if they would ship as much oil as Rockefeller, Andrews and Flagler, they would be given the same rebates.[36] To the refiners, then, it was a simple case of the survival of the fittest. The era of ruthless competitive warfare had begun. Every refiner realized that his days were numbered unless he could outdo his competitor. Flagler had put his firm way out in front. He and Rockefeller were destined to win the race.

Both Rockefeller and Flagler realized the importance of expansion. The possibility of merging or combining with weaker refineries had already been considered by the two men. Their business was foremost in their thinking; their planning was constant. These perfectly mated partners studied very carefully the methods which the Western Union Telegraph Company had used in forming its combination,

[34] John T. Flynn, *God's Gold, The Story of Rockefeller and His Times,* 145.
[35] *New York Tribune,* December 23, 1906.
[36] I. M. Tarbell, "Rise of the Standard Oil Company," *loc. cit.,* XX (December, 1902), 117.

and they watched also the methods used by the railroads in the process of combining and forming large systems.

Flagler first mentioned to Rockefeller the possibility of combining with smaller refineries one morning as they were walking to work. Rockefeller thought about the idea and replied, "Yes, Henry, I'd like to combine sóme of these refineries with ours. The business would be much more simple. But how are you going to determine the unit of valuation? How are you going to find a yardstick to measure their value?" In a few minutes Flagler answered, "John, I'll find a yardstick." [37]

That very same afternoon Flagler went hunting for refineries and found an operator on the lake front who was about ready to quit. The man said that oil was not his game, and, after a little while with Flagler, he was convinced that he would never make any money at it. Flagler bought him out for $4700. This was the first move towards combination, or perhaps the first step towards the creation of what was later the Standard Oil Company. By 1869 Rockefeller, Andrews and Flagler had out-distanced all the other refineries in Cleveland.[38] In all of these earlier purchases, Flagler used his "yardstick"; he determined the value of the refinery and set the price which he and Rockefeller would pay for the property. His aggressiveness often caught his seller off guard, and the "bargains" he obtained on his purchases warmed the cockles of Rockefeller's heart. He was more adept at meeting people than Rockefeller. This trait of Flagler's served well to enrich himself and his partners. Rockefeller later stated that Flagler was always on the active side of every question, and that his energy was responsible for the rapid growth and progress of the partnership, and later for the Standard Oil Company; Flagler's faith in the future of oil production often boosted his partner's spirits. Said Rockefeller, "His courage

[37] J. K. Winkler, *John D., A Portrait in Oils*, 78.
[38] *Ibid.*, 80–84.

in acting up to his beliefs laid strong foundations for later years." [39]

In these early years of the partnership, Samuel Andrews did only the technical work. Rockefeller commented later that "he had nothing whatever to do with the office affairs, or the oil freighting business, and would not have had as much knowledge about these questions as the clerks in our office." [40] But chubby, friendly Samuel Andrews made a definite contribution to the partnership which bore his name.

In the opinion of the scholars who have studied the men connected with the rise of the petroleum industry, Flagler stands very high. Allan Nevins comments that "next to John D. Rockefeller," Flagler counted for most in industry in Cleveland.[41] John T. Flynn maintains that Flagler did a great deal of Rockefeller's thinking, and that the "two men were admirably suited to each other," and that Flagler, "a bold, unscrupulous self-seeker . . . could be relied upon to propose the needful course. . . ." [42] John Winkler believed that Flagler was "fully as capable an organizer" as Rockefeller and did most for the rapidly expanding monopoly.[43] Ida M. Tarbell declared that when the Standard Oil Company was formed Flagler, next to Rockefeller, was the strongest man in the firm. He was untiring in his efforts to increase the business. Miss Tarbell believed that he "had no scruples to make him hesitate over the ethical quality of a contract which was advantageous." She continued, "He was not a secretive man, like John D. Rockefeller, not a dreamer, but he could keep his mouth shut when necessary and he knew the worth of a financial dream when it was laid before him." [44]

[39] J. D. Rockefeller, "Random Reminiscences of Men and Events," *loc. cit.,* 10885.

[40] Rockefeller to Allan Nevins, quoted in Nevins, *John D. Rockefeller,* I, 274.

[41] Allan Nevins, *John D. Rockefeller,* I, 274.

[42] J. T. Flynn, *God's Gold, The Story of Rockefeller and His Times,* 172.

[43] J. K. Winkler, *John D., A Portrait in Oils,* 74.

[44] I. M. Tarbell, *Rise of the Standard Oil Company,* I, 50.

Florida's Flagler

There can be no doubt that Henry M. Flagler was an important figure in the infant petroleum industry. As the industry expanded the more important he became and the richer he grew. His sights were fixed on the future.

FIVE

The Standard Oil Company

THE petroleum industry was booming by 1870. The center of most of the activity dealing with oil was in northwestern Pennsylvania around Titusville and Oil City. This section, which had become popularly known as the oil regions, was not more than fifty miles in length. Not only were the oil wells located there, but also some of the petroleum was refined there. Earlier the oil regions were unimportant, but after 1860 no other section of the country was more famous. Cleveland, Ohio, was not far away, and it, too, soon became prominent in the petroleum industry as a refining center. Pittsburgh and Philadelphia gave promise as refining towns, but because of Cleveland's location on the shores of Lake Erie, the Ohio city soon took the edge over other refining towns. More and more crude oil was shipped from the oil regions to Cleveland for the refining process because of transportation facilities and the aggressiveness of the refiners there. It was due largely to the efforts of Henry M. Flagler and John D. Rockefeller that the city became so prominently known for its refining activities.[1]

Rockefeller and Flagler had been very successful in their efforts to take over or combine most of the small refineries in Cleveland. Their own organization had grown considerably during the years 1867–1870, but they were now on the threshold of further expansion by means of the combining

[1] G. H. Montague, "The Rise and Supremacy of the Standard Oil Company," *loc. cit.*, 272–273.

and unifying process. The historian might point, however, to the fact that the late sixties and seventies were a period in which a great deal of unifying was being done in the economic world. Several big combinations were in the making. There was the realization that more could be accomplished with a bigger, stronger organization than with one smaller and weaker. Rockefeller said later that there was always the possibility of making more money with a larger organization.[2] Both Rockefeller and Flagler were bent on making money. That was the motive behind most of their actions.

Rockefeller, Andrews, and Flagler decided to incorporate their partnership in 1869 because they needed more capital to accomplish all they had planned. It is safe to say that Henry M. Flagler conceived the plan for incorporation. Later when John D. Rockefeller was asked if the Standard Oil Company was the result of his thinking, he answered, "No, sir. I wish I'd had the brains to think of it. It was Henry M. Flagler." [3] Rockefeller thought at first the idea was farfetched, and that it probably would not work, but Flagler proved to him that it would. Many times later Flagler's imagination and ingenuity were responsible for the continued growth of the business.[4]

The Standard Oil Company became a reality on January 11, 1870, when the partnership was incorporated as a joint stock company.[5] The *Cleveland Leader*, which became very friendly to the Standard Oil Company, had this comment to make several days after the incorporation:

On the 11th inst., one of the most flourishing oil companies of this city, commencing business with a full paid capital of

[2] John Moody, *Truth About the Trusts*, 112.
[3] Edwin Lefèvre, "Flagler and Florida," in *Everybody's Magazine*, XXII (February, 1910), 183.
[4] William H. Allen, *Rockefeller, Giant, Dwarf, Symbol*, 188.
[5] The act of incorporation was signed on January 10, 1870; however, the *Cleveland Leader* claims January 11, 1870, as the day for incorporation.

one million dollars, was incorporated under the name of the 'Standard Oil Company.' The corporators are John D. Rockefeller, Henry M. Flagler, Samuel Andrews, Stephen V. Harkness and William Rockefeller. The company has purchased of Rockefeller, Andrews and Flagler all their real estate, factories, offices, etc., in Cleveland, Oil City and New York. Their real estate in Cleveland amounts to about fifty acres in the heart of the city. The offices and factories possess all the requisites found in business establishments of the highest order.

A meeting of the directors of the company was held on the 13th inst., and the following officers were elected: President, John D. Rockefeller; vice-president, William Rockefeller; secretary and treasurer, H. M. Flagler; superintendent, Samuel Andrews.

The general offices are in the Cushing block, and are connected with the refinery by telegraph. The branch office is at 181 Pearl Street, and the warehouse is at Hunter's Point, New York.[6]

The act of incorporation under laws of Ohio was signed by Rockefeller, Flagler, Andrews, and Stephen V. Harkness, all of Cleveland, and by William Rockefeller, of New York. The amount of the capital of the new corporation was one million dollars. It was divided into ten thousand shares, valued at one hundred dollars each. The largest stockholder was John D. Rockefeller who took 2,667. This amount represented new investments in the corporation as well as his old holdings in the partnership of Rockefeller, Andrews and Flagler. The second largest stockholder was Stephen V. Harkness, the silent partner in the old firm, who subscribed for 1,334 shares. Flagler, along with Samuel Andrews and William Rockefeller, took 1,333 shares each. The old partnership of Rockefeller, Andrews and Flagler bought 1,000 shares as a unit, and the last 1,000 shares were subscribed by a new-

[6] *Cleveland Leader,* January 19, 1870.

comer, O. B. Jennings, brother-in-law of William Rockefeller, from New York. It was a new corporation but nine-tenths of the stock was owned by those people who had invested in the partnership in 1867. Jennings, the only new person in the group, was there because of William Rockefeller's influence.

Standard Oil was born as a big enterprise. It had cut its teeth as a partnership and was now ready to plunge forward into a period of greater expansion and development. It soon was doing one-tenth of all the petroleum business in the United States. Besides its two refineries and a barrel plant in Cleveland, it possessed a fleet of tank cars and warehouses in the oil regions as well as warehouses and tanks in New York.[7] The new organization, which gave Rockefeller and Flagler better opportunities for flexibility, was planned to make easy the entrance of new capital into the business. At the same time Flagler and Rockefeller did not intend to relinquish leadership in the new firm. The two Rockefellers, Flagler, and Harkness owned nearly seven-tenths of the corporation. There was no question about Rockefeller and Flagler continuing as the leading figures in the new organization.

In order to control completely the production in Cleveland, Rockefeller and Flagler made no secret of their plans to buy or force out of existence all the refiners there with whom they had not already combined. Their chief competitors in Cleveland were Clarke, Payne and Company; Alexander, Scofield and Company; Hanna, Bashington and Company; Westlake, Hutchins and Company; Cleveland Petroleum Refining Company; and Critchley, Fawcett and Company. In addition to these, there were a number of small plants—a total of twenty-five in Cleveland in 1870. Some of them were producing only a barrel or two of oil a day, and most of them were being very inefficiently operated. Flagler and Rockefeller studied the situation as if playing chess or checkers. Their next move was important because of their determina-

---

[7] Allan Nevins, *John D. Rockefeller*, I, 292.

tion to control all the refinery interests in Cleveland. Shrewdly, they moved forward.[8]

Several of the smaller refineries closed their businesses in anticipation of what was to come. The refiners talked among themselves about their future. Theirs was a feeling of terror and despair. Since there was nothing that could be done against this strength that opposed them, within a few months after the Standard Oil Company was incorporated twenty of the twenty-five refiners were in the hands of Rockefeller and Flagler.[9] The public was getting a good taste of the corporation, which, up to 1870, was less prominent than the partnership, but which was to become vastly more powerful in the years to come. There was some little criticism, but people were too stunned by the suddenness of the Standard's actions to realize what had happened.

Flagler always denied that the "freezing-out" process was Standard Oil's only method. When a competitor was approached on the subject of combining with the corporation, he was given his choice of accepting cash or stock in the firm. Most of the small oil men, realizing they could not stay in competition with Standard Oil in Cleveland, sold out for cash, and retired from the business in disgust. This group became violent critics of the rising corporation, as naturally they would.[10] No matter how much they wanted to justify their actions, Rockefeller and Flagler could not convince the public that they were right. Opposition to the corporation began to mount, and hate was rapidly engendered for the two Standard leaders. Rockefeller and Flagler contended that any "killing" of a competitor's business was always done in a cheerful way. Flagler tells about one victim of the Standard Oil who was considered a "freeze-out" case, as follows:

[8] Ida M. Tarbell, "The Rise of the Standard Oil Company," in *McClure's Magazine*, XX (December, 1902), 121.
[9] John T. Flynn, *God's Gold, The Story of Rockefeller and His Times*, 160.
[10] "He Made Florida," *Literary Digest*, XLVI (May 31, 1913), 1241.

When I was selling flour and grain in Cleveland, I had a certain German for a customer. He owned a bakery in the suburbs, and I often trusted him for a barrel of flour when collections were slow and money was scarce. One day I met him on the street, and he surprised me by saying that he had sold his bakery and was running a little oil refinery. Usually Mr. Rockefeller and I walked downtown in the morning to talk over private matters. Next day I told him about the little German baker who had gone into the oil business without my knowledge. We bought the refinery for $5,200. The German owed $5,000. At my suggestion he took $2,700 in money, with which he pacified his creditors for the time being, and $2,500 in Standard stock. We made him superintendent of our stove department and sent him into the woods, where he arose to a salary of $8,000 a year. I was pleased later to ask him for his $2,500 in stock and to issue in its stead $50,000 of stock in the larger corporation. Still later he received $10,000 more in a stock dividend.[11]

On another occasion Frank Arter, small Cleveland refiner, was being threatened by Standard Oil. Flagler offered him $4,000 in stock for his business, but Arter held out for $25,000 in cash. The trade was deadlocked for some time, but soon the small refiner realized that he could not buck the larger corporation; he yielded and let his refinery become absorbed by Standard Oil. Frank Arter died a rich man a number of years later.[12] Perhaps these cases were exceptional ones. Other smaller refiners were not so lucky. There can be no question of Standard Oil's ruthlessness. To Flagler their methods were just good business; Rockefeller agreed. By 1872 Standard Oil had bought out most of the larger as well as the smaller refiners in Cleveland and many new stockholders appeared in the Company, among them being Amasa Stone, Benjamin Brewster, J. A. Bostwick, P. H. Watson, and O. H. Payne.[13]

This process of concentration among the stronger concerns

[11] *New York Tribune*, December 23, 1906.
[12] Conversation with Harris Gillespie.
[13] *New York Tribune*, December 23, 1906.

and extermination of the weaker ones continued for several years. No refinery could stand up under the savage competition of such organizations as the Standard Oil unless it had a capital of at least $500,000. Through its process of concentration and its superior efficiency, the Standard Oil Company became larger than all its competitors in Titusville, Pittsburgh, Oil City, and New York. The first round in the battle for the survival of the fittest was over. From this time on instead of each refiner's being primarily interested in the efficiency of production, he was interested more in cheaper transportation, in order that he might survive competition and stay in business. The advantage each sought was in favorable rebates.[14]

Flagler's experience in securing rebates since 1867 gave him an advantage over most of the refiners. He played the game shrewdly. The Standard Oil Company's first concession in the field of rebates came from the Lake Shore Railroad. Flagler secured for Standard Oil a better freight contract than the one previously granted to the old partnership. At this time the Company was shipping some of its oil to New York and other eastern points by water, which was a slow method. Since the bad feature about water transportation was the inability to use it the year round, Flagler agreed to ship oil by Lake Shore Railroad all through the year, and guaranteed a volume of sixty carloads of oil each day, whether business was good or bad. Of course, a heavy rebate was asked for this consideration on the part of Standard Oil. Competitors of Standard Oil also asked Lake Shore for the same favors granted Standard Oil. They were told that they would receive the same consideration only when they shipped as much oil as Standard Oil Company.[15] Standard Oil managed to stay out front. They had established their advantage and did not mean to relinquish it.

Other railroads began to lower their rates, and soon a real

[14] Gilbert H. Montague, *The Rise and Progress of the Standard Oil Company*, 11.
[15] Allan Nevins, *John D. Rockefeller*, I, 296, 297.

freight war was on for traffic to points both east and west of Cleveland. The New York Central, the Erie, and the Pennsylvania Railroad had completed connections all the way to Chicago and they fought each other bitterly for traffic. Even though they met once each year and agreed on certain freight rates, they regularly broke their agreement in order to get a larger volume of business. This reckless competition extended into the oil regions. The Pennsylvania Railroad hauled oil to Pittsburgh and to Philadelphia. The Erie Railroad, which entered the oil fields by a connection with the Atlantic and Great Western road, hauled oil to New York, as did the New York Central, which bought out the Lake Shore Railroad. So well were the Standard Oil Company's traffic affairs managed by Henry M. Flagler that he could ship oil 740 miles to New York by New York Central at precisely the same rate the Pittsburgh refiners were charged for a haulage of 400 miles.[16]

In 1872 Rockefeller and Flagler became involved in a scheme known as the South Improvement Company which created much opposition and criticism, especially in the oil regions. It is not known if Rockefeller or Flagler actually had anything to do with creating the South Improvement Company. Flagler said later that neither he nor Rockefeller believed in the idea at first, but they were forced to join under pressure. He said in testifying before a House Committee investigating trusts that it originated with Peter H. Watson and W. G. Warden. This may or may not be true. John Flynn, however, states that the scheme had all the earmarks of Flagler's mind and experience, despite the fact that he denied any responsibility for its origination.[17] Other scholars in the field have also accused Flagler of conceiving the idea.[18] The one thing that looked a bit suspicious was the fact that no

[16] G. H. Montague, *op. cit.*, 269–271.
[17] J. T. Flynn, *God's Gold, The Story of Rockefeller and His Times*, 151.
[18] Herbert Asbury, *The Golden Flood*, 300.

one admitted having begun the South Improvement plan, and all blamed different people.

The name of the scheme was a misnomer. In fact, the South (or Southern as it was correctly written) Improvement Company had no significance at all, for the gist of the whole plan was to bring together secretly all the refiners and shippers, and to force the railroads to give special rebates and drawbacks. In other words, the South Improvement Company was set up to do throughout Ohio, Pennsylvania, and New York what the Standard Oil Company had done in Cleveland— exterminate all opposition and competition that would not yield to the monstrous corporation. The price of oil had decreased over a period of several years, because of overproduction and the falling off of the foreign market; so the producers felt that a larger combination would tend to force prices up at least fifty per cent. By controlling the refining interest they could also fix their own price on crude oil shipped from the oil regions. Since they would be the only buyers and sellers, the speculative aspect of the business would not exist. The plans looked perfect on paper—they would put the entire petroleum industry in the hands of a few persons. The combination was projected on January 2, 1872, in Philadelphia; however, no new charter was secured from the state for the organization. By an act of the Pennsylvania legislature on May 1, 1871, the South Improvement Company had been created and had been vested with all the powers given by a previous act of April 7, 1870. The secondhand charter with which the oil men formed the new combination had power "to construct and operate any work or works, public or private, designed to include, increase, facilitate, or develop trade, travel, or the transportation of freight, livestock, passengers, or any traffic by land or water, from or to any part of the United States." [19] This very indefinite charter had no connection with what the oil men were trying to do. The name was

[19] G. H. Montague, *op. cit.*, 272.

so misleading that the officers talked of changing it to the American Cooperative Refining Company, but they never got around to doing it.[20] By no means were they as vague about their business as was the charter. There were 2,000 shares created in the South Improvement Company; of that number, 900 were owned by Henry M. Flagler, John D. and William Rockefeller, O. H. Payne, and H. Bostwick. The fact that all these men were prominent in the Standard Oil Company gave rise to speculation as to the part that that corporation played in the newly created enterprise.

The South Improvement Company lost no time in making preliminary plans for its operations. It completed contracts on January 18, 1872, with the Pennsylvania, the New York Central, and the Erie Railroad, by which the South Improvement Company was to ship forty-five per cent of all its oil by Pennsylvania, and to divide equally the rest of its shipments between the Erie Railroad and the New York Central Railroad. The company also agreed to furnish adequate storage facilities for the oil both en route and at its destination, and to keep an accurate check on all the petroleum shipped over the railroads both by itself and other parties. The three railroads in return were to allow the South Improvement Company rebates on all shipments carried by them. They agreed to charge all other refiners, who were not affiliated with the South Improvement Company, not less than full rates and to protect the South Improvement Company from any loss or injury by competition. The spider was in the process of winding his web a little tighter around the helpless independent refiner.

The agreement between the South Improvement Company and the railroads supposedly went into effect on February 26. Up to this time much secrecy had shrouded the developments; in fact, not much was known about the new company, but word got around among the producers in the oil regions

[20] *Cleveland Leader,* April 11, 1872.

as to the purpose of the organization. On February 27 the oil
regions, and especially Titusville, became thoroughly aroused.
At first the producers did not believe what they heard, but
they were soon seeing for themselves. The oil drillers in the
regions realized what the South Improvement Company
would mean for them, and they did not intend to fall in line
with any such proposition. An impromptu mass meeting was
held in the Titusville opera house to throw up some sort of
defense against the newly organized combination. Producers
from all over the oil regions were there ready to take some
sort of action. They were not rough nor rowdy but they
were angry and were determined not to yield to the refiners,
headed by Rockefeller and Flagler. The meeting resulted in
the formation of the Petroleum Producers Union, whose sole
purpose was to fight the South Improvement Company. That
was the most important thing accomplished; however, several
other actions were taken. A committee was chosen to ask the
legislature of Pennsylvania to revoke the charter of the South
Improvement Company, and another committee was appointed to ask the Congress of the United States to investigate
the whole situation. It also ordered that a review of the conspiracy against them be written and that a list of names of the
persons involved be made ready. A lengthy report was prepared and 30,000 copies were distributed. This review told an
extremely ugly tale about Rockefeller, Flagler, and their associates. They were dubbed traitors to the industry. For
weeks all the producers in the oil regions abandoned regular
business and surged from place to place speaking and holding
demonstrations. The whole section was awakened to action.
They were intent on destroying the "Monster" or the "Great
Anaconda," as the South Improvement Company was called,
and its "Forty Thieves" as Rockefeller, Flagler, and the other
refiners were referred to. The producers expected nothing
but robbery from the railroads, for, after all, they were accustomed to that; but they refused to be robbed by men in

their own business like the refiners. In other words, they would not sit idly by while the railroads and refiners teamed up against them. The leader in this movement against the South Improvement Company was John D. Archbold, who, strangely enough, later became vice-president of the Standard Oil Trust.[21]

It was open warfare for some time between the Petroleum Producers Union and the South Improvement Company. The controversy lasted for about forty days before anything was actually accomplished. The Producers Union headed by William Hasson refused to let oil supplies leave the wells. This action antedated the modern strike. The industry was at a standstill, since as long as it could get no oil from the wells, the refiners and the railroads might as well not have been in business. In most refining cities the plants were closed, and in Cleveland mass meetings for the relief of workmen were held. There was much excitement; strangely enough, though, very little vandalism was committed. Cooler heads prevailed. On April 15, 1872, the refiners gave in, and promised to dissolve their scheme of combination. The South Improvement Company had failed, but its actual origin remained in darkness.[22]

Throughout the conflict, public sympathy lay with the Producers Union. Most of the newspapers helped out the fight against the combination of refiners and railroads. The *New York Tribune* insisted that the combination was trying to choke the life from the producers. The *Derrick* of Oil City went so far as to publish a black list of all the refiners involved in the conspiracy. Fortunately for Henry M. Flagler, his name was omitted from the first list, but he was just as deeply involved as any on the list which included Watson, Rockefeller, Bostwick, Warden, and others.[23] The *Cleveland Herald*

[21] I. M. Tarbell, "The Oil War of 1872," *loc. cit.*, XX (January, 1903), 248.
[22] *Ibid.*, 252.
[23] *Ibid.*, 249.

opposed the combination but knew little about what it was. The editor assured the refiners that he doubted the organization was for their benefit.[24] The *Herald's* competitor, the *Cleveland Leader*, however, took an opposing view. The *Leader* tried to make the Cleveland refiners think the new company would solve all their problems, but it was about as vague in trying to do so as the charter of the combination.[25] On April 11, 1872, the *Leader* published a lengthy statement signed by the Standard Oil Company and four other refineries in which they tried to justify the existence of the South Improvement Company. Their attempt to make the producers like it was feeble, and they failed miserably.[26]

During the heat of battle between the producers and the refiners, the House of Representatives started an investigation of the giant scheme, as the producers had requested. President U. S. Grant, well known for the scandals in his administration about this time, was interested in the conspiracy which was trying to take root in Pennsylvania and urged that some official action be taken. Nothing immediate came of the investigation, though in an indirect way it perhaps helped to influence the refiners to yield. At any rate, the South Improvement Company never did a dollar's worth of business. Because of all the opposition it could never get started and soon died in embryo.[27]

Instead of losing from the South Improvement scheme, the railroads actually gained. General George B. McClellan, president of the Atlantic and Great Western Railroad, started the ball rolling when he made overtures to the producers while the oil war was in process. He told the producers that he was not interested in becoming allied with the refiners. It was not long before the railroads revoked their contracts with the South Improvement Company, and one by one made contracts

[24] *Cleveland Herald*, March 2, 1872.
[25] *Cleveland Leader*, February 27–April 10, 1872.
[26] *Ibid.*, April 11, 1872.
[27] Henry D. Lloyd, *Wealth Against Commonwealth*, 59.

with the producers. But the victory for the producers was not to last, for some of the refiners still had plans to alter the situation.

Rockefeller and Flagler were impressed with the possibilities of such an organization as the South Improvement Company and did not mean to let the scheme die. They planned to create another combination very similar to the former one. Both Flagler and Rockefeller had faith in their ability to get the railroads on their side. Flagler knew if he could give them enough traffic they would do anything or sign any contract he offered them. Consequently, their next move was to carry their racket to other refiners. They went to Pittsburgh and talked their plan over with several men who they thought would be interested, and then journeyed on to Titusville where they hoped to sell it to other refiners there. The scheme became known as the Pittsburgh plan, since it originated in that city.

In early May, 1872, Flagler and Rockefeller appeared on the streets in Titusville. They talked with Jacob J. Vandergrift, one of the oil region refiners. Then they went calling on other refiners in the region. They even convinced John D. Archbold, the leading refiner of the oil regions, of their plan. They argued that their new scheme was void of any of the objectionable features of the old scheme, in that it was not clouded by secrecy and suspicion. Finally a public meeting was called on May 15 and 16, at which time the new Pittsburgh plan was explained. Henry M. Flagler acted as spokesman for the visiting refiners, and he did a creditable job in trying to explain the new scheme to the local refiners, and later in trying to defend it. The organization, called the Central Association of Refiners, would cater to all refiners. He explained that it was a scheme to save the oil industry rather than destroy it. There was to be an organization to manage the oil business throughout the United States, and all refiners were allowed to become stockholders. There was to be a board of directors, which was to handle the buying of crude oil and all arrangements for transportation. It was assumed that the parent organization was to be the Standard Oil Company. The audience, which was filled with hundreds of producers as well as refiners, listened very attentively to Flagler's speech, but they had not forgotten that he was connected with the South Improvement scheme, and the producers greatly distrusted him. After Flagler finished, both John D. Archbold and J. J. Vandergrift, oil regions refiners, tried to speak in favor of the new scheme, but the patience of most of the audience had been worn threadbare. Neither Archbold nor Vandergrift was allowed to speak. They were howled down by all sorts of uncomplimentary remarks and were dubbed traitors because of their current affiliation with Flagler and Rockefeller. Several producers made impromptu speeches, denouncing the plan as "rotten" and "overbearing." Flagler and Rockefeller were greatly embarrassed, to say nothing of their associates. The meeting was adjourned in an uproar. Flagler and Rockefeller went back to Cleveland beaten men. They had walked into an open trap, set for them by their enemies in Titusville and the oil regions.[28]

Neither Rockefeller nor Flagler was the kind to be discouraged by a setback. They were convinced that a large-scale combination could be perfected, and they were determined to carry their point. Their next attempt was to organize the National Refiners Association, which was a scheme very similar to the Pittsburgh plan, but it, too, failed before very long. Then another attempt to organize the refiners came in the summer of 1874, the result of a well-planned scheme. As two of the biggest refiners outside of Cleveland were Charles Lockhart and W. G. Warden, the new plan was to include them both. Lockhart and Warden were asked to be the guests of Rockefeller and Flagler at a fashionable hotel in

[28] I. M. Tarbell, "An Unholy Alliance," *loc. cit.*, XX (February, 1903), 390–391.

Saratoga, New York. The gathering of the four men involved a few social activities, but the main purpose of their short stay in Saratoga was to sell their two guests on the idea of consolidating with the Standard Oil Company. Saratoga had been the planning grounds three years before for the first big consolidation plan, the South Improvement Company. Their plan for wholesale consolidation was certain to work this time. As the four men dined and talked together, Rockefeller and Flagler revealed to their guests the success they had achieved in bringing all the refiners in Cleveland together under their direction. They explained that the Standard Oil Company at that time had such a monopoly there that their profit in 1873 was over a million dollars. It was the result of combination in one city. The hosts went ahead to prove that they could do nothing by an open association. It had to be a closed affair. Lockhart and Warden were impressed by Standard's record of achievement in Cleveland, and they had visions of a larger combination in which they might figure prominently. Rockefeller and Flagler made it plain that in any new arrangement Standard Oil Company would continue to take the lead; however, the four men present—Rockefeller, Flagler, Lockhart, and Warden—would become the nucleus of the new company which would gradually acquire control of all refiners everywhere. Their scheme also included a mastery of the railroads in the matter of freight rates.[29]

The conference lasted for six hours, and at the conclusion Warden and Lockhart were thoroughly sold on the plan. They agreed to transfer their refineries, which were located in Philadelphia and Pittsburgh, to the Standard Oil Company in Cleveland. In exchange they took stock in the organization and continued to operate their respective plants as if no change had taken place. No doubt Rockefeller and Flagler were elated that evening as they returned to their room in the United States Hotel. No doubt a celebration dinner was held with all

[29] *Ibid.*, 495–96.

the trimmings. At any rate these two canny, money-lustful, yet pious, men were happy. They were definitely on the right road to the control of a vast industry which would lead to enormous wealth. All this transaction was done in secrecy, because of the popular disapproval of such action. Public opinion had been partially responsible for the defeat of the previous plans. Lockhart and Warden also agreed to help in the process of absorption of smaller refineries. They were to start a campaign of persuasion as soon as they reached their respective homes. This they did most effectively. Further consolidation took place very soon. On October 15, 1874, in secret purchase, the Standard Oil Company engulfed Charles Pratt and Company of New York. This brought into the fold Charles Pratt and H. H. Rogers, two of the shrewdest oil men in the business. Pratt and Company continued to operate under its own name, ostensibly the chief rival of the Standard Oil Company in New York. With Warden, Lockhart and Pratt now in the company, Rockefeller and Flagler had as their allies the most successful men in the business. Added to this advantage was the fact that the new associates in the business were located in three of the best refining centers in the country outside of Cleveland—Philadelphia, Pittsburgh, and New York.[30]

Their next move was to invade the oil regions and become entrenched in such towns as Titusville and Oil City; accordingly, they approached John D. Archbold and J. J. Vandergrift. Both men had at first violently opposed any such action with the Standard Oil Company, but they realized that no progress in the future could be made without some connection with the firm. They, too, agreed to absorb all of the small oil companies in that region. The Standard Oil Company increased its stock on March 10, 1875, to $3,500,000 in order to take care of these new purchases. Ten thousand shares were added and Warden and Lockhart secured 6,250 of them.

[30] *Ibid.*, 496.

71

Charles Pratt received 3,125 and the remaining 625 were subscribed by S. V. Harkness.[31]

In addition to this monstrous growth, the Standard Oil also had a monopoly with the railroads and pipe lines. The pipe lines, which were rapidly being used for the transportation of oil, were falling under the control of one or the other of the great systems which were being created. This battle, which the Standard Oil finally won, was centered against the Empire Transportation Company. By 1878 the Standard Oil Company controlled most of the pipe lines carrying petroleum from the oil regions.[32] Rockefeller and Flagler were also dictating the rates they were to receive from the railroads. The New York Central, the Erie and the Pennsylvania railroads were not hard to convince. This practice of fixing rates continued despite rising opposition from the public against discrimination on the part of the railroads.

The story of how the Standard Oil Company and its affiliates drove all the other refineries out of business is an interesting one. There was not any stopping of the rampaging organization. Among the many new subsidiaries of the Standard Oil Company in the late seventies were the following: the Standard Oil Company of Pittsburgh, the Atlantic Refining Company of Philadelphia, the Acme Oil Company, the Imperial Oil Company, Charles Pratt and Company, J. A. Bostwick and Company, the Sonce and Fleming Company, the Camden Company, and the Baltimore United Oil Company. All these companies worked faithfully in their respective communities, which extended from New York to Cleveland, in bringing smaller refineries into the fold. Their connection with the parent organization, the Standard Oil Company located in Cleveland, was never mentioned; it was supposed to be a secret at first, but Rockefeller and Flagler both realized that the true

[31] Allan Nevins, *John D. Rockefeller*, I, 478.
[32] I. M. Tarbell, "Death of the Pennsylvania," *loc. cit.*, XX (April, 1903), 612–621.

nature of such a powerful organization could not be kept from the public for any great length of time. By 1879 these corporations, which became known as the Standard Alliance, controlled 95% of the petroleum industry of the country. They made almost a clean sweep of the field. Rockefeller and Flagler had accomplished in about four years what no other oil concern had ever done. They used outright coercion by underselling those smaller concerns which balked at their offers. So well did they control the field that they could force the railroads to raise freight rates on the smaller refiners who would not yield. Throughout the oil regions, where Rockefeller and Flagler were despised most, an especially thorough job was done. John D. Archbold and J. J. Vandergrift were exacting and hard on the little refiners there. It was not unusual to observe such signs on closed refinery doors as, "Sold Out," "Dismantled," and "Shut Down." By 1879 practically nothing was left in the oil regions but the Imperial Oil Company of Oil City and the Acme Oil Company of Titusville, both subsidiaries of Standard Alliance. The Standard Alliance was nothing more than an informal substitute for the trust which was to come a few years later.[33] Henry M. Flagler's part in this combination process was very important. His official position was that of secretary of the parent organization. He was also considered the "lawyer" of the company. He had a keen legal mind despite the fact that he had not been trained for this work. Cold and remorseless, he was a shrewd analyst of delicate matters. His decisions were invaluable, and Rockefeller depended upon his judgment as much as he did his own. One of his greatest achievements of the late 1870's was his work in bringing the James N. Camden Oil Company into the Standard Oil fold. The Camden Company faced an uncertain future, a point on which Flagler capitalized. After some time the Camden Company was consolidated with Standard. The output of its refineries at Parkersburg, West Virginia, was re-

[33] G. H. Montague, *The Rise and Progress of the Standard Oil Co.*, 66.

duced and a large refining plant was established at Baltimore.[34]

James N. Camden was one of the few men connected with the Standard Alliance who sought public office. He was elected to Congress for several terms, and, as was to be expected, he favored the growth of big business. After he went to Washington, Camden kept Flagler posted on matters in Congress pertaining to their own business. He reported in December, 1878, about an anti-discrimination bill, "I have the ear of some half dozen Senators that I will see. I can't think there is the least probable danger of such a bill getting through the Senate. . . ."[35] A good many of the messages between the two men were written in code, giving evidence to the fact that their transactions were in deepest secrecy. For some time in 1878 Camden had been trying to buy out a small refinery belonging to a Mrs. Hunt in Maryland. His first report to Flagler concerning this deal was unfavorable. It looked as if the owner of the plant would not give in to pressure.[36] But several days later a telegram from Camden to Flagler no doubt bore good news. It read as follows: "Mix with Taint. Saved has Macron Saxon and Meat to—Nailer put in force Kingdom over Sirup Maze. St. Louis Rail Road Meduse to have it Martyr. Rivers frozen up tight."[37] Another addressed to Flagler later bore this message: "Macar Kiss, but no Malted Marshal Maslin will be Spring King evening if you advise."[38]

In the late 1870's there were a number of investigations made of the workings and operations of the Standard Oil Alliance. There was a growing feeling on the part of the public that this ever-expanding monster should be curbed. More and more demands were being made of Congress to do something. The State legislatures were also being aroused to action. James N. Camden was brought before a Senate com-

[34] Festus P. Summers, *James N. Camden*, 185.
[35] James N. Camden to Henry M. Flagler, December 13, 1878.
[36] *Ibid.*, May 20, 1878.
[37] Telegram, James N. Camden to Henry M. Flagler, May 26, 1878.
[38] *Ibid.*, May 25, 1879.

mittee in the West Virginia legislature in January, 1879, but nothing resulted from the investigation. The queries were mostly about rebates and special favors which the corporation was receiving from the railroads. Camden was noncommittal and replied, "We have had no rebates . . . for a long time, and we are having none at this time." [39] About this same time the Pennsylvania legislature was bringing suit against several members of the Alliance, and the Hepburn Investigation was taking place in New York. The Ohio legislature also instituted an investigation at which time Henry M. Flagler gave a very interesting testimony concerning rebates; however, none of his answers were satisfactory. Other Standard associates testified, too, but their statements were vague and proved to be truculent and unsatisfactory. The investigation in Pennsylvania was as unsuccessful as the one in Ohio. The two Rockefellers, Bostwick, Warden, Lockhart, Vandergrift, Camden, and Flagler were all under fire.[40] The public knew well that the Standard Oil Alliance was simply a revival of the old South Improvement Company, a conspiracy in every respect. The public was not to be denied, and a rocky road lay ahead for the leaders of the Standard Alliance in their battle against the people. A short message from Camden to Flagler in 1879 indicates the end of the first round of investigations. He wrote that "the legislative investigations of the Alliance have fizzled out in West Virginia; How are you getting along with the legislative investigation in Pennsylvania?" [41]

[39] James N. Camden to Henry M. Flagler, January 29, 1879.
[40] John K. Winkler, *John D., A Portrait in Oils,* 124.
[41] James N. Camden to Henry M. Flagler, February 6, 1879.

⚏ SIX ⚏

Retirement from Oil

NEW York was destined to become the site of the Stand-ard Oil Company, as well as the home of its secretary, Henry M. Flagler. That city, America's largest by 1870, was rapidly becoming the center of much of the nation's industrial and banking interest, and many persons of note and wealth made their homes there. For one, there was Cornelius Vander-bilt, who ranked high among the railroad builders. His fortune had grown quite out of proportion with that of the average American. Then there were William B. Astor, of fur fame, and Alexander T. Stewart, department store mogul, who made New York their home.[1] Flagler's fortune, as yet, could not compare favorably with the largest in New York, but he soon established himself as one of the city's most promising citizens.

New York was a gay city, claiming nearly two million in-habitants in the seventies. Visitors came from all over the world to see the sights. Sober Philadelphia and puritanical Boston were sometimes shocked at the goings-on in New York. Stage shows with their scantily dressed girls and old-fashioned saloons with their alluring waitresses were the talk of the East. From Manhattan to Coney Island one could find entertainment of various sorts.[2] The Flaglers had looked with anticipation to their future home in this setting. Though Flagler himself had visited there on several occasions, the

[1] Allan Nevins, *Emergence of Modern America*, 91.
[2] *Ibid.*, 93.

family first got a glimpse of New York in the winter of 1877. Mrs. Flagler and the two children, Jenny Louise and young Harry, accompanied him to the metropolis, and for a time made their home at the Buckingham Hotel.[3]

The same year that the Flaglers moved to New York, much history was being written in America. Rutherford B. Hayes assumed the duties of President of the United States, after the hotly disputed election of 1876 in which the Republicans out-maneuvered the Democratic candidate, Samuel J. Tilden. The last of the federal troops were removed from the South and home rule was once again enjoyed by the one-time Confederate states. The new South had been conceived, but it had by no means matured. The smoldering embers of the Civil War had not completely died out, and certainly the wounds of Reconstruction would have to be nursed by the South for a long time. Political leadership, both in the North and South, was far below normal. But the nation had reason to be encouraged. The road to reunion and better days lay ahead. The Panic of 1873 which caused a halt in the economic progress of America was over, and the Republican party was trying to live down the misconduct of several persons in the Grant administration.[4]

The Flaglers, who had every reason to be happy over their steadily rising fortune, liked New York. Flagler's wife continued in poor health; consequently, she was advised by her physician to spend part of the next winter in Florida. After a visit to Cleveland in the summer, where they still maintained their home, Flagler decided to have his wife spend the coldest part of the next winter in the South. Despite the pressure of his business Flagler accompanied his wife on the trip. They went no farther in Florida than Jacksonville because of the lack of transportation south of that point. Flagler noticed with concern the need of hotel facilities and travel accommoda-

[3] Conversation with Harry Harkness Flagler.
[4] L. M. Hacker and B. J. Kendrick, *The United States Since 1865*, 54, 55.

tions in the state which boasted of magic curative qualities for invalid persons. Mrs. Flagler rested well in Jacksonville, but after a few weeks her restless husband felt that he must return to his business in New York. He found it hard to relax; so Mrs. Flagler and the two children returned north with him. She refused to remain without her husband. The responsibility of the children in a strange place would have been a great burden for a person who was not well.

The Flaglers changed their New York residence to the Windsor Hotel and with the exception of several long visits to their home in Cleveland, remained at that hotel until Flagler purchased a house in the city on the corner of Fifty-fourth Street at Fifth Avenue.[5] Mrs. Flagler's bronchial trouble grew steadily worse, and the cold weather seemed to aggravate her condition considerably. Her husband insisted that she go alone to Florida each winter, but it was a long wearisome trip to Jacksonville and, besides, she refused to be away from her husband and children. He was in the midst of a busy life creating a fortune, and could not spare the time to take her to Florida himself. Sometime during the winter of 1880 he realized the inevitable. Her condition became critical, and by this time not even the warm Florida sunshine could make her better. Flagler insisted that she be allowed to go, but the doctor advised against the trip, and for the first time the wealthy Flagler realized that money was not the key to one's happiness. On May 18, 1881, Mary Harkness Flagler died.[6] Her death had a profound influence on Flagler. He determined to direct some of his attention towards himself and his children. These sobering effects began slowly to make a new man of him. He was sad and lonely, but for the sake of the children he tried not to give in to his feelings. Harry Flagler, who was a youth of eleven at the time, needed more than his father's

[5] This was the only home in New York City that Flagler ever owned. He did not sell it until after he moved his residence to Florida in the 1890's. Conversation with Harry Harkness Flagler.

[6] Flagler Family Records, File II of Flagler Collection.

influence; so Flagler persuaded his devoted half sister, Carrie Flagler, to come to New York and preside over the home at Fifth Avenue and Fifty-fourth Street. She soon won the confidence of young Harry, and filled admirably the vacancy left by the death of his mother. Jenny Louise, the older of the Flagler children, had been married for several years to John Arthur Hinckley. Her frequent visits to the Fifth Avenue home in New York were a source of pleasure for her father as well as for young Harry, who was devoted to his sister.[7]

Realizing the need for a change in his surroundings, Flagler rented a large house at Mamaroneck, New York, on Long Island Sound, in the summer of 1881, which was accessible by both water and rail from New York City. Situated on a narrow extension of land, almost surrounded by water, the estate, which was fittingly called Satan's Toe, consisted of thirty-two acres of land. A beautiful forty-room frame house graced the peninsula estate. Frequent guests, mostly relatives, shared in the pleasures of the summer home. Flagler visited his office in the city regularly but spent most of his time during the summer with Harry, Jenny Louise, and "Aunt Carrie" at Mamaroneck.

They all liked the summer home so well that Flagler was determined to buy it from the owner, Leonard Jacob. The transaction took place on June 1, 1882; and the property became Flagler's for the sum of $125,000. During the next few years many improvements were made in the house and surroundings. By January 2, 1885, Flagler had spent $330,992.51 on the Mamaroneck property.[8] The house was completely renovated inside and out. New fixtures were installed throughout the dwelling and attractive furniture was bought. Even the chandeliers were according to Flagler's own ideas. One chandelier, designed of solid brass with crystal hangings, weighed more than a thousand pounds. The new owner con-

[7] Conversation with Harry Harkness Flagler.
[8] From Flagler ledger on Mamaroneck property, Kenan Collection.

79

structed a sea wall around most of his property and had his own private breakwater extending for two hundred yards into the Sound. Sand was brought from the New Jersey coast for the transformation of the rocky muddy shores into a smooth bathing beach.[9] Flagler enjoyed his role as a creator of this place of beauty, for Lawn Beach, as he now called his summer home, was one of the most attractive vacation places in New York. Its wide verandas and big halls became the scene of many social functions. Lawn Beach did its part in creating within Flagler a desire for more leisure time, and it helped him to forget the pressing duties of the Standard Oil Company.

Flagler's influence in the Standard Oil Company and with John D. Rockefeller steadily diminished after 1882. Though he remained a vice-president of the company until June, 1908, John Dustin Archbold, a younger man, gradually took Flagler's place in the upper ranks of the business. In many respects Archbold was a much more aggressive man than Flagler and attracted John D. Rockefeller's attention from the start. He was born July 26, 1848, in Leesburg, Ohio, the son of a Methodist preacher. He had a very hard time during his early life, but after a steady climb, he became a petroleum producer in the oil regions, organizing the Acme Oil Company, which expanded later into the Standard Alliance. He was a real genius in the new firm of which he was one of the vice-presidents. No task was too great for him to undertake. He frequently called upon men in high government positions to do favors for him and his company and they always responded favorably. From 1882 until he died in 1916, he helped to dominate the policy and counsels of the Standard Oil Company.[10] Though he took Henry M. Flagler's place in the inner circle of the Standard Oil magnates, Flagler did not withdraw completely from the great organization. There was

[9] *New York Times*, February 10, 1924.
[10] William B. Shaw, "John Dustin Archbold," in *Dictionary of American Biography*, I, 337.

no break between Rockefeller and Flagler; the latter merely decided to retire slowly from the business. He maintained an office at 140 Pearl Street in New York, though by 1888 not more than half of his time was spent there. He seemed to find a new zest in life after he became interested in his developments in Florida, and by 1895 he was spending more time in the Southern state than he was in New York. By 1908 he was virtually inactive as far as the Standard Oil Company was concerned. It was in that year that he resigned the vice-presidency; however, it was not until 1911 that he gave up his membership in the Board of Directors.[11]

Flagler always manifested an interest in the Standard Oil Company and was one of the largest stockholders in the company until his death. His wealth multiplied more rapidly perhaps between the years 1880–1900 than during all the other years in his life because of these large holdings. It was during that time that the Standard was experiencing its period of greatest development. The Company had enjoyed unusual growth prior to 1882. From 1870 to 1882 its capital was increased from one million to fifty-five million dollars. In seven years it had paid some eleven million dollars in dividends, and at the same time it had laid by forty-five million dollars in new assets.[12]

To keep pace with the growing concern a new organization was formed on January 2, 1882, known as the Standard Oil Trust.[13] It brought in all the existing stockholders in the various enterprises which had been taken over by the old Standard Oil Company. These included refining, piping, buying and selling oil. There were thirty-seven stockholders interested in Standard and all the subsidiary and allied corporations. They merely conveyed their shares in the various companies into the hands of nine trustees. These nine men had all been

[11] *New York Times*, May 21, 1913.
[12] John Moody and George K. Turner, "The Masters of Capital in America," in *McClure's Magazine*, XXXVI (March, 1911), 565.
[13] *House Reports*, IX, 308.

prominently connected with the old concern.[14] They were John D. Rockefeller, William Rockefeller, Henry M. Flagler, O. H. Payne, Charles Pratt, John Archbold, W. G. Warden, Jabez Bostwick, and Benjamin Brewster. The trustees controlled two-thirds of all the shares and became the direct stockholders in all the various companies connected by the system. The other stockholders controlled one-third of the shares, receiving trust certificates in one-hundred-dollar denominations in return for the shares which they had deposited in the newly created trust.[15] The trustees were to receive salaries of twenty-five thousand dollars each, with the exception of the president, who was voted a salary of thirty thousand dollars. The principal office of the trust was to be located in New York.[16]

With a capital of fifty-five million dollars and properties valued at seventy-five million dollars the Standard Oil Trust was the biggest business concern in America. It soon became notorious. Public sentiment at once began to form against the monstrous organization. Wave after wave of criticism broke over the heads of Rockefeller, Flagler, and their associates. The public began to demand that governmental action be taken which would curb the growth of the Trust. As early as December, 1882, Flagler, Rockefeller, and Benjamin Brewster were summoned to appear before a United States Senate Committee which was inquiring into certain practices of the new business. The inquiry was held at the Metropolitan Hotel in New York, but all efforts to extract from the witnesses any information as to the exact workings and nature of the Trust failed. The committee also was determined to find out the

[14] John Moody, *Truth About the Trusts,* 119. See also C. M. Destler, "The Standard Oil, Child of the Erie Ring, 1868–1872," *Mississippi Valley Historical Review,* XXXIII (June, 1946), 100. Professor Destler maintains that the Standard Oil Trust was nothing but a gigantic offspring of the Erie ring, 1868–1872. Five of the nine trustees appointed had been connected with Jay Gould in the old Erie oil ring.
[15] Matthew Josephson, *The Robber Barons,* 277.
[16] *House Reports,* IX, 311.

reasons for its formation and the size of the dividends that were paid, but the witnesses said virtually nothing that would throw light on the new organization. Flagler waxed adamant, and became furious at the committee's attorney who kept reminding the group about the rising tide of public sentiment against the organization. At one point he demanded that Flagler answer a certain question.

Refusing, Flagler shouted, "It suits me to go elsewhere for advice, particularly as I am not paying you for it."

Quickly rejoined the attorney, "I am not paying you to rob the community, I am trying to expose your robbery." [17] Needless to say, the hearing ended in failure.

As monopolies began to be formed in other areas, some definite plans were soon made to curb the consolidation of big business. The public was not only disturbed over the consolidation, but it became thoroughly aroused at the methods of dishonesty in competition. These dishonest methods were often responsible for the success of the corporation. Henry George's *Progress and Poverty* (1879), Edward Bellamy's *Looking Backward* (1887), and Henry Demarest Lloyd's *Wealth Against Commonwealth* (1894) were all directed against the growth of monopoly. In politics, too, there was considerable opposition. Both the Republicans and Democrats opposed railroad corporations and monopolies as early as 1872. In 1880 the Greenback party condemned monopolies, and in 1884 an Anti-Monopolistic party was created for the purpose of preventing further gains by the corporation. In 1888, the platforms of the Republican, Democratic, Prohibition, and Union Labor parties all opposed the growth of monopolies. Many states had definitely banned monopolies by this time, but the federal government had not taken any effective action.[18]

The committee on manufacturing of the House of Repre-

[17] Allan Nevins, *John D. Rockefeller*, II, 60, 61.
[18] Harold U. Faulkner, *American Economic History*, 446, 447.

sentatives began an investigation in 1888, and in the same year the Senate of the state of New York began a similar inquiry. The inquiry made by the House committee was the most important since the investigation made by the Hepburn Committee. The Standard Oil Trust and the Sugar Trust were the concerns under fire. The chairman of the committee, Henry Bacon, started the hearings on April 6, 1888. Franklin B. Gowen, the attorney who had exposed the Molly Maguires, was the chief questioner, and he was anxious to treat the Standard Oil Trust as he had the Maguires. Gowen was a fiery, energetic person, who more than once drew anger from his witnesses. Among the Standard executives whom he questioned were Henry M. Flagler, John D. Rockefeller, and John D. Archbold. Flagler came to the stand on April 27, and explained his early connections with the Standard Oil Company as secretary. He let it be known that he had ceased to be secretary of the Standard Oil Company of Ohio when the Trust was formed in 1882, and since that time he had served as one of the nine trustees.[19]

Flagler was deliberate and calm with his answers, but at times evasive. Several questions were asked him pertaining to the history of the Standard Oil Company, which he answered with much brevity. Gowen queried him about the old South Improvement Company, but Flagler appeared to know very little about it. He disclaimed any part in the organization of the South Improvement Company; however, his critics place a good bit of the responsibility on his shoulders. He insisted that neither he nor Rockefeller had any confidence in or respect for the organization.

"We did not believe in it, but the view presented by other gentlemen was pressed upon us to such an extent that we acquiesced in it to the extent of subscribing our names to a certain amount of the stock, which was never paid for. The company never did a dollar's worth of business and never had

[19] *House Reports,* IX, 287.

any existence other than its corporative existence, which it obtained through the charter. Through its president it negotiated certain railroad contracts, which, as I remember now, were signed by the company and by the officers of the railroad. Those contracts were held in escrow a few weeks and were destroyed or canceled by mutual consent." [20] Many of Flagler's answers concerning the South Improvement Company were made in short terse remarks, such as, "No, sir," "Yes, sir," or "I do not remember."

The oil magnate was questioned thoroughly on the make-up and workings of the Trust Company. He argued that the Trust was not a corporation, saying that it derived its existence by virtue of a contract "entered into by and between the individuals who created" the Trust. He admitted that the Trust was a combination of the Standard Oil Company of Ohio, Standard Oil Company of New York, Standard Oil Company of New Jersey, Standard Oil Company of Pennsylvania, Standard Oil Company of Minnesota, Standard Oil Company of Iowa, and Standard Oil Company of Kentucky. Since each of these companies was chartered in different states, persons who were stockholders of these several companies were parties to the agreement. His contention was that the Trust simply became the custodian of the stock and that the state corporations remained intact as independent combinations.[21] He also admitted that the National Transit Company was a part of the Standard Oil Trust, and that the Trust owned the company which possessed pipe lines to the board.

As to the control of railroad rates and pipe lines, Flagler defended the combination by saying that it was a necessity to get control of the medium of transportation. He admitted that the Standard Oil Company went all out to kill the Empire Transportation Company because it was in competition with the Standard Oil Company. In each case the witness was not

[20] *Ibid.*, 289.
[21] *Ibid.*, 302, 303.

consistent with remarks which he had made earlier. For instance, in 1880, Flagler had admitted that the Standard Oil Company owned properties in Ohio and New Jersey. He swore that his company did not own, operate, or control any other refineries in the United States. But on the witness stand on April 27, 1888, he declared that the Standard Oil Company owned refineries in Pittsburgh as early as 1874.[22]

Gowen kept harping on the subject of railroads, trying to draw from Flagler some fact concerning the Trust's interest in that field. In answer to these questions Flagler insisted that the Standard Oil Trust was not interested in railroads. He admitted that, personally, he was connected with three different railroads. He said that he was a director of the "Chicago, Rock Island, and Pacific Railway," also that he was president of the "Jacksonville, St. Augustine, and Halifax River Railway." He was also a large stockholder in the "Tampa, Jacksonville, and Key West Railway." [23]

Flagler's testimony revealed that the Standard Oil Trust had increased its capital to about ninety million by 1888. The market value of all the shares was estimated at about one hundred fifty-four million dollars. Annual dividends of 7% had been paid the stockholders since 1882. This was indeed a very good showing for any concern.[24]

The hearings lasted for several months, with a mass of facts and information being gathered from all the executives. Flagler was called back to the stand in Washington on July 20, 1888, at which time the query was limited to railroad rates and rebates.[25] Actually, very little substance was gained by the committee from either of Flagler's appearances, and perhaps less from his associates'. The Standard Oil Trust was a hard nut to crack.

Prior to the hearings held by the committee from the House

[22] Ida M. Tarbell, *History of the Standard Oil Company*, II, 139.
[23] *House Reports*, IX, 298.
[24] Allan Nevins, *John D. Rockefeller*, II, 131.
[25] *House Reports*, IX, 768–790.

of Representatives, the New York State Senate also made an investigation of trusts. The hearings took place in February, 1888, with the Standard Oil Trust as its principal target. It gathered a report of 1500 pages, 1,000 of which were devoted to the creation and early history of the company. Flagler was in Florida during most of the investigation but returned to New York on February 28 to serve as witness. His remarks included an explanation of the early history of the company, information about the South Improvement Company, the ten-cents rebate Standard received from all the railroads in 1875, and the purchase of the Empire Transportation Company.[26] The investigation led to nothing definite or specific; in fact, it proved a disappointment to the people of New York. Public hatred for the continued growth of these combinations was intensified. One indirect result was the passing of the Sherman Anti-Trust Act in 1890, but, like the Interstate Commerce Act of 1887, it was far from effective during the first few years of its existence.

The first effective and energetic effort to dissolve the Standard Oil Trust came from Ohio in 1890. David K. Watson, attorney general of that state, filed a proceeding in *quo warranto* on May 8 in the Ohio Supreme Court against the Standard Oil Company of Ohio. The court rendered a decision depriving the company of the right to remain a part of the trust.[27] The case was followed by critics of the trust all over America. Politicians who leaned towards the large combinations tried to discourage Watson in his fight, but he would not be stopped. Mark Hanna, who had always approved the tactics of the Standard Oil Company, wrote to the attorney general as follows: "You have been in politics long enough to know that no man in public life owes the public anything." [28]

[26] I. M. Tarbell, *History of the Standard Oil Company*, II, 139.

[27] This decision was rendered in the case of State *ex rel.* Attorney General *vs.* Standard Oil of Ohio. See Ryan, *History of Ohio*, IV, p. 398.

[28] Carl Wilkins, *History of the State of Ohio*, 212.

The movement started by Watson led to vigorous action by the United States Supreme Court, and the Standard Oil Trust was accordingly dissolved on March 2, 1892. Henry M. Flagler, who was still the secretary, though mainly in name, called a meeting of the holders of Standard Oil Trust certificates for March 21, 1892, at the central office, 26 Broadway, New York, for purposes of liquidation. The Trust was apparently dissolved into twenty constituent companies with a capital of $102,233,700, and an evaluation of $121,631,312. However, the trustees continued to exist under the new name of "liquidating trustees." The dissolution process was not actually carried out at this time. In fact, the unity of action among the several companies was changed very little. It did not take long for the public to realize that the monopolistic power of the Standard Oil Trust had yet to be broken.[29]

The old guard in the firm had, to a large extent, passed off the scene. Not only had Flagler retired, but Samuel Andrews, one of the original partners, lost interest in the growing concern and sold all his shares in 1880. Charles Pratt died in 1891, and Jabez Bostwick passed away in 1892. O. H. Payne and William B. Warden withdrew from the combination in the eighties. H. H. Rogers and William Rockefeller found other interests as Flagler had done.

The changed line-up in the Standard Oil saw some interesting faces, including young John D. Rockefeller, Jr., who appeared at 26 Broadway fresh from his graduation at Brown University in 1897. He carried much of the burden for his father, to say nothing of John D. Archbold, who by this time had become an old hand at the business. There was complete revamping of the company in 1899, but it had no effect upon the management. Actually there had been very little change in the continuity of the Standard's management since the early seventies. John D. Rockefeller continued as the president of the Standard Oil of New Jersey and John D. Archbold as the

[29] I. M. Tarbell, *History of the Standard Oil Company*, II, 151–52.

vice-president. The stockholders numbered 3500.[30] The board of directors had considerable power, and it was fairly well known that they collected the dividends of all the other constituent companies, and then divided them among the stockholders, just as the dividends had been divided by the trustees after 1882, and by the liquidating trustees after 1892.[31]

In 1911 the Standard Oil Company of New Jersey, the parent organization, was finally dissolved into thirty-five units.[32] This was what had been attempted since the trust was formed in 1882. All those who held old Standard Oil Company stock were issued the same percentage of stock in all the new corporations. The dissolution of Standard Oil Company brought about many changes, and an entirely different organization, but by this time Henry M. Flagler was only an interested spectator on the side lines. His interests in Florida had long since overshadowed completely any attachments that he might have had for the Standard Oil Company.

[30] *Ibid.*, II, 356.
[31] *Ibid.*, II, 266.
[32] "The Standard Oil Melons," *The Literary Digest*, LXXV (October 28, 1922), 6. This has good description of the "melon-cutting," as breaking up of Standard Oil Company was called.

SEVEN

A Florida Honeymoon

WEDDING bells rang for Flagler in 1883. On June 5 of that year he was married to Ida Alice Shourds at the Madison Avenue Methodist Church in New York City.[1] It was not a marriage that was entirely pleasing to the Flagler and Harkness clans, but there was nothing that could be done about it. The fact that she was eighteen years younger than he seemed to make no difference to either of them. She was thirty-five and he was fifty-three. The friendship which grew into courtship had begun in the Flagler home where Miss Shourds had been an attendant to his first wife during her years of declining health. Prior to becoming a practical nurse Alice aspired to be an actress, but her dramatic ability was not sufficient to gain for her a secure place in that field.[2]

The second Mrs. Flagler's background was greatly different from that of her husband, despite the fact they were both reared in the home of clergymen. She was born in Philadelphia on July 4, 1848. Her father, who was an Episcopal minister, died when Alice was very young and her mother, Margaret B. Shourds, moved to New York. The two sons, Charles and Stephen, were employed in the city; but Mattie, an older sister, soon married and moved away. Alice's formal education was very limited, as she was not inclined to follow intellectual pursuits. Her husband was a self-educated man and reflected

---

[1] *New York Herald-Tribune*, June 6, 1883.
[2] Conversations with Theodore Pomar, Anna Fremd Hadley, and Belle Dimick Enos.

a certain amount of culture and refinement which she could not appreciate. Flagler was a habitual reader whereas his wife's tastes ran much to the contrary.[3]

Nevertheless, there is no doubt about Flagler's love for his new wife regardless of her shortcomings. His deep love for her apparently gave them some basis of understanding. He thought she was an exceptionally beautiful woman, and never hesitated to let her know that he thought so. Without question Alice Flagler was an attractive woman, and her husband was not the only man who shared that view. She was small in stature and possessed a profusion of red hair which she usually rolled on top of her head. Her eyes were a bright blue, and her complexion was very fair. She had a small face and delicate features, but underneath was a violent temper which was virtually uncontrollable at times.[4] However, Flagler was aware of her faults when he married her.

It was not with too much enthusiasm that the new Mrs. Flagler was welcomed to the family home in New York. The groom was engrossed in a business deal that would not permit him to leave town at the time of the wedding; so it was decided to postpone the honeymoon until fall. Consequently a couple of trunks containing Alice's personal belongings were delivered to the Flagler home on the day after the wedding, followed soon by the newly-married couple themselves. Carrie Flagler, the half sister who had mothered young Harry and looked after the home for two years, returned to Cleveland to live. She was asked to stay but she felt as though her duty to her brother's family was finished. Young Harry's stepmother tried earnestly to fill the vacant place in the home; but as far as the boy was concerned she never succeeded.[5]

From the outset, Alice Flagler was impressed with her husband's wealth; his fortune, as far as she was concerned,

[3] *New York Times*, May 21, 1913.
[4] *Ibid.*
[5] Conversation with Harry Harkness Flagler.

was one of his most engaging features. With an almost un-
limited bank account, she launched a spending spree that
would have astounded a man of modest means. It was a case
of "from rags to riches." Within a few months after she was
married, her wardrobe contained some of the most beautiful
and elaborate clothes the fashion shops in New York could
afford. She tried hard to bridge the gap between herself and
her husband with his money. She worked hard at being the
wife of a millionaire, realizing all the while that she was living
in a world different from anything she had ever experienced.
Most of all she wanted New York society to recognize her,
but try as hard as she could, that goal was never reached.

The belated honeymoon was begun in December, 1883.
Flagler disliked cold weather very much; so for months he
and his wife had been planning a trip to Florida. Aside from
the trip to Florida in 1878, he had never been very far away
from his work.[6] But now at the age of fifty-three, he was
worth between ten and twenty million dollars and he was
ready to retire from his strenuous labors. He made no definite
plans about when he would return to New York. The trip
from New York to Jacksonville required ninety hours of
travelling, involving many changes and delays, because of
the different gauges of tracks along the way. The Flaglers
could have gone via boat from New York to Savannah, and
from there to Jacksonville, but they chose the overland route
by rail. Savannah was probably the most important of the
Southern seaport towns, and railroad lines concentrated there
from all parts of the country.[7]

Arriving in Savannah, the oil magnate and his wife paused
only a short time before making the remainder of the trip.
Jacksonville was not far, but the trip was more uncomfortable

[6] *Ibid.*
[7] G. W. Nichols, "Six Weeks in Florida," *Harper's Magazine*, XLI (October, 1870), 655.

than the journey from New York to Savannah. One contemporary traveller expressed it in these words:

> There are two ways of getting to Jacksonville [from Savannah], and whichever you choose you will be sorry you had not taken the other. There is the night train by railroad, which brings you to Jacksonville in about sixteen hours; and there is the steamboat line, which goes inland nearly all the way, and which may land you in a day, or you may run aground, and remain on board for a week.[8]

Most people chose the journey by steamboat, despite the chance they took of being stranded before they reached their destination. It is more than likely, however, that the Flaglers continued their journey by rail. The route did not run directly to Jacksonville, but the unlucky traveller rode from Savannah to a junction not far from Valdosta, Georgia, called Dupont. From Dupont, he took a bumpy little road to Live Oak, and from there he went directly to Jacksonville. It was perhaps three or four times the direct distance from Savannah to Jacksonville.[9] Whichever mode of travel the Flaglers decided upon, there can be one thing certain: it was not a comfortable journey.

Jacksonville was a thriving little resort town. Its history dated back to 1822 when it was surveyed and laid out, and named for Andrew Jackson, who was the first governor of the territory. Its early growth had been slow, for the Seminole Indian War, 1836–1842, stunted the expected growth of the town. By 1847 there were less than a thousand inhabitants in Jacksonville.[10] After the Civil War, it became a commercial center, an outlet for the transportation of lumber and cotton. Located a few miles inland on the St. Johns River, Jacksonville gave promise of being an important seaport and railroad

[8] *Ibid.*
[9] *Florida Dispatch* (Live Oak), July 3, 1878.
[10] T. Frederick Davis, *History of Jacksonville*, 82.

terminus. Several hotels were constructed, especially for the winter visitors, who came from the North seeking either pleasure or improved health. Among the finest of these hotels was the St. James, and it was at this fashionable place that the Flaglers stayed. The building had been completed only about four years. Constructed of brick and wood, it was one of the most famous hotels in the South. For the guests it had many amusements, such as bowling alleys, billiard rooms, and sun parlors.[11]

Flagler and his bride stayed only a few days in Jacksonville, deciding to go on to St. Augustine by way of the St. Johns River. All of the winter visitors in Jacksonville usually took a river trip on the St. Johns. It was a historic water highway to inland Florida and newcomers were always charmed with the beautiful scenery which was made up of orange groves and small settlements along both banks of the lazily flowing river. Flagler was impressed with the entire area.[12] At Tocoi, about thirty miles up the river, the honeymooners left their steamer and boarded the St. Johns River Railroad, a short line of fifteen miles, which until 1870 had been horse drawn. After that time it operated with a little "coffee mill" engine. The road was built in 1858 by John Westcott, but had been sold to William Astor, who rebuilt the line and operated it more efficiently. The fare from Tocoi to St. Augustine was two dollars per person, and it took several hours to complete the trip.[13]

Needless to say, the Flaglers were anxious to reach their destination. It is not known exactly where they stayed on their first trip to St. Augustine. There were no large hotels. They both were charmed with the ancient city, despite the fact that it was run-down. Nearly 2,000 persons lived in the town, and they always thought in terms of the past, very

[11] *Ibid.,* 487.
[12] Conversation with Harry Harkness Flagler.
[13] Harry G. Cutler, *History of Florida,* I, 61.

seldom speaking of the future. Flagler was astounded at the lack of development, but he was delighted with the weather and the numerous orange groves which were in and around the town. Their stay in St. Augustine was an enjoyable one, and they remained longer than they had planned. A cold wave gripped the North around the first of the year, while flowers bloomed in profusion in St. Augustine. On January 4, the thermometer dropped to twenty-seven degrees below zero in several places in the East; in St. Louis it was twenty-three below zero; in Cleveland fourteen below.[14] It was a prolonged cold spell, lasting until late in February. As the editor of the *New York Herald-Tribune* stated, it was a "phenomenal winter."[15] The Flaglers were glad to be away from it all, and remained in the Florida sunshine until nearly March 1, 1884.

This trip to Florida did something to Flagler; it convinced him that St. Augustine was an ideal place to retire. It made him determined to come often to the land where the thermometer seldom reached as low as the thirties, and where flowers bloomed the year round. Definite plans to return were made before he left for New York.[16] One thing worried him, however. Why did St. Augustine not have better facilities for their winter visitors? Why did not someone build an attractive hotel there so as to entice winter-weary Easterners? To say that Flagler had any intention of playing the role of a developer this early would be a mistake. His thoughts, however, were soon to turn in that direction. He began to have visions of what St. Augustine might be if only a little money were lavished on her. Destiny had set in to shape a new career for the oil magnate; a career which, in the end, helped to prove that Ponce de Leon must have found the famed fountain of youth somewhere on Florida's east coast.

Florida was long overdue in the realm of development and

---

[14] *New York Herald-Tribune*, January 6, 1884.
[15] *Ibid.*, February 24, 1884.
[16] Clarissa Anderson Dimick to author, February 28, 1946.

expansion. She seemed to be waiting for the magic touch of a great benefactor like Flagler. There were dormant possibilities which were not obvious to the average eye, yet to the keen perception of men like Flagler much could be seen. This southernmost state had been the site of the first permanent settlement in the United States.[17] From the days of Pedro Menendez in 1565 until 1763 the Spanish had dominated there although development had been negligible during the period.[18] Much more progress had been made in the English colonies to the north. At the close of the French and Indian War in 1763 Spain was forced to cede Florida to the English; so from 1763 until 1783 Florida was a part of the British Empire. At the close of the American Revolution Britain lost Florida along with the other American colonies but under different circumstances. The colonies received their independence, but Florida was given back to Spain, as a part of her settlement in the American Revolution. Accordingly, Spain took up where she had left off in 1763. Spanish Florida was a thorn in the flesh to the southern American states. There were border troubles involving both the Seminole Indians and the slaves, and to make matters much more complicated there was a growing feeling among many Americans that their country should acquire the Spanish territory, thereby settling all controversies. The sentiment persisted for some time. Finally as a result of the Onis-Adams treaty, which was ratified in 1821, Florida became an American territory.[19]

1949
1821
128

The period from 1821 until 1845 was one of adjustment and preparation for statehood. American customs, habits, and ways of life slowly displaced those which had been brought

[17] St. Augustine, Florida, the first permanent settlement in the United States, was made by Pedro Menendez de Aviles in 1565. See Kathryn T. Abbey, *Florida, Land of Change*, 33, 34.

[18] Many Spanish explorers had visited Florida before Menendez made his settlement at St. Augustine, the first being Ponce de Leon, who landed in Florida in April, 1513, and named the peninsula *Pascua Florida*, because it was discovered "in the time of the Feast of Flowers." See *Ibid.*, 6.

[19] Sidney Walter Martin, *Florida During the Territorial Days*, 44.

in earlier by the Spanish. After a time the territory became a political unit, and was finally admitted to the Union on March 3, 1845.[20]

Florida shared with her sister Southern states the bitter dregs of Civil War and Reconstruction. Up to the time of the War very little advancement had taken place in Florida; her population remained small, and she was still primarily a land of swamps, rivers, and marshes. The Reconstruction years, despite hardships and adversities, produced some rather decided material gains. The population grew rapidly from 1860 to 1880; in the latter year the state claimed 269,493 persons, a ninety per cent increase over the twenty-year period.[21]

There were several reasons for the rise in population, most of which was in the northern part of the state. In the first place, many of the soldiers who had been sent to Florida during the Civil War found the state a very livable place, much to the surprise of many of them. They liked it so well, especially during the wintertime, that they returned to build homes and make a living. There were no factories in the state; though there were a few saw mills and perhaps a few banks, there was little business anywhere. Orange growing as an investment had just started in a small way in the northern and central sections. A limited amount of northern capital was used in the infant citrus industry.[22]

As early as 1880 Florida was known in various parts of the country for her warm sunshine, her mild winters, her long winding rivers, her virgin forests, and her desirability as a place for invalids, especially consumptives. The modern American tourist was unknown, but some few stout hearts made the long journey from the North to enjoy the pleasures that Florida had to offer. Edward King in his series of articles on the South soon after the Civil War called Florida "Our

[20] Dorothy Dodd, ed., *Florida Becomes a State*, 426.
[21] Rembert W. Patrick, *Florida Under Five Flags*, 79.
[22] J. E. Ingraham, "The Story of the East Coast," *Picturesque Florida*, I (January, 1910), 3.

American Italy," and became very enthusiastic over the possibilities of the southernmost state. He stated that many Northerners went to Florida each year as early as 1874. He continued, "It is not invalids who crowd Florida now-a-days, but the wealthy and the well. One-fourth of the annual visitors are in pursuit of health; the others are crusading to find the phantom 'pleasure.' Fully one-half of the resident population of Jacksonville is northern, and has settled there since the [Civil] War." [23] Other contemporaries put more emphasis on Florida as a health resort. *Harper's* Magazine maintained that by 1870 Florida had become the winter home of many thousands of persons having "pulmonary complaints." Most doctors advised their patients to go to St. Augustine; however, others settled in Jacksonville or along the St. Johns River. [24]

The St. Johns River flowed through one of the most attractive areas in Florida, and along its banks people found ideal places to settle. Towns and villages grew up, and were served by picturesque river steamers, which were most commonly used for travel. The St. Johns River was the chief highway for transportation for northeast Florida. As early as the sixties several steamers made weekly trips from Charleston and Savannah down the coast to Jacksonville, which was only a few miles inland from the mouth of the river. From Jacksonville the boats proceeded on up the river to Tocoi, Palatka, Federal Point, and Enterprise. The steamers used fat pine which could be bought at various places up and down the river. [25] The steamboat era in Florida preceded the railroad era by many years. Passengers, as well as freight, were transported by boat, and the importance of the waterways, especially the St. Johns, cannot be overemphasized.

Most of the population in Florida during the seventies and

[23] Edward King, "The Great South," *Scribner's Monthly*, IX (November, 1874), 3.
[24] G. W. Nichols, "Six Weeks in Florida," *loc. cit.*, 661.
[25] Branch Cabell and A. J. Hanna, *The St. Johns, A Parade of Diversities*, 239, 242.

eighties was situated in the northern part of the state, between Jacksonville and St. Augustine on the east and Pensacola on the west. Of the 269,493 people in Florida in 1880, the counties touching the east coast, including the St. Johns River area, had 39,935. The gross valuation for taxes for these counties in 1884 was $12,166,134, whereas the gross valuation for taxes for the whole state of Florida at the same time was $60,042,655. Jacksonville's population was about 15,000, but there was no bridge across the sprawling St. Johns, connecting the city with points to the south. Daytona, a settlement of about 200 people, was 40 miles south of St. Augustine on the Atlantic Ocean.[26] It was on the fringe of the frontier; however, its ideal location gave it many possibilities.

A contemporary Florida newspaper in 1877 noticed with interest the attention the region around Daytona was receiving, and said that a considerable amount of land was being sold in the New Smyrna area. During the winter months stages had been put into operation between Enterprise on the St. Johns and New Smyrna on the coast. The small villages of Port Orange, Volusia, and New Britain also figured in the stage route.[27] The rich Indian River section just south of New Smyrna was virtually untouched. Melbourne was in existence, but that was about all. Around the shores of Biscayne Bay there were a few more scattered families. The little village of Key West was completely isolated from the mainland. Dade County, which extended in 1888 from St. Lucie River to Key West, had a population of only 257. Ten years later the county claimed 861 inhabitants.[28]

Life up and down the Florida east coast was extremely simple: there were few luxuries and conveniences. For a living, people fished, hunted, and perhaps raised some fruit and vegetables. Their products, however, were mainly for home

[26] *A Brief History of the Florida East Coast Railway*, 4.
[27] *Florida Dispatch* (Live Oak), September 26, 1877.
[28] J. T. Van Campen to author, March 2, 1946.

consumption because a market for such perishables was limited. Livestock, especially cows, was almost unknown. It was virtually impossible for a person to get milk. Fresh meat, except for fish, was a rarity.[29]

Transportation in Florida in 1880 was very limited, but a few roads had been built before that time. Perhaps the first railroad in Florida was a short line from Tallahassee to St. Marks built in 1834. This road, completing a distance of 23 miles, was not only the first railroad in the state but also was one of the earliest in the United States. The road, which was very crude, served as an important factor in the growth of Middle Florida. In 1834 several other companies were incorporated for the purpose of building railroads, but the beginning of the Seminole Indian War in 1836 and the Panic of 1837 put an end to most of these ventures.[30]

During the next twenty-five years several hundred miles of railroads were constructed in Florida. By the time the Civil War broke out, the following roads, comprising 416 miles, were in operation: the Florida Railroad, from Fernandina to Cedar Keys, which covered a distance of 155 miles; the Pensacola and Georgia Railroad, from Lake City to Tallahassee, a distance of 114 miles; the Florida, Atlantic and Gulf Central, Jacksonville to Lake City, sixty miles in length; the Florida and Alabama Railroad, which ran from Pensacola to the Alabama line, a distance of forty-seven miles; the St. Johns River Railroad, fifteen miles long; and the Tallahassee Railroad, twenty-three miles in length.[31]

During the Civil War the railroad mileage in Florida increased to 485 miles, but from 1866 until 1880 there were only two additional miles of railroads laid in the state. Railroad mileage in Florida increased rapidly in the early eighties,

[29] *A Brief History of the Florida East Coast Railway*, 5.
[30] Rowland H. Rerick, *Memoirs of Florida*, II, 167.
[31] *Ibid.*, 180.

with a considerable portion of this construction taking place in East Florida.[32]

But Florida was not to be denied much longer. The early eighties witnessed some development in the field of transportation, industry, and agriculture. This was true of the entire South, and Flagler could not help noticing. A new spirit was beginning to pervade most of the Southern states. They were not thinking so much in terms of the past as they were the future. Henry Grady, Atlanta newspaper editor, was gaining fame as a prophet of the New South, which meant industrialization and development. In 1881 Atlanta held an exposition for the purpose of showing the nation her advantages. Cities of the New South included Atlanta, Birmingham, Chattanooga, and Knoxville. Older towns which received a new impetus from industrialization and development were New Orleans, Richmond, Charleston, Columbia, and Savannah. In Florida, the spirit of development also prevailed strongly. In 1880, William D. Bloxham was elected governor with a promise to help develop Florida by draining many of the swamp lands and making them inviting to settlers. Hamilton Disston, a saw manufacturer from Philadelphia, was given large areas of reclaimed land in South Florida; in addition he bought four million acres of swamp land at twenty-five cents an acre, and began to make it fit for settlers. About the same time other builders were at work in Florida too. H. H. DeLand, a New Yorker, settled in Middle Florida, and laid out a town which bore his name. Henry B. Plant, a Connecticut Yankee, contributed much to the upbuilding of the state through his railroad construction and development on the west coast. The discovery of phosphate deposits near Tampa and the cultivation of citrus fruit through Middle Florida brought many new people into those regions.[33] By 1885, Florida was on the way

[32] R. H. Rerick, *Memoirs of Florida*, II, 187.
[33] W. B. Hesseltine, *The South in American History*, 560–564.

towards an era of progress and development. Economic advancement was definitely on the way. Flagler pondered over these things long after the warmth of the sunshine from his first winter in Florida had left his system.

EIGHT

Permanent Stakes in Florida

THE Flaglers did not forget Florida. The thought of their
pleasant stay in Jacksonville and St. Augustine in 1883–
1884 gave rise to plans for another trip the next winter.
Flagler had pleasure and perhaps a little business in mind. He
had hoped to spend part of the fall, 1884, in St. Augustine
but certain business obligations kept him in New York until
after Christmas. In fact, they did not leave the city until
February 17, 1885. New York was experiencing its coldest
weather of the year—a very good time for them to be going
South. Travelling in their private railroad car which Flagler
had purchased the year before, they arrived in Jacksonville
only two days after their departure. Travel between New
York and Jacksonville had been speeded up within the year,
and the trip was not so long and tiresome as it had been in
the past.[1]

They renewed many acquaintances at the St. James Hotel,
but remained there only a week. Flagler heard while there
that a new hotel had been constructed in St. Augustine, and
that many of the Jacksonville visitors were going on to the
old town for long periods of stay since accommodations there
were much better. Naturally the millionaire was anxious to
see the new building. On February 25, the couple left Jacksonville on the newly constructed Jacksonville, St. Augustine,

---

[1] Henry M. Flagler Diary, February 19, 1885, St. Augustine Historical
Society Library.

and Halifax River Railway.[2] They left their private railroad car in Jacksonville, and were ferried across the St. Johns River from Jacksonville to South Jacksonville to the beginning point of the new road.[3] The trip to St. Augustine required the greater portion of one day, and he was a hearty soul indeed who made it without loss of spirit or appetite. The Flaglers were happy to reach their destination; happier still was he to see the new San Marco Hotel and to talk with its manager.[4] Flagler had visualized such a venture and predicted it would do a good business.

With a luxury hotel now in operation, St. Augustine had changed considerably in the twelve months they had been away. The San Marco, though not extremely large, was an up-to-date place. It had been completed to the point of taking guests, but more work was yet to be done. A group of New Englanders had put up the money for the construction of the building and had hired Osborn D. Seavey, with whom Flagler became very friendly, to manage it. This same group of men had built the Magnolia Springs Hotel in Green Cove Springs, on the St. Johns River halfway between Jacksonville and Palatka. Seavey, an experienced New England hotel man, had managed the Magnolia Springs before coming to St. Augustine. It was through his efforts that more Easterners spent the winter of 1885 in St. Augustine than ever before.[5]

There were several other building projects in St. Augustine which claimed Flagler's attention also. Among the most pretentious pieces of construction was the Villa Zorayda, the handsome residence of Franklin W. Smith. Smith, who had been in St. Augustine for some time, had become interested in a building scheme for the town. The Villa Zorayda was

[2] *Ibid.*, February 25, 1885.
[3] J. T. Van Campen to author, March 2, 1946.
[4] *Ibid.*
[5] Seavey later became manager of Flagler's hotels in St. Augustine, remaining in that position until March, 1894, when he resigned. *Tatler*, February 17, 1894.

new construction material

constructed with the use of a new kind of material made from a mixture of cement, shells, and water. The structure, which was considered the loveliest private dwelling in St. Augustine, was an exact miniature reproduction of one of the palaces of the Alhambra, once occupied by a famous Moorish princess. This oriental palace was square in shape with a court in the center onto which opened several balconies. Around the building was a flower garden. At night the place was lighted by colored lamps which were placed on the outside. The windows were of stained glass so that the light on the inside blended beautifully with the lamps outside.[6] Franklin W. Smith also had in mind building a resort hotel not far from his home. He told Flagler about his plans, but he did not begin to build the Casa Monica, the name of his new venture, until 1886, and it was not completed until January, 1888.[7]

Flagler was also impressed with the accessibility of St. Augustine as compared with several years before. Much had been said and written concerning the new road from South Jacksonville to St. Augustine, but more advertisement was being given the extension which William Astor was building from Tocoi Junction, just west of St. Augustine to East Palatka, on the St. Johns. Astor, who owned the little line from Tocoi to St. Augustine, completed his new extension in 1886, and called it the St. Augustine and Palatka Railroad.[8]

Other railroad construction in the St. Augustine area was taking place in the middle eighties. U. J. White constructed a short logging road from the St. Johns River at East Palatka to San Mateo, a distance of only about four miles. With the financial aid of S. V. White, a Wall Street operator, the road

---

[6] *Florida Times-Union* (Jacksonville), January 13, 1888.

[7] After Franklin W. Smith finished his Casa Monica in 1888, he operated it for only a short time. Flagler purchased this hotel in 1889, and for several years operated it independently from his others. He renamed it the Cordova. In 1894 he built a connection between this hotel and the Alcazar, and operated it in connection with the latter. William R. Kenan to author, March 8, 1946.

[8] R. H. Rerick, *Memoirs of Florida*, II, 201.

was extended slowly across the deserted area from the St. Johns River to Ormond and Daytona on the coast, about fifty-one miles in distance. Before the road reached Daytona, the construction was delayed many times because of marshy land. In other spots it was necessary to cut through coquina rock, since it was not subject to blasting, in order to lay the road bed. At this time, as there was no machinery available for cutting the rock, the work had to be done by hand. A bridge across the Halifax River was necessary, but building it was relatively easy compared to many of the other obstacles in construction.[9]

All of these short railroads around St. Augustine were unrelated, and to some extent unimportant, but they were an indication of better transportation facilities which were soon to come if ample hotel accommodations could be provided. Realizing, as Flagler did, the importance of St. Augustine as a resort center, he began to do a little figuring and also a little talking. His friends said he had always wanted to own a hotel; some said he had always been fascinated by the duties of a hotel manager. Be that as it may, he was becoming more interested every day in the future of St. Augustine; so he postponed any idea of returning to New York in March as he had planned. To build a hotel or not to build a hotel seemed to be the burning issue in his mind.

One thing that helped to hasten his decision and activate his interests in St. Augustine was the celebration of the landing of Ponce de Leon in March, 1885. The celebration was an elaborate one, put on especially for the winter visitors, and it impressed Flagler deeply. The name Ponce de Leon kept playing back and forth in his mind.[10] There was the name for his first structure—a hotel, the Ponce de Leon. Another thing which helped Flagler to declare his good intentions was his

[9] The *Observer* (Daytona Beach), January 4, 1936.
[10] Henry M. Flagler Diary, March 27, 1885.

acquaintance with Andrew Anderson, prominent and influential St. Augustine citizen, whom he met soon after he arrived in February, 1885. Anderson, a practicing physician, was born in St. Augustine, March 13, 1839, when Florida was still a territory of the United States. His parents had moved there several years earlier from New England. Anderson graduated from Princeton in 1861 and from the College of Physicians and Surgeons, New York City, in 1865. Upon receiving his medical training he returned to St. Augustine to practice his profession.[11] Dr. Anderson owned a considerable amount of property in the St. Augustine area, and as soon as he learned that Flagler was interested in making some investments in the city, he went to see him. They talked at great length.[12] The discussion continued for several days, and it can be safely asserted that Anderson's influence was largely responsible for the first of Flagler's investments in St. Augustine. The decision was reached, and Flagler hastened his return to New York. He left on April 1, 1885, but not until he had purchased several acres of land from Dr. Anderson on which to build a magnificent hotel. As he bade his newly-made friend good-bye, he promised to return within six weeks to get his plans under way.[13]

Flagler kept his promise, and on May 15 returned to St. Augustine with more definite ideas about what he wanted to do. Mrs. Flagler did not come with him, but in her stead was a business associate, Benjamin Brewster, known especially for his ability to evaluate men, property, and materials. Brewster's presence was not without reason. Flagler needed his advice on many matters concerning his proposed plans. Also accompanying Flagler was Thomas Hastings, a young but promising architect from New York. The three New Yorkers were

[11] Clarissa Anderson Dimick to author, February 28, 1946. Dr. Anderson died in St. Augustine, December 1, 1924.
[12] Sworn statement to court by Andrew Anderson, 1923.
[13] Flagler Diary, April 1, 1885.

guests of the Andrew Andersons, and the doctor worked tirelessly with them on plans for a new hotel.[14] The actual plans and details, which were finished early one morning after an all-night session, were all worked out in Dr. Anderson's parlor. Hastings, who had sketched off a rough drawing of the building, returned to New York to make further study of Spanish architecture before the blueprints were made. Flagler and Brewster followed on May 22, leaving Dr. Anderson highly enthusiastic over the proposed building program. No one knew more than he what added capital would mean to St. Augustine. His untiring efforts in getting Flagler to make the decision were crowned with success. His job was not finished yet; in fact, it had just begun. He had promised to act as Flagler's agent in St. Augustine when the millionaire himself was not there.[15]

The news of Flagler's proposal to build the Ponce de Leon Hotel in St. Augustine spread rapidly. People began to speculate in land, and Flagler was deluged with all sorts of offers of property, some good and some bad. Some people tried to sell to Dr. Anderson, and when he would not buy, they sent their letters directly to Flagler in New York. A small land boom ensued. To one prospect the millionaire wrote, "I have no desire to speculate in St. Augustine property. I only want to buy certain property which will be needed for the new hotel." [16] The enthusiasm over Flagler's coming to Florida was not confined to St. Augustine. People in Palatka, twenty-eight miles away, tried to interest the millionaire in purchasing land from them too. Dr. Anderson assured the Palatka people that Flagler was interested only in building a hotel in St. Augustine, and that it was not his purpose to set off a wave of land speculation. Becoming somewhat indignant over what

[14] Sworn statement to court by Andrew Anderson, 1923. Flagler visited in the Anderson home from time to time thereafter.
[15] Flagler Diary, April 22, 1885.
[16] Henry M. Flagler to G. W. Atwood, June 9, 1885.

they called his lack of attention, they determined to send a delegation of Palatkans to New York for the purpose of calling on Flagler concerning their interests. Anderson warned Flagler of their proposed trip, to which he answered, "I note what you say about the Palatka people. If I can only be advised about their coming to New York, I will take pains to be out of town when they arrive." [17] Hearing of Flagler's attitude, the Palatka delegation cancelled plans for the trip.

The summer of 1885 was a busy one for Flagler. He remained in New York, spending much of his time at his summer home, Mamaroneck, but he was in constant touch with Dr. Anderson. There was almost daily correspondence between them. Anderson spent most of the summer getting detailed matters cleared up in preparation for the actual building of the hotel. In the first place, a large portion of the land on which the hotel was to be built was low and marshy and had to be filled in with sand and dirt. This was a long, hard job, but Dr. Anderson did it well. Another rather tedious task which Flagler turned over to his representative in St. Augustine was the securing of permission from the government authorities to quarry coquina from certain areas in that region. They planned to use coquina rock to build the proposed structure. A third task which Anderson undertook for Flagler concerned the moving of the tiny railroad depot from the grounds of the San Marco Hotel. Naturally, Flagler wanted the depot to be situated at some central point in St. Augustine. There was another reason, too, why he wanted it moved: he believed that St. Augustine was destined to become a railroad center; therefore, she deserved a better depot. The new St.

---

[17] Henry M. Flagler to Andrew Anderson, June 18, 1885, Dimick Collection. The story is told that later Flagler tried to buy some property in Palatka in connection with his railroad which ran through East Palatka, but the Palatkans involved refused to sell it to him, because of their earlier treatment. This story is perhaps true, though the author has not been able to authenticate it.

Augustine enthusiast promised to give the land for a new depot, if it should be moved. His offer was accepted, and he provided the town with better facilities.[18]

Flagler gave Dr. Anderson free access to his purse strings. No task was too great or expensive. If Anderson thought something should be done, Flagler saw to it that the task was accomplished. In one letter in June, 1885, the doctor suggested to his friend in New York that between them they were spending a lot of money, and ended by saying that if he did not stop, they would both soon be in the poor house. Flagler answered jocularly, "If I crowd you too rapidly on improvements, you must lean back; I guess, between us, we can manage it." [19] There was one thing certain: after this, the St. Augustine doctor never worried about how much he spent.

Only once during this period of preparation did Flagler become pessimistic and think of giving up the program. The occasion was in July, 1885, when he learned that much more work would be needed in building up a fill or low portion of the grounds on which the Ponce de Leon was to be constructed. The land was an ideal location for the proposed structure, but there was a creek running across it. The Sebastian River was dredged, and the displaced earth was used to fill in the creek bed. At the same time the problem of filling the creek was being solved, Dr. Anderson was having an extremely hard time clearing the titles to some of the land Flagler was trying to purchase in connection with the hotel. Flagler did not remain discouraged long, however, and sent the following message to his friend in St. Augustine, "It will be a disappointment, of course, if we have to stop operations, but you and I are too old and tough to be killed off by a thing of this sort [clearing the land titles]." [20] The Standard Oil magnate was too well schooled in the Rockefeller principles

[18] Henry M. Flagler to Andrew Anderson, June 27, 1885.
[19] *Ibid.*, June 30, 1885.
[20] *Ibid.*, July 29, 1885.

to let one or two obstacles stand in his way. Had he given in and stopped at this point, his Florida developments perhaps would never have become a reality, but he had great determination to accomplish what he had set out to do. That was one of the secrets of his success.

By midsummer, it was the hope of both Flagler and Anderson that the actual work on the foundation of the Ponce de Leon could take place in August or September. They wanted to have the building ready for use for the season, 1887, but there was much work to be accomplished before the realization of their dreams came true. One thing in which Flagler was intensely interested was the reaction of the officials of the city of St. Augustine to his plans. Making sure that everything was in readiness when the time came to build, Flagler instructed Anderson to see that the board of aldermen had no objection to his proposed program. Said Flagler, "We should be well advised on these points, for if I contract with the builders to do this work, and don't give them the ground at the time agreed upon, it may prove a very serious matter to me, as well as delay the completion of the hotel a year longer." [21] Another question which entered Flagler's mind at this time concerned malaria. The disease was uncontrollable in certain places and Flagler feared that the digging of the foundation might create a malarial epidemic in St. Augustine. Anderson, however, being a physician, quieted his friend's fears by assuring him that if lime were freely used by the workmen while digging, the possibility of spreading the disease would be minimized.

Locally, much encouragement was given the Flagler movement. Almost everyone wanted to cooperate. President Green of the Jacksonville, St. Augustine, and Halifax Railroad consented to extending his road farther into the city so that the materials being hauled could be placed nearer the scene of construction. Permission was immediately granted by the city

[21] *Ibid.*, July 16, 1885.

officials for the use of coquina rock from Anastasia Island which was just across the Matanzas River from St. Augustine; however, that permission had to be approved by the United States government. Flagler was a personal friend of Secretary of State Whitney, who secured permission for him through the Treasury Department to use as much of the coquina as he needed.[22]

While Anderson and Flagler figured diligently on details pertaining to the building program, the architects, Thomas Hastings and John M. Carrere, worked constantly on the blueprints. They remained at their office in New York all summer consulting with Flagler almost daily.[23] The two young architects realized this was their opportunity to make a reputation for themselves. They knew Flagler had plenty of money; so they tried hard to reproduce, as far as possible, the atmosphere of old Spain in the structure which was the builder's wish. As the architects finished the plans for each floor, a photograph was sent to Dr. Anderson. Flagler's letters to Anderson carried a note of eagerness as the blueprints neared completion. He was putting much of his time, money, and energy into the hotel which he hoped to be the most beautiful in the world. As he wanted it to be a surprise, he requested the drawings of the building not to be made public and no indication of how much he was spending to be made known. He had estimated that the work, if begun by September, 1885, would be finished by January 1, 1887, but the many particulars involved in the huge undertaking were not completed on scheduled time, and the construction was delayed for several months.

After learning that the work could not be finished on schedule, Flagler invited Dr. Anderson to visit him at his

[22] *Ibid.*, August 5, 1885.
[23] Some sources state that Flagler sent Hastings and Carrere to Spain to study the architecture of that country, but this is untrue. They studied Spanish architecture, it is true, but from secondary sources. *Ibid.*, June, July, August, 1885.

summer home at Mamaroneck for a two-weeks vacation. The trip was made in August and the two men, who had already become very friendly, enjoyed the many activities which Mamaroneck offered, including several ocean trips on Flagler's yacht, the *Columbia*. Their two weeks together gave them a better understanding of each other, an understanding which continued to grow as long as they lived.[24]

During Anderson's visit with Flagler they talked at great length about St. Augustine's future and what the resulting effects from a building program in that town might mean. After seeing all of the splendor and wealth displayed at Mamaroneck, Anderson asked Flagler why he had become interested in a musty old place like St. Augustine, when he had such beautiful surroundings at his New York home. Flagler's reply, in effect, was that his place at Mamaroneck was complete; it was finished, and there was very little to be done to enhance its value. But there was St. Augustine with all sorts of possibilities for development and he wanted to see what could be done with it.[25] It was Anderson's firm belief that his rich friend looked on the Ponce de Leon Hotel, his first undertaking in Florida, not wholly as a commercial enterprise, but largely as a pleasure for himself, a plaything perhaps, or a means of satisfying his desire to see what he could create in the quaint old town. He set out on his Florida enterprises without any idea of being able to obtain from them an income commensurate with his investment. The entire scheme seemed to be essentially a hobby. Sustaining his hobby, too, was another motive. Henry M. Flagler was a religious man imbued with a firm belief in a personal Deity. It was Dr. Anderson's belief that Flagler felt obligated to use his wealth in such a manner as to create opportunities for others to help themselves. He regarded furnishing large numbers of persons with employment as the highest form of charity. This desire was,

[24] Clarissa Anderson Dimick to author, February 28, 1946.
[25] Sworn statement to court by Andrew Anderson, 1923.

113

to a large extent, influential in shaping Flagler's efforts in Florida. Though Anderson was never officially connected with any of the Flagler enterprises, he was one of the oil magnate's most enthusiastic boosters.[26]

Anderson returned to St. Augustine in September to finish minor details before construction got under way. Flagler made a short visit to St. Augustine on October 22, but returned to New York on October 31.[27] The trip was merely to make routine inspection of what was going on, and to finish arrangements for digging the foundation. The excavation began on the Ponce de Leon on the morning of December 1, 1885, with the majority of the two thousand St. Augustine inhabitants on hand to see the initial stroke take place. Flagler arrived again on December 2 from New York and seemed satisfied with his project. He remained for nearly three weeks, going back to New York in time for the Christmas holidays.[28] All the information that had been kept secret concerning the hotel was now made public, and, as the great structure began to rise slowly from what had been wasted marsh lands, people throughout the East talked of the tremendous undertaking. Many people questioned Flagler's judgment in the matter, but the millionaire himself looked at the proposition from an entirely different angle. En route to Florida on one of his many trips in 1886 to see how the work was progressing, he was asked by a travelling companion why he was building that hotel in St. Augustine. Illustrating his answer with a story, Flagler replied, "There was once a good old church member who had always lived a correct life until well advanced in years. One day when very old he went on a drunken spree. While in this state he met his good pastor, to whom, being soundly upbraided for his condition, he replied, 'I've been giving all my days to the Lord hitherto, and now I'm taking

[26] *Ibid.*
[27] Diary of Henry M. Flagler, October 22–October 31, 1885.
[28] *Ibid.*, December 2–December 17, 1885.

one for myself.' This is somewhat my case. For about four-teen or fifteen years, I have devoted my time exclusively to business, and now I am pleasing myself."

Flagler's answer was typical of him, and was no doubt one of his motives for beginning the development. The companion, however, answered jokingly, "You have been looking for a place in which to make a fool of yourself, and you've finally chosen St. Augustine as the place." [29] This statement expressed the views of many of his close friends, but they knew that once Flagler had his mind set there was no way for anyone to change it.

For a while it seemed to Flagler that the work was going terribly slow, but it took time to get everything thoroughly organized. The building was one of the first large structures in the country to be made of poured concrete. St. Augustine offered no natural building stone other than the coquina, which in many instances was too soft. Ton upon ton of coquina gravel was brought over from Anastasia Island across the bay and was mixed with cement. Twelve hundred Negroes were engaged to tramp this mixture as it was poured into the forms. Hundreds of other laborers, both black and white, were employed to do the many other duties connected with construction. Slowly the four-foot-thick walls rose cast in one solid piece. Certainly one of the biggest problems was the transporting of materials to the scene of construction. The short railroad from South Jacksonville to St. Augustine did a Herculean job. Some of the lumber was secured from the banks of the St. Johns River in the Palatka area, being brought to Tocoi by river barge, and then transported to St. Augustine by rail. Coastal schooners were used in bringing heavy materials from Jacksonville via the Atlantic Ocean. Finished material as well as unfinished material had to be moved long distances. A great portion of the magnificently carved and dressed oak finish for the interior of the building

[29] L. C. Frohman, "From the Florida East Coast Files." MS., 3.

was prepared in New York, and was shipped to St. Augustine by water.

Despite all the effort, Flagler soon realized that the gigantic task of completing the hotel would not be finished in time for the 1887 season. The architects had insisted from the beginning that it would be difficult to meet his proposed deadline. The contractors for the Ponce de Leon Hotel were James A. McGuire and Joseph E. McDonald. Both men were prominent New England contractors, each having come to Florida because of the rich field in construction. McGuire had been brought down from Boston by Isaac Croof, a wealthy merchant, who proposed to build several hotels throughout the state. McGuire built for Croof the beautiful Magnolia Hotel at Magnolia Springs.[30] After this hotel was completed, McGuire was assigned to build the San Marco Hotel in St. Augustine. McDonald, who had just come to Florida, was also hired by Croof to work on the San Marco Hotel. The two men seemed suited to each other in their work, and did a magnificent job in building the first modern hotel in St. Augustine. It was at the San Marco Hotel that McGuire and McDonald first met Flagler. He admired their work from the beginning, and after a short conference with the two men, they agreed to do the work on the Ponce de Leon. McGuire and McDonald became Flagler's official contractors, just as Hastings and Carrere were called upon to make the plans for Flagler's building program in Florida.

Flagler carefully supervised the construction of the Ponce de Leon, and spent much time between his office in New York and his first project in Florida. He received with enthusiasm news from the contractors that the huge building would be ready for occupancy by January 1, 1888. So anxious was Flagler to see the hotel completed and furnished that this story which bears the impress of truth was told about him later: The furniture of the hotel was delayed several days,

[30] Magnolia Springs later became Green Cove Springs.

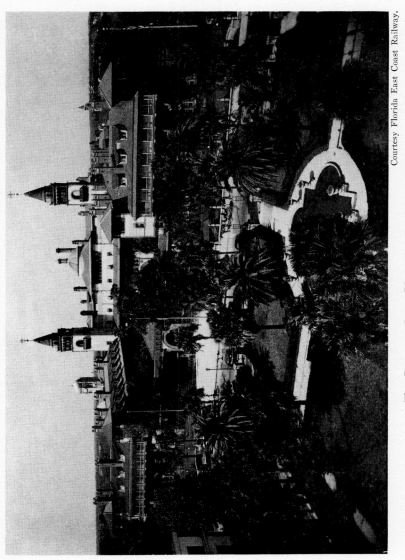

THE PONCE DE LEON HOTEL AT ST. AUGUSTINE

and finally when the schooners arrived at St. Augustine harbor, Flagler took off his coat and worked diligently to help transport the new furnishings to the newly constructed hotel. He liked to mix with the laborers; sometimes they were unaware of his presence. On this particular day, in conversation with a worker who thought Flagler was a day laborer also, one employee said, "This Flagler is a pretty good fellow." [31] It was worth the day's efforts for Flagler.

Another story is told about Flagler's being refused entrance to the Ponce de Leon grounds while the structure was being built. He often walked about the unfinished building smoking a cigar. There were "No Smoking" signs placed here and there for the attention of the workers. One day Flagler tried to enter, smoking his cigar, when he was stopped by a watchman. The millionaire quickly informed the watchman that he was Mr. Flagler, the owner of the hotel. The watchman replied, "I can't help that. There have been a good many Flaglers trying to get in here," and he did not get in until one of the contractors, James McGuire, came by and rebuked the guard for not recognizing his boss. Flagler, however, complimented the young man on his efficiency.[32]

The Ponce de Leon Hotel was finished on May 30, 1887, but was not formally opened until January 10, 1888, the beginning of the next season. The first dinner ever to be served in the $2,500,000 structure was given in an air of celebration and gaiety.[33] Hundreds of visitors crowded the spacious rotundas, corridors, and the tropical court, viewing perhaps the most beautiful decorations ever introduced in any hotel in the world. A prominent band from New York was brought

[31] *The Tatler*, January 21, 1893.
[32] Louis Larson to Barron Bridges, undated letter in Florida Historical Society Files.
[33] Printed Menu, January 10, 1888, St. Augustine Historical Society Library. The *Times-Union* gives the impression that the opening did not take place until January 12, but that was perhaps the day the newspaper reporter arrived on the scene. Several souvenir menus, dated January 10, 1888, for the formal opening dinner are in existence.

down for the first season, and merry-makers celebrated at great length the first of Henry M. Flagler's developments in Florida.

As the visitor approached the hotel, he was impressed by the size of the mammoth structure which covered most of a five-acre lot. The Ponce de Leon, with its medieval towers overlooking the Atlantic Ocean, was situated not far from the center of quaint old St. Augustine. It was fitting that the great structure should be named in honor of the discoverer whose romantic quest had made his name symbolic of the adventurous spirit of his age. The architects had truly preserved the spirit of Old Spain. They envisioned not merely a big hotel, but a pleasure palace, embodying the characteristics of Spanish Renaissance architecture, with sunny courts and cool retreats, fountains, and towers, and decorations suggestive of the history of the city.[34] The hotel was not a tall building in the modern sense of the word, being only four stories high, but it was big and sprawling. The grounds were beautifully arranged with tropical gardens, overhanging palms, and appropriate shrubbery. Adjacent to the grounds were a large orange grove and a woodland section which served as a back drop of dark green against the sandy tan color of the building.

The front entrance was arranged with verandas running along the street on each side of the main gate. On the grand arch were mermaids supporting the shields bearing the name of Ponce de Leon. There was definitely a theme of the sea displayed at all of the entrances. At the east entrance and west entrance there were fountains with water flowing from the mouths of dolphins. These were not only typical of the sea

[34] Charles B. Reynolds, *Architecture of the Hotel Ponce de Leon*, 3–4. The Ponce de Leon set a new standard in American architecture. It gave Carrere and Hastings a place in the forefront in the profession. From that time the firm exercised a preeminent influence in its field. Among its works were the interior of the Metropolitan Opera House, the New York Public Library, the Senate and House office buildings in Washington, the home of the Carnegie Institution of Washington, and the Memorial Ampitheater at Arlington.

but had local significance as well, for the name of the River of Dolphins was bestowed by the Frenchman, Laudonnière, when he anchored in Florida in 1564. The dolphins and the shells were motives repeated again and again throughout the hotel. Even the door knobs were modeled after shells.[35]

Inside the front gate was an interior court, covering an area of ten thousand feet, surrounded by vine-clad verandas. In the center there was a multi-colored fountain, around which was planted the most unusual evergreens. Directly across this court from the main entrance, the visitor entered the rotunda through the grand archway, which was twenty feet broad and above a number of smaller arches supported by pillars of terra cotta of spiral shape. The rotunda was a spacious area, being the center of operations of the building. It was inlaid with richly colored mosaic work. High above was the great dome supported by pillars of massive oak. The figures and ornaments, all of Spanish Renaissance, treated of eight subjects. Here were found allegorical representatives of the elements, fire, water, air, and earth. The other four figures, typical of adventure, discovery, conquest, and civilization, were located on the pendentives of the ceiling of the second story. These figures were very elaborate. Adventure wore a cuirass and on her helmet an eagle's crest. She held a drawn sword. Discovery was robed in drapery of the blue of the sea. In her right hand was half a globe; the other rested upon a tiller. Conquest, clad in martial red, with helmet and cuirass, firmly grasped an upright sword, significant of might and war-won supremacy. Civilization was clothed in white and wore a crown. In her lap was an open book, symbol of knowledge. Her face had the repose of dignity and benevolence.[36]

To the right of the rotunda were found the offices and parlors, and to the left was the grand parlor, decorated in keeping with the beauty of the hotel. Back of the rotunda

[35] *Ibid.*
[36] *Ibid.*, 5, 6.

was the grand dining hall. The stairs on the right and left walls leading up to the dining room were solid polished marble. The paintings here represented the Landing of Columbus, the Conquest of Charlemagne, and the Introduction of Christianity. Upon entering the dining hall, the visitor was impressed with the stained glass windows, the magnificent columns of antique oak, and the highly polished floors. The room was an oval in shape, seventy by 150 feet in size, and had a seating capacity of seven hundred people. Two galleries were in front and one in the rear overhanging the room. The ceilings were handsomely decorated with designs of the sixteenth century. Here was told the tragic story of St. Augustine's first years. It began with the persecutions of the French Huguenots, who in turn sought refuge in the New World. The pictured story continued, to show how Jean Ribaut explored the coast of Florida in 1562, under a commission given by the Admiral of France, searching for a location to plant a colony. He entered a river which he named the River of May (the St. Johns) and erected a stone pillar as token of possession. Later René de Laudonnière came with French colonists who built the fort at the mouth of the River of May. By a more definite claim, however, Florida belonged to Spain; so King Philip II sent his boldest Spanish adventurer, Pedro Menéndez, to drive out the French. Menéndez destroyed the French settlement and then moved southward to the mouth of the River of Dolphins and established a settlement for the Spanish. The paintings further told the story of a bloody massacre which Menéndez performed shortly thereafter at an inlet south of St. Augustine. He killed a large band of Frenchmen there who had been shipwrecked for some time. The inlet became known as Matanzas (Spanish for "slaughter") Inlet. Later Dominique de Gourges got revenge for the bloody acts of Menéndez, but by this time the Spanish were so well entrenched in Florida that it was impossible to uproot them.

This picture-writing was done by one of the most prominent artists of the day, Virgilio Tojetti. It was one of the most unusual of its kind in America. The general scheme was an adaptation of the picture-writing of the American Indian.[37]

Within the hotel there were 450 sleeping apartments: some were suites of rooms, some single rooms, and some were bridal chambers with most luxurious furniture. The furnishings in each room were worth approximately one thousand dollars. Electric lights, which were something of a novelty to most of the guests, were installed. Facilities for steam heat, seldom used in Florida, were also included in the building. There were numerous private parlors, reading rooms, game rooms, and refreshment rooms throughout the building. The furnishings in every room were most luxurious, including exquisite draperies, imported rosewood, walnut, and mahogany furniture, and Brussels carpet. There were two miles of halls and corridors, serving as avenues, all leading either directly or indirectly to the main rotunda.[38]

When Henry M. Flagler began the construction of the Ponce de Leon Hotel, he did not know that it would lead to further development. He soon realized, though, that the Ponce de Leon would need a sister hostelry catering to people who were not quite so wealthy. Accordingly, the Alcazar Hotel was built across the street to accommodate this group. The Alcazar was begun early in 1887 by McGuire and McDonald, contractors, the plans having been drawn by Carrere and Hastings. For a while both hotels were being built by virtually the same workmen. Materials and furnishings came from a common source, and many of the same ideas were used in both buildings. Both were in the Spanish Renaissance style, though the Alcazar had a distinctive Moorish stamp on it. It was opened with seventy-five furnished rooms late in 1888,

[37] *Ibid.*
[38] *Florida Times-Union,* January 13, 1888.

121

but it was not fully completed until the next year, when its formal opening was held.[39]

The Alcazar, an Arabic word meaning "royal castle," embraced some of the most beautiful specimens of architectural decorations from the castles of Seville. It rounded out perfectly the picturesque group of buildings on King Street— the Ponce de Leon, Alcazar, and the Casa Monica, which was built by Franklin Smith. The Alcazar was somewhat smaller than the Ponce de Leon, the dimensions being 250 feet by four hundred feet. The structure was four stories high, and was built around a court. Leading from the court were arcades similar to the Palais Royal. Stores, restaurants, shops, and salons opened upon the court. Above were two floors of rooms supported by handsomely carved columns and symmetrical arches. The façade was a reproduction of that of the famous Alcazar in Seville, one of the royal palaces of the kings. In front of the building was a large tropical garden with flowers, trees, and fountains. In the rear of the hotel was a large casino which was built at the same time. This part of the hotel was the "sporting section" and included sulphur and salt water pools for bathing, indoor amusement courts, and game rooms. It was one of the most popular places in Florida, and served many times as the scene of elaborate balls and parties. It was regularly used every season.[40]

Although the Alcazar did not accommodate as many guests as the Ponce de Leon, and had no rotunda nor dining hall as famous as that which could be found across the street, many people felt that it was just as beautiful as any of the Flagler structures. The cost of the Alcazar, including the casino, was only about half that of the larger hotel, but Flagler, himself,

[39] Conversation with William R. Kenan, Jr.
[40] *Florida Times-Union*, January 28, 1893. The casino was destroyed by fire on January 24, 1893, but was rebuilt immediately, and was used until the hotel closed. The Alcazar stood idle for a long time, but recently was converted into a hobby museum. The Ponce de Leon is still open a few months each winter.

felt that the Alcazar was equally as pretty. European travellers in this country usually spoke of the Alcazar in terms more glowing than those used for the Ponce de Leon.[41] The difference was simply a matter of taste.

As soon as the Ponce de Leon and Alcazar hotels were opened, they were filled with visitors from the North. Thousands of tourists poured into St. Augustine annually, and the news of Flagler's work there spread throughout the United States. Flagler became more pleased over the prospects, and by 1888 there was no doubt in his mind about spending more money in Florida. To add to his holdings he purchased the Casa Monica Hotel, which was located adjacent to the Alcazar, on the right. This hotel was under construction from 1886 to 1888. When Flagler purchased it in 1889, he renamed it the Cordova, and until 1894 operated it as a separate hotel. Later he built a connection between this hotel and the Alcazar and operated it in conjunction with the latter.[42]

Since Flagler's business interests in Florida were increasing rapidly, he spent a considerable part of his time in the state. There was always time for pleasure even though he was busy and the warm climate of St. Augustine made winters there pleasant. He and his wife loved St. Augustine and the gaiety which the old town offered. Mrs. Flagler usually was with her husband each time he went South. After the hotel opened, their suite at the Ponce de Leon was occupied each winter by the family and guests whom they brought from New York.

The private railroad car of the Flaglers, named Alicia for Mrs. Flagler, made travelling delightful. It was large and commodious, having several bedrooms, a spacious sitting room, dining room, and kitchen, with all of the conveniences of the homes of that day. Flagler made so many trips from New York to Florida he turned down opportunities to go to

[41] *Florida Times-Union*, January 16, 1893.
[42] *The Tatler*, December 15, 1894. This building is no longer a hotel, though the connection between it and the Alcazar was only recently removed.

other places and resorts. Travelling was not a pastime with him. Outside of a trip to Jamaica, and a business visit to the Bahamas, he was never out of the country. He had no desire to go abroad nor to visit distant places in the United States.

Since both of the Flaglers liked Florida so well, it was not long until they were planning to build their own home in St. Augustine. The building was begun in 1892, but they did not move in until March 1, 1893. Located only about two blocks from the Ponce de Leon Hotel, the newly-built Kirkside, as it was called, was a structure of much beauty. It was especially designed for winter living, and was spacious and roomy and fitted for entertaining. Pure colonial architecture prevailed throughout the fifteen-room structure. The front elevation was two stories high, the roof being supported by Ionic pillars. The capitals of the pillars were extremely rich and beautiful, corresponding with the cornices, brackets, and mouldings. The dwelling was white, with pale green blinds. Inside was exquisite furniture. Through the house ran a big hall with brightly decorated rooms on each side. The salon, which was usually considered the prettiest room, was suggestive of Versailles in all of its splendor. Added features to all the bedrooms were connecting baths and dressing rooms. The specially designed chandeliers furnished electric light. The grounds of Kirkside were artistically laid out. Plants and palms grew around the concrete walks and drives. The entire lot was enclosed by a coquina wall four feet high.[43]

Life was good to the Flaglers throughout the eighties and early nineties. His fortune was increasing by the millions, because of his large holdings in the Standard Oil Company, and she enjoyed to the fullest being married to a man of great wealth. During the winters in St. Augustine she entertained lavishly at the Ponce de Leon Hotel and in her own home; and although her husband cared little for social life, he usually tried to please her by participating freely in all of her enter-

[43] *The Tatler*, March 4, 1893.

tainments. St. Augustine was always a gay place during the winter months. It had come to be recognized as a vacation center for wealthy people of the East. Hundreds of them came each year. Alice Flagler tried diligently to lead the social life of the town but had only moderate success.[44]

One of her most elaborate entertainments for the winter society of St. Augustine was given on February 3, 1892, at the Ponce de Leon Hotel. She called it the "Hermitage Ball," the festival being commemorative of Andrew Jackson and his contribution to the state of Florida. Present were nearly a thousand persons, including many dignitaries who were guests at the hotel. President and Mrs. Benjamin Harrison received special invitations but were unable to attend. Ex-Governor Porter of Indiana, at that time United States minister to Italy, represented the President. Governor and Mrs. Francis P. Fleming of Florida were among those in attendance.

Mrs. Flagler wore a beautiful gown of white tulle, *en traine*, the front bodice being embroidered in mother of pearl and gold and the skirt was bordered with pearl fringe half a yard deep. The bodice was decolleté, the neck being finished with white ostrich. Bows of broad white velvet caught up the short sleeves. Her necklace was many strands of pearls, and a spray of marguerites formed a fillet for the hair. Alice Flagler made herself the center of attraction throughout the evening.[45]

On two other occasions during the same month the Flaglers were hosts at lavish social affairs, one of which was a colorful military ball on February 22, invitations to which were suggestive of great wealth. Over seven hundred of these expensively engraved letters were mailed. Dinner was served to the guests, after which brilliant fireworks were set off from the roof and grounds of the Ponce de Leon Hotel. Again Alice Flagler's gown and her actions during the evening attracted

[44] Conversation with Amy McMillan.
[45] *The Tatler*, February 6, 1892.

125

attention from every guest.[46] Though some of her guests did not approve of her conduct, she was usually the center of attention.

The winter of 1893 saw even more entertainment by the Flaglers than the year before. *The Tatler*, social sheet in St. Augustine, listed five formal affairs given by the Flaglers between January and March. Many small parties given at Kirkside were not listed. On March 23, 1893, Mrs. Flagler gave a dance at the Ponce de Leon which was called by *The Tatler* the "pearl dance" because of the unusual size and beauty of the pearls which she wore.[47] To Mrs. Flagler, St. Augustine was a playground. Her gait was too fast for her husband, and before long he began to withdraw from so much social activity.

Flagler's investments in Florida became so great that he invited his son Harry to come to Florida and help him bear some of the responsibility.[48] Young Flagler went reluctantly. It was the father's plan for Harry to learn the hotel and the railroad business and gradually succeed him in the work. Flagler needed greatly all the aid his twenty-three-year-old son could give him. The young man tried for two years to make himself a business executive; but none of the work was pleasant. His father could not understand why the son disliked the business world, but Harry Flagler was determined to follow a career more suited to his tastes. In the end, he returned to New York where he became prominent in musical circles.[49] Probably Flagler was a little overbearing in his dealings with his son; he did not realize that the youth was

[46] *Ibid.*, February 27, 1892.
[47] *Ibid.*, March 25, 1893.
[48] Conversation with T. V. Pomar.
[49] Harry Harkness Flagler gave much time and money to the Symphony Society of New York, and later became its president. Leopold Damrosch organized the society, and was its first conductor; later his son, Walter Damrosch, succeeded him. Harry Flagler was also president of the Philharmonic Symphony Society of New York. Conversation with Harry Harkness Flagler.

sincere in his distaste for the life that had been chosen for him. Nevertheless, the misunderstanding caused a breach between the two which never fully healed.[50] The youth's alienation from his father was not easy for the latter to accept because Harry was the only living child.

Jenny Louise Flagler, his only daughter, had died on March 25, 1889. Her first husband, John Arthur Hinckley, had died; and on October 6, 1887, she married Frederick Hart Benedict, a Wall Street broker. On February 9, 1889, she gave birth to a baby girl, but the child lived only a few hours. The mother's condition did not improve as expected; so her physician recommended that she be carried to Florida for rest and recuperation.[51] Her father-in-law, E. C. Benedict, who was well-known in yachting circles, offered his finest yacht, the *Oneida*, for the trip. The doctors felt that the cruise down the coast would be less strenuous than the trip by rail; then, too, the salt air from the ocean was thought to have certain healing qualities. Several days after the yacht put to sea, Jenny Louise became much worse. Complications set in; and before the yacht could reach Charleston, the nearest port, she died. Her husband and her brother Harry were with her at the time. Her father, who was in St. Augustine with his wife, went to Charleston and accompanied the party back to New York, where his daughter was buried in Woodlawn Cemetery. Several years later the Memorial Presbyterian Church was built in St. Augustine; and her remains, along with those of her mother and her infant child, were moved to a vault adjoining the church.[52] The passing of his daughter was a great source of sorrow to Flagler, and he determined to make the church a fitting memorial to her. Costing $200,000, it was completed in 1890, and the name changed from the First Presbyterian Church. The building was located at the rear of the Ponce de

[50] Henry M. Flagler to Andrew Anderson, August 19, 1896.
[51] Conversation with William R. Kenan, Jr.
[52] Harry Harkness Flagler to author, November 26, 1945.

Leon Hotel and was designed in the style of the Venetian Renaissance. The edifice was one of the chief adornments of the city, the dome contributing its dignity and grace to St. Augustine's picturesque skyline. Adjoining the church was the beautifully constructed mausoleum. Space for Flagler's tomb was also provided within the mausoleum. The dedicatory services were held in the new building on March 16, 1890. The church, which contained six hundred seats, was completely filled and running over for this occasion. Eight ministers were in charge of the services, and an imported choir from New York provided the music. Among the many notables present were the wife of the President of the United States, Mrs. Benjamin Harrison; the Vice-President of the United States, Levi P. Morton, and his wife; the John Wanamakers; the Henry M. Flaglers; Harry Flagler; and Frederick Benedict, husband of the young woman in whose memory the church was built.[53]

Flagler also befriended the Methodist and the Catholic congregations in St. Augustine. A disastrous fire almost destroyed the Catholic cathedral in the early nineties, and his contribution assisted in large part in the rebuilding of the structure.[54] In the case of the Methodist Church, Flagler wanted the lot on which their church stood; so he offered them a new building and parsonage only about five blocks from the old church. The new church cost $84,000, whereas he got property in return valued at $4,000.[55] Such action was typical of Flagler. If he wanted a thing bad enough, no price was too high to pay.

Flagler was interested in the betterment of St. Augustine, as well as her progress and development. On many occasions he rendered great service to the town, one being the construction of a modern hospital. He built it and then deeded it to a

[53] *Florida Times-Union*, March 17, 1890. The imported choir cost $6,000.
[54] *St. Augustine Evening Record*, May 20, 1913.
[55] Edwin Lefèvre, "Flagler and Florida," *Everybody's Magazine*, XXII (February, 1910), 178.

local board of trustees in 1889 at a very impressive ceremony. The hospital, too, was named Alicia for his wife.[56] Mrs. Flagler was greatly interested in this particular undertaking by her husband.

The structure consisted of a main building and two large pavilions. Flagler furnished it completely with beds, mattresses, and all the other necessities but he suggested the formation of an association of women to assist in maintaining it. This organization was perfected in 1888, before the hospital was finished, and by 1900 had earned more than thirty thousand dollars by holding benefit balls, teas, sewing parties, and other functions. The hospital handled a great number of charity cases, for which the county paid a small fee.

Among the other projects in St. Augustine to which Flagler contributed financially were the building of the City Hall and the Negro school, the paving of the streets, the establishment of a water works and electric lights, the laying of sewers, and the construction of a number of comfortable homes for his own employees. He also built there his car shops, which gave steady employment to hundreds of men.[57]

By the early nineties Flagler was St. Augustine's most prized resident. He had done more there in five years than most people had done in a lifetime. St. Augustine liked him and he liked St. Augustine. There was something about Florida he could not shake off. There was a challenge he could not let go unheeded. At the age of sixty he had carved a new career for himself. He looked to the future with anticipation and enthusiasm.

[56] *The Tatler*, February 3, 1900. About ten years before Flagler's death, the name was changed to Flagler Hospital; later a large sum of money was promised by the third Mrs. Flagler for a new plant, but she died (June, 1916) before the building became a reality; so the trustees of the estate gave $175,000 for the new hospital which still bears his name. Conversation with William R. Kenan, Jr.
[57] J. E. Ingraham, "The Story of the East Coast," *loc. cit.*, 4.

NINE

Penetrating the Florida Frontier

FLAGLER was not born a railroad builder; and there is but little evidence that he was ever interested in hotels until he saw the need for better accommodations in St. Augustine. The great need for a luxury hotel in the old city spurred him into action. Transportation facilities were equally as poor as the hotels, and because of this fact most of the visitors who came to Florida travelled by boat on the St. Johns River, patronizing hotels along its banks. But St. Augustine, located some distance from the river, was not affected directly by increased water transportation.

Flagler was well aware of Florida's poor railroads, but it was brought to his attention very distinctly when he began construction of the Ponce de Leon Hotel. The Jacksonville, St. Augustine and Halifax River Railroad ran from South Jacksonville to St. Augustine and was in position to serve St. Augustine effectively. However, it was a rickety little narrow-gauge railroad that gave poor service to St. Augustine and consequently was of little value to Flagler in his program of construction. He tried without success to get the owner to improve the road. His next move was to try to buy it and run schedules as he saw fit. Soon after the Ponce de Leon construction was begun Flagler began negotiations to purchase the short road. His efforts were successful and the property became Flagler's on December 31, 1885; whereupon the road was immediately improved.[1]

The narrow-gauge tracks, consisting of thirty-pound rails,[2] were speedily torn up and replaced with sixty-pound rails. New equipment was provided for the trains, and within a year material for Flagler's building program in St. Augustine was being shipped much faster than ever before. Tourists also began to use the new route, and the Ponce de Leon was filled to overflowing almost immediately on being opened to the public.[3]

During the next few years Flagler became interested in acquiring other railroad property connecting St. Augustine. The fact that he owned the road from South Jacksonville to St. Augustine made him indirectly interested in other roads. In 1888 he purchased two other short roads. The first was the St. Augustine and Palatka Railroad, which ran from St. Augustine to Palatka; and later he acquired the St. Johns Railroad running from Tocoi on the river to St. Augustine. Both trains used the same tracks from St. Augustine to Tocoi Junction, a distance of about six miles, but separated there, one track going to Tocoi and the other to East Palatka. This totaled more than forty miles of railroad, and gave Flagler access to the St. Johns River at Tocoi and East Palatka, as well as a depot at South Jacksonville. His building program at St. Augustine continued, and Flagler's fame began to spread. His railroad purchases claimed considerable attention, and he began to wonder if he should stop here. Late in 1888 he acquired the logging road that had been constructed from East Palatka to Daytona via San Mateo and Ormond by S. V. White. This acquisition gave him a direct line from South Jacksonville to Daytona, and he began at once to remodel the portions which had not already been improved. While

---

[1] Speech by Scott Loftin, July 8, 1935, Florida East Coast Files.

[2] Thirty-pound rails weigh thirty pounds per yard.

[3] E. S. Luther, "The Transformation of the Florida East Coast," *Banker's Magazine* (February, 1909), 259.

road crews were busy along the route, no schedules were interrupted. Standard-gauge tracks were completely laid by 1889, and the entire road from South Jacksonville to Daytona was as modern as could be found anywhere in the South.[4] It was with this accomplishment that Henry M. Flagler entered the field of railroads.

There were other developments which Flagler anticipated in connection with his railroad. Since his tracks touched the banks of the St. Johns River at Jacksonville, Tocoi, and Palatka, he realized the need of building bridges at those points. Tocoi, however, was soon eliminated from his plans because of the nature of the river at that particular place, but the actual work of bridging the St. Johns at Palatka was soon under way. The bridge was completed in 1888, and the millionaire then anticipated carrying his program of development into Palatka.[5] He made several visits to Palatka, but received little encouragement from the civic leaders. Their actions were perhaps prompted by their failure to get him interested in purchasing land there in 1885. At any rate, he was refused right to purchase lots on the river front for a hotel, and land farther from the river was so advanced in price that he became disgusted with his treatment and left.[6] At that time Palatka had two hotels, the larger one being the Putnam House, known far and wide for its splendor and beauty. It had served visitors to North Florida for a number of years, its popularity being due chiefly to the convenient location on the river. The Flagler touch on Palatka would have set off rapid growth in the little town.

Flagler did not let his setback in Palatka stop his efforts in that section. The bridge which he built was laid with tracks, and though the depot was built in East Palatka, cars were

[4] George M. Chapin, *Official Program, Key West Extension of the Florida East Coast Railway*, 5.
[5] Edwin Lefèvre, "Flagler and Florida," in *Everybody's Magazine*, XXII (February, 1910), 176.
[6] Conversation with the late Sims W. Rowley.

shuttled back and forth across the river, serving both communities. He liked Putnam County, and often visited East Palatka, San Mateo, and Hastings. He purchased a considerable amount of land in the latter two places. With the Hastings land he established a model farm, and helped in giving that place a name in the potato world. In San Mateo he turned his land into orange groves, and became a friendly competitor to all the other citrus growers in that section. Not only Flagler, but his railroad as well, was appreciated in San Mateo. On one occasion he favored all residents of San Mateo, several hundred in number, with a free train trip to St. Augustine and dinner at the Alcazar.[7]

Soon after the bridge at Palatka was built, Flagler made plans to bridge the St. Johns at Jacksonville. Passengers who were going by rail to St. Augustine and other points south had to be ferried across the river to South Jacksonville, where they boarded the train. To eliminate this inconvenience, Flagler began construction of an all-steel bridge in 1889. When it was opened for traffic on January 20, 1890, it was one of the finest of its kind ever built in the South, remaining in use until 1925.[8] The completion of the bridge meant that through trains could be operated between New York and St. Augustine, assuring the Ponce de Leon and Alcazar hotels of more guests during the winter season than ever before. These all-Pullman vestibule trains had been operated between New York and Jacksonville for a year or so. At the end of each car there was a closed vestibule, and one could go throughout the train without being exposed to the wind and weather. Perhaps the greatest wonder in connection with the new train was that it was electrically lighted throughout. So widely heralded was this new route to Florida that Grover Cleveland, then President of the United States, yielded to an urge for fast travel and made a visit to Jacksonville and St.

[7] *Florida Times-Union*, March 1, 1892.
[8] *A Brief History of the Florida East Coast and Associated Enterprises*, 12.

Augustine in the winter of 1888, stopping at the newly-constructed Ponce de Leon in the latter city.[9]

In order better to accommodate his passengers, Flagler built a modern railway depot in St. Augustine, not very far from the Ponce de Leon Hotel. It was a two-story structure, 106 by fifty feet, and included all the conveniences the late eighties could afford. The depot was built on a thirty-acre lot which had been filled in because of its marshy nature.[10] Another bit of expense which Flagler undertook as a railroad promoter was the laying of a continuous wire fence on both sides of the tracks for almost the entire distance from Jacksonville to Daytona. Cattle claims proved so numerous those first few years that something had to be done to keep them off the tracks. But even the fence failed to clear the tracks completely of the roving cattle which seemed anxious to have the run of the woods as well as Flagler's trains.[11]

During the late eighties both St. Augustine and Jacksonville claimed Henry M. Flagler. Each place felt honored to have his presence or his money. Jacksonville became so aroused over him and the attention he was giving Florida that the Board of Trade made an all-out effort to get him to sponsor a drive to bring tourists to that city. They appointed him on a local committee to plan and arrange a "Sub-Tropical Exposition," as they called it, for Jacksonville. The purpose was to attract people from all over the nation and advertise Jacksonville as the foremost Florida city.[12] Flagler took only moderate interest in the movement and the scheme never developed as completely as the Board of Trade hoped it would. In many respects Flagler was conservative in his spending and did not open up his purse to everyone who called upon him.

[9] *Ibid.*, 10.
[10] *Florida Times-Union*, April 22, 1888.
[11] J. T. Van Campen to author, March 2, 1946.
[12] *Florida Times-Union*, April 15, 1887.

By 1889 Flagler had thoroughly embarked on his new career as a builder and a developer. His railroad, which served Florida as far south as Daytona, made connections with steamers on the Halifax River which penetrated farther into the rich citrus belt. The expenditures had run to a figure fully ten times that originally contemplated almost without realization by the promoter himself. One thing called for another. Each time he looked around his energetic mind found new possibilities for development. His interest continued to lead him southward in Florida into the heart of an undeveloped country. In this respect he was a frontiersman—a nineteenth century pioneer.

His next move was to purchase an interest in the small hotel at Ormond, a town on the coast north of Daytona. It was erected by John Anderson, a native of Maine, and Joseph D. Price, from Kentucky. The construction of the hotel was done with money lent the builders by the same S. V. White, long-famed Wall Street operator, who financed the construction of the railroad from East Palatka to Daytona. The venture did not prove profitable to Anderson and Price; so Flagler bought them out in 1890. The Flagler touch was all it needed. He enlarged the building and beautified the grounds. The hotel was well located, between the Halifax River and the ocean, but not far from either. One visitor declared that it was an extremely comfortable place and "more home like than any other Flagler Hotel, and the grounds have a more exotic look than those hotels in St. Augustine." [13] Among the many features at the Ormond Beach Hotel were the golfing facilities. A new eighteen-hole course was constructed, and though Flagler cared nothing for golf himself, he foresaw what an attraction a good course would be. Automobile racing fans also crowded the Ormond Beach Hotel to enjoy that sport which soon made Ormond and Daytona beaches famous.

[13] Edwin Lefèvre, "Flagler and Florida," *loc. cit.*, 171.

Much enthusiasm was also shown in bicycling, special equipment being furnished for those engaging in this and water activities.[14]

Down the coast was Daytona, another hopeful prospect for the magic touch of Flagler. But Daytona, like Palatka, was not very cordial; consequently he did not leave there such an imprint as he had in Ormond or St. Augustine. Daytona was the terminal point for the Flagler railroad for a number of years. South of Daytona the east coast of Florida was not very inviting. Only a few travellers ventured into that region. Nevertheless a few settlers inhabited the banks of the Indian River. The Indian River, Lake Worth, Biscayne Bay, and other waterways provided the main thoroughfare of travel. The mode of transportation was sail boats and other small craft, which were subject to the uncertainties of wind and weather. This entire section showed much promise as an agricultural region. Oranges and pineapples were already being shipped by boat from the Indian River region.[15] It is doubtful if Flagler had any intention of extending his railroad south of Daytona in 1890. His interest, as it had been since 1885, was in the construction of hotels. He talked considerably about further hotel construction, and the rumor got about that he was thinking of building a big hotel in every Florida city. Enthusiastically, the *Weekly Floridian* insisted from the capital city of Tallahassee, "Come right along, Mr. Flagler: Tallahassee is the very place to locate one of them [hotels]." [16] But Flagler was not interested in building hotels in places except possible resort centers.

It is not known exactly when Flagler made up his mind to push his railroad into Florida's frontier. Prior to 1890, he had never built a mile of railroad. All he had done was to buy old railroad properties, improve them, build bridges, and in-

[14] *The Tatler*, December 23, 1889.
[15] *A Brief History of the Florida East Coast and Associated Enterprises*, 13.
[16] *Weekly Floridian* (Tallahassee), June 4, 1890.

crease the equipment. From 1890 to 1892 his road did a good business in connection with the Indian River steamer traffic. He bought a few small boats himself for the purpose of running regular schedules up and down the Indian River, making connections with the Jacksonville, St. Augustine, and Halifax River Railroad at Daytona. This road, which was a consolidation of all the properties that Flagler had bought to this time, was doing good business. Flagler was the president of the company, and Charles C. Deeming was the secretary and treasurer. They owned eleven locomotive engines, seventeen passenger cars, five baggage, mail and express cars, and ninety freight cars—a total of one hundred twelve cars. The capital stock of the road amounted to $200,000.[17]

Much demand was soon made on Flagler to push his road on into the Indian River section. People pointed out that a direct railroad line down the coast would be a better proposition to control and develop traffic than the existing route up the Indian River by steamer and from there by rail. Landowners offered some inducement, and many promised a right of way for the railroad extension. Flagler studied the matter for two years, after which time he was thoroughly convinced that he had gone too far with his developments to stop at this point. In 1892 he obtained a charter from the state of Florida authorizing him to build a railroad along the Indian River as far south as Miami.[18] It is rather certain, however, that Flagler had no ambition for a railroad that far. His immediate plans called for the road to go to Rockledge; and perhaps, if things worked out right, he might build on down the coast to Lake Worth, which was one of the most desirable spots on the east coast.

Preliminary plans were hurriedly made, and Flagler hastened to New York to make the necessary financial arrange-

---

[17] *Poor's Manual, Railroads of the United States*, XXIII (1890), 636.
[18] J. E. Ingraham, "The Story of the East Coast," in *Picturesque Florida*, I (January, 1910), 4.

ments. Land was purchased, equipment gathered, and laboring crews assembled for the great task. On June 17, 1892, Flagler telegraphed to his superintendent to begin the construction of the railroad from Daytona to Rockledge.[19] Working under favorable conditions, the railroad was completed to New Smyrna on November 2, 1892, and on that same day the first train puffed into the little village which had been founded by Andrew Turnbull in 1707, but had about dwindled from the map.[20] It was a significant day in the history of the east coast because it stamped Flagler as a builder and developer of railroads as well as hotels. About the same time a more appropriate name was given the railroad, the Jacksonville, St. Augustine and Indian River Railroad, after which time construction was pushed with even greater rapidity into the heart of Florida's undeveloped east coast.

On February 6, 1893, Flagler's train rolled into Titusville, and on February 27, 1893, the little towns of Cocoa and Rockledge were gaily decorated to greet the iron horse. Very few people ever dreamed of seeing a railroad running south of Daytona. Little children clung to their mothers' skirts and grownups stared in amazement to see the little engine move slowly towards a make-shift depot. Flagler's name became a byword. He could not stop now. Over eighty miles of new railroad had been constructed and put into operation in less than a year. The Standard Oil magnate received a big thrill from watching the two ribbons of steel roll southward; he had employed more than fifteen hundred men to complete the task. But the task was only half completed, and Flagler's nature would never allow him to stop until a thorough job was done. Along the southern banks of the Indian River there were more pineapples and oranges which could be marketed much better if fast railroad freight service were available. The

---

[19] *Weekly Floridian*, June 25, 1892.
[20] *Florida Times-Union*, April 24, 1893.

cultivation of this fruit was expanding rapidly, spreading farther south along the coast.[21]

Flagler could not resist the urge for further action. He gave orders to continue with the construction towards Palm Beach. He saw hidden possibilities in this seemingly crude land. There was a considerable amount of work to be done in laying the rails, because Flagler wanted the road to follow the coast as nearly as possible. Marshy places were filled in and built up while at others the track was laid on graded sandy soil. The rails weighed sixty pounds to the yard, though these were later replaced with ninety-pound steel tracks.[22]

The track was finished to Eau Gallie on June 26, 1893, and by January 29, 1894, trains were operating to Fort Pierce. The little settlement at Palm Beach waited anxiously for the coming of Flagler's train to their community. But much planning and building were necessary before that section could feel the magic touch. On March 22, 1894, workmen completed construction of the tracks to a point across Lake Worth from Palm Beach, which was to be the terminus of the Flagler railroad.

II

Palm Beach was only a small community but settlers had inhabited the narrow strip of land just off the Florida coast for many years. It was separated from the mainland by an arm of the ocean, which was called Lake Worth, having been named for General William J. Worth by United States soldiers who had been sent there before the Civil War to settle Indian troubles. In October, 1867, George W. Sears was cruising southward along the Florida east coast from the Indian River to Miami when he noticed what looked like an inlet to the ocean. Upon exploring the inlet he found that it

[21] J. T. Van Campen to author, March 2, 1946.
[22] *Ibid.*

led inside a shallow pass into a beautiful tropical lake, the shores of which were lined with overhanging trees, jungle vines, and foliage. Sears was astounded at what he saw, a paradise virtually untouched. The only living beings in the Lake Worth area at this time were one or two deserters from the Confederate Army who did not know that the war had been over for two years.[23] Sears revealed with enthusiasm the story of Lake Worth to his friends. Soon others came to visit the place, and it was not long before a small community had grown up on the island. Some drifted there for one reason or another, perhaps because land was cheap, or the winters were balmy, or neighbors scarce. By 1878, there was not much promise that the settlement would ever develop into a thriving town.

Among the early settlers who came during the late seventies was Robert R. McCormick, Chicagoan of harvester fame. He bought several large tracts of land and built a winter home on Lake Worth. He was considered the first developer of Palm Beach. His tropical gardens contained almost every tree, shrub, and flower that could thrive in the soil and climate. Another early resident of Palm Beach was Captain O. S. Porter, who early saw the advantages of the tropical lake area. As years passed other people learned of the beauty of Lake Worth, and winter homes increased there, all of them being built on the east side of the lake. The first post office was established in 1878 and the name of "Lake Worth" was given to the community. The first postmaster was V. O. Spencer, who used a row boat to visit the settlers around the lake in quest of signatures for the petition to the Post Office Department.[24]

The name of "Lake Worth" did not become permanent. Within a few years there was a move led by E. M. Brelsford to re-name the settlement "Palm City," but the Post Office

[23] Unidentified clipping, Welsh Scrapbook, Vol. 48, 6.
[24] J. W. Travers, *History of Palm Beach*, 4.

Department in Washington refused to accept that name. There was much protest made because "Palm City" was rejected, but a compromise was soon effected. Gus Ganford, a visitor from Philadelphia, who was prospecting in the wild jungle country of South Florida, heard about the rejection of the name and suggested that the community submit the name of "Palm Beach" since there was no other city in the United States with this name. Thereupon a petition was immediately dispatched to Washington, requesting the change. Three weeks later, in March, 1886, the name of Palm Beach, Florida, was confirmed by the Post Office Department.[25]

Within a few years more people learned about Palm Beach, situated between the lake and the ocean. The fertile soil and near-perfect climate made possible many kinds of tropical plants including the coconut palm and the royal poinciana. It made an ideal resort, but it needed the touch of a man who had the vision to see its possibilities, and the will and resources to do something about it.

In the meantime, Flagler visited Palm Beach on one of his trips to St. Augustine. It was in the early nineties. There were not more than a dozen or so houses in Palm Beach at the time. It was a good three days travel from Jacksonville and unless one desired frontier conditions he did not choose these surroundings. But Flagler was charmed with South Florida, and the Palm Beach section was much to his liking. He decided to make further investigations. In April, 1893, he made another trip to Palm Beach, and after consultation with some of his lieutenants, decided to buy some of the McCormick property for seventy-five thousand dollars and build another typical Flagler hotel.[26] The community was electrified when it heard that he intended to construct his railroad as far south as Palm Beach. He announced that work on the hotel would begin im-

[25] *Palm Beach News* (Souvenir Edition), 1903. Lake Worth later became the name of a community several miles down the coast.
[26] *Palm Beach Post-Times*, November 17, 1940.

mediately and that the railroad would be extended as soon as possible. Flagler's purchase of land in Palm Beach was publicized far and wide. Prices of real estate increased to incredible figures. Land that had been virtually worthless was immediately priced from one hundred fifty to one thousand dollars an acre. The boom was on. Homesteaders, who had come to Palm Beach several years earlier, suddenly found themselves rich.[27]

Flagler and his lieutenants moved swiftly to locate hundreds of workmen in Palm Beach. There were no housing facilities; so they were all put into a community of tents and shanties which was given the name of the "Styx." On May 1, 1893, work was begun on a new hotel, already named the Royal Poinciana. Here again, as in the case of the Ponce de Leon Hotel, the transporting of materials to the scene of construction was the biggest problem. Work on the railroad was progressing simultaneously with that on the hotel; therefore Flagler had to provide other means for shipping materials to Palm Beach. Most of it was brought by railroad to Eau Gallie, and from there to Jupiter it was sent by boat. But from Jupiter to Juno, a distance of about eight or ten miles materials were shipped by way of a little railroad called the "Celestial Line." From there on to Palm Beach water transportation was used. Some of the lumber for the Royal Poinciana Hotel was shipped by way of river steamers down the coast of Florida to Palm Beach. Several Mississippi steamers were purchased by Flagler for this purpose.[28]

As late as the spring of 1893, there were virtually no settlers on the west side of the lake where West Palm Beach now stands. However, Flagler saw the possibilities of establishing a commercial town there, leaving the east side, or Palm Beach,

[27] *A Brief History of the Florida East Coast and Associated Enterprises,* 4.

[28] Conversations with J. Borman and T. V. Pomar.

142

to the winter visitors. In April, 1893, he purchased several hundred acres of land, largely from Captain O. S. Porter, and laid out the town site for West Palm Beach. His idea was to terminate the oncoming railroad in that place.[29] He moved the Styx across the lake, so that his workmen were all housed in the newly-created town. The Styx grew rapidly, and consequently West Palm Beach soon became a thriving town. Tents and shacks continued to spring up as more and more workmen poured into the area. West Palm Beach resembled a mining camp similar to the frontiers of the far West, suffering some of the rough elements that pervaded those towns. The only difference was in the location. The workmen rowed across Lake Worth each morning to their jobs at the Royal Poinciana and then back across the lake in the afternoon.[30]

The town of West Palm Beach, as it was laid out in August, 1893, extended from the waters of Lake Worth some distance westward to Clear Lake. J. E. Ingraham, one of Flagler's most able assistants, was placed in charge of the construction in the infant town. The streets were given the names of trees, fruits, and flowers common to the area. The east and west streets were called Clematis, Fern, Datura, Banyan, and Althea. The north and south avenues Lantana, Narcissus, Olive, Poinsettia, Rosemary, Sapodilla, and Tamarind. One of the first city organizations was the fire department. Ingraham thought such an organization was specially needed since many of the shacks and huts of the new town were highly inflammable. These fire fighters were called the "Flagler Alerts." A bell atop a building used for a city hall summoned the fire fighters to duty. When the bell was sounded, the "Alerts" jumped on bicycles, rushed to the city hall, donned helmets and coats, and then sped away to the flaming structure with a cart-like hose-reel and hand engine, hoping that the fire would not be

[29] *Florida Times-Union*, April 10, 1893.
[30] *Miami Herald*, August 5, 1944.

burned out when they arrived. The day of the horse drawn fire engine was yet to come to West Palm Beach.[31]

The new city grew much faster, in comparison, than Palm Beach. Wooden stores were erected, one of the first merchants being George S. Maltby, a furniture dealer and undertaker, from McPherson, Kansas. Another newcomer was E. M. Hyer from Orlando, who operated a small store. Captain E. M. Dimick opened the first drugstore. The next step for West Palm Beach was to become an incorporated town, and several of her first citizens worked diligently to that end. After a number of mass meetings the town was duly incorporated on November 10, 1894. John S. Earman was elected mayor of West Palm Beach by seventy-eight voting citizens. George W. Potter, E. H. Dimick, J. M. Garland, J. F. Lamond, George Zapf, H. T. Grant, and H. J. Burkhardt were elected aldermen. For their city clerk the citizens elected Eli Sims, and W. L. Torbett was made city marshal. West Palm Beach came into existence with comparative ease and a population of about one thousand people. The laws of Florida provided that when two-thirds of the voters within a certain area decide to become incorporated, they could file a request with the clerk of the circuit court for immediate action, and this was done without sanction from the state legislature. West Palm Beach was situated in Dade County at the time of its incorporation, the county seat being located at Juno.[32]

Henry M. Flagler was the benefactor of early West Palm Beach. He helped in many of the civic projects, as well as undertaking large private developments there. Houses were built for his employees, and the temporary dwellings were slowly torn down. Flagler contributed to public funds and helped in the construction of several of West Palm Beach's prominent buildings. He gave a plot of land for a municipal cemetery, and at one time expressed a desire to be buried in

[31] *Ibid.*
[32] *Palm Beach Tropical Sun*, March 5, 1937.

West Palm Beach. He also built the Catholic Church in the city because a large number of his employees, including Joseph McDonald, were Catholics.[33]

Largely as the result of Flagler's efforts, Palm Beach County was created out of Dade County in 1909, West Palm Beach becoming the county seat. The newly-created county seat had a population of 1,700 people, and had outgrown its sister-city, Palm Beach, both in size and commercial importance. Palm Beach continued to cater to resort activities and did not become a separate municipality until 1911. This act marked the passing of the Flagler era in both of the Palm Beaches.

III

Flagler's greatest contribution to the Lake Worth region was the extension of his railroad down the east coast, and the construction of the Royal Poinciana and Breakers hotels. The railroad was completed to West Palm Beach on April 2, 1894, and the Royal Poinciana was finished in record time and opened on February 11, 1894, having been started on May 1, 1893.[34] It was located on the eastern shore of Lake Worth and embraced about one hundred acres of the most beautiful land in that section, the grounds being covered with perhaps the greatest variety of tropical growth found in Florida.[35] Though the hotel's frontage was on the lake, the ocean was only several hundred yards in the rear. The structure was one of the largest wooden buildings in the world used exclusively for hotel purposes. It required 1400 kegs of nails; 5,000,000 feet of lumber; 360,000 shingles; 4,000 barrels of lime; 500,000 bricks; 240,000 gallons of paint; and more than a million dollars to build. The hotel had 1200 windows and 1300 doors. One of Flagler's heaviest expenses was transportation, since his own road had not at that time been completed. The lumber cost from $13.50

---

[33] Conversation with J. Borman.
[34] *Miami Herald*, August 5, 1944.
[35] *Florida Times-Union*, April 10, 1893.

to $16.00 per thousand; shingles from about $2 to $3 per thousand; bricks about $12 per thousand; and lime about $1.35 per barrel. The wages for carpenters and other laborers ran from $1.50 to $2.25 a day.[36]

It was necessary to build up part of the land on which the Royal Poinciana was constructed, but filling in swamps and hammocks was not unusual for the millionaire. His engineers dumped thousands of carloads of earth on marshy lands which later became a magnificent golf course adjacent to the hotel. Avenues of Australian pines were planted to enhance the dignity of the building and tropical shrubs and trees lent grace and beauty to the surroundings. The hotel was named for the royal poinciana tree, a native of Madagascar and common to the tropics. It is a beautiful umbrella-shaped tree and produces a scarlet and orange flower. It is extremely delicate, and stands very little cold weather.

The building itself was a huge sprawling structure with 540 bedrooms, accommodating 800 at the time it was opened in 1894. The building was enlarged from time to time, the final capacity being around 1200 guests. The dining room had a seating capacity for 1600 people. At the time the hotel was constructed, it was considered the largest resort hotel in the world. Though it was only six stories high, it covered several acres of ground. In the center of the building was a large rotunda from which ran several miles of hallways. There were spacious drawing rooms, lounges, parlors, and a casino. A large veranda ran across the front of the building.[37] The furniture was chosen with utmost care and taste, attracting the most fastidious traveller. The color scheme on the inside was green and white. The chairs were upholstered in green velvet and there was a light green carpet on the floor. The walls and ceilings in the more prominent rooms were painted in light green with trimmings of white. The outside of the hotel was

---

[36] *Florida East Coast Homeseeker*, June, 1916, 10.
[37] J. W. Travers, *History of Palm Beach*, 6.

painted yellow with white trimmings.[38] The building was enlarged in 1899 and again in 1901.[39]

The Royal Poinciana was the gathering place for wealth, fashion, and society. It was known throughout the United States for its service and food. Some seasons, wealthy patrons paid more than $100 a day for a double room, including meals; however, much cheaper rooms were available and the price differed from season to season. As in the other Flagler hotels there could be found a great variety of accommodations, depending entirely upon one's desires and ability to pay. Approximately 1400 employees were kept busy during the months when the hotel was open, usually from December to April. There was a waiter for every four diners, a chamber maid for every few rooms, and a bell man in every hall. Highlighting the social season each year was the Washington Birthday Ball, held on February 22. This event was always the most brilliant and the most anticipated of the year. Thousands of dollars were spent in preparing for the affair each year. Among other social activities engaged in each season were cake walks, teas, balls, and dinners. The gay nineties were perhaps nowhere gayer than in Palm Beach.

Outdoor activities were probably more popular than the social affairs on the inside. Each evening found people on the lawn and in the gardens, or strolling informally along the lake front. They were picturesque in their conservative attire. The ladies wore dark skirts and white blouses with leg-of-mutton sleeves. The men were dressed in light trousers or tight-fitting knickers, dark coats, stiff collars, and caps. Golf was the popular sport among the visitors, and two eighteen-hole courses were available. Numerous tennis courts, motor boats, wheel chairs, bicycles, and courteous well-trained attendants furnished by the hotel for the exclusive use of its guests com-

[38] Conversation with Lillian Bradstreet.
[39] It was condemned in 1928 and the frame structure was torn down soon thereafter. Conversation with J. Borman.

pleted the various other forms of amusement. A regular trolley car drawn along the track by a donkey between the Poinciana and the ocean several hundred yards away was provided to carry guests to and from the beach. The little cart was a special treat for the children.

There were certain cultural features, too, provided for the guests at the Poinciana. Perhaps the most stressed was religious worship. Guests frequently heard religious discourses by the Reverend E. B. Webb, who came to Palm Beach in 1895. Flagler engaged Mr. Webb to lecture weekly, and built an annex to the Royal Poinciana where people might assemble. Guests at both hotels, regardless of their religious affiliations, visited the chapel regularly. After Webb's death, in 1900, Flagler remodeled the little chapel and prevailed on George M. Ward, who was at that time president of Rollins College, Winter Park, Florida, to become the minister. Ward, who became an intimate friend of Flagler, served in this capacity for thirty-one years.[40]

The second of the Flagler hotels in Palm Beach was the Breakers, though it was not always called by this name. For a number of years it was known as Palm Beach Inn. The building was begun during the summer of 1895, and was located one quarter of a mile east of the Royal Poinciana on the ocean shore. It was opened for the first time in January, 1896. The Inn had a most unusual history. From the start, it was not as pretentious as the Poinciana; however, after the first few seasons the building was enlarged and beautified and the name changed to the Breakers. A modern structure was completed in 1900, and it gave promise of rivaling the Royal Poinciana but in 1903 the building was completely ruined by fire. It was replaced in 1906, and was as luxurious and popular as any of the Flagler hotels.[41]

[40] *Palm Beach News* (Souvenir Edition), 1936.
[41] This building burned in 1925 but was soon thereafter rebuilt, and made into one of the finest hotels in the world. The new Breakers is today one of the finest resort hotels in the United States, being located on the ocean shore in Palm Beach. See William R. Kenan, Jr., *Incidents By the Way*, 81.

Flagler also built a number of cottages along the ocean in Palm Beach, as well as his own home which was situated on Lake Worth. In 1896, he built a railroad and footbridge across Lake Worth, connecting the two Palm Beaches. This made it possible for visitors to come to West Palm Beach on his railroad and have easy access to either of his hotels in Palm Beach. The tracks across the lake reached the Palm Beach side at a point just south of the Poinciana Hotel. From there they were continued on to the Breakers, and for several years trains deposited passengers at the south door of both hotels. The railroad across the lake later became a street car line and Flagler's railroad was terminated in West Palm Beach. It remained the terminus for several years while Flagler took stock of his Florida developments.

Much speculation ensued. Would Flagler go farther south with his developments? Those who knew him best contended that he would never be satisfied until he had reached the southernmost tip of Florida. He did not give any indication of what he proposed to do, but Flagler was a man of action, and it was not long before he gave his answer.

The City That Flagler Built

HENRY M. FLAGLER was the father of Miami. The little settlement which was located on the point where the Miami River empties into Biscayne Bay gave very little promise of growth, despite its beautiful location, until the Standard Oil magnate touched it with his magic millions. For many years the spot had attracted a few frontiersmen. As early as February 27, 1808, the Spanish government, which then dominated in Florida, granted one hundred acres of land to one John Egan on the Miami River, the name being an Indian word meaning "Sweet Water." Egan, who was a hardy pioneer himself, persuaded a few settlers to join him in making a home on the banks of the beautiful river, in view of the bay. This was the beginning of Miami.

After Florida was transferred to the United States in 1821, James Egan, a son of John Egan, laid claim to a large portion of the land in the Biscayne Bay area because of the grant which his father had been given by the Spanish government in 1808. Young Egan went through the formality of presenting his petition to the United States Commissioners at St. Augustine. The Commissioners deemed his claim valid and he was given deeds to 640 acres of choice land along the shores of Biscayne Bay by the federal government.

Egan found a few brave settlers in the vicinity, but others came with the outbreak of the Seminole Indian War in 1836. Much more activity took place as the settlers in the surrounding area sought protection from the savage Indians. The federal government established Fort Dallas at the mouth of the Miami River and war activities in the area radiated from that point. Hundreds of troops got a taste of early Miami long before it was ever developed. The war itself helped to open up other portions of the Miami River to settlers.[1]

There was no effort made to advertise Fort Dallas, as the settlement was called, or South Florida to the outside world before the Civil War. After the Civil War was over the Biscayne Bay Company and several other land companies bought up tremendous tracts of land, including the Egan grant. Their purpose was to develop the region, and one syndicate had the idea of raising bananas along the Miami River. It made extensive plans, and hoped to make millions of dollars from the sale of Florida bananas. At the time, Cuban bananas were selling for one dollar per bunch plus transportation, and the syndicate felt that they could raise bananas as well as the growers in Cuba. But their hopes were doomed to failure. The bananas in Florida would not grow the size of the Cuban bananas; consequently the whole plan was abandoned, and the future of Fort Dallas lay in her possibilities as a commercial and resort center rather than a banana plantation.[2] In the meantime the Biscayne Bay Company continued to sell land around the mouth of the river. There were a few other settlements growing up in the area also. At Coconut Grove, six miles south of the Miami River, a lighthouse keeper and several families had located, and a few fishermen lived along the bay. One of the first settlers to buy land from the Biscayne Bay Company was William B. Brickell. In 1871 he moved to Fort Dallas and located south of the river. He was a hearty venturer, and depended at first on fishing and salvaging for a livelihood. Later he established a trading post at the mouth of the river very near the old fort, which had virtually become abandoned by this time. Brickell traded mostly with the In-

[1] Florida Press Association, *Bulletin*, March 22, 1901.
[2] Harry Hargis, *Miami in Your Pocket*, 14.

dians and fishermen, living the life of a typical pioneer in a section whose possibilities had not yet been opened up to development.[3]

The next pioneer to settle at Fort Dallas was Mrs. Julia D. Tuttle, who came to south Florida with her husband and her father, Ephraim T. Sturtevant, about the same time that William D. Brickell located there. Julia Tuttle was fascinated with everything about south Florida. She liked the Miami River and beautiful Biscayne Bay. Her father and her husband returned to their native home, Cleveland, Ohio, but Mrs. Tuttle decided to remain in Florida for a time. She purchased 640 acres of land from the Biscayne Bay Company on the north bank of the Miami River, built a small cabin and enjoyed the backwoods life of a wilderness region. In the meantime her husband died and she returned to Cleveland, but only for a short while. She came back to Fort Dallas on November 13, 1891, and remained there until her death on September 14, 1898.[4]

Mrs. Tuttle bought and remodeled the old fort and made a very comfortable home out of it. She liked Fort Dallas but for several years she was unable to attract many permanent settlers there to buy her land. She was on the north side of the river and Brickell was on the south side of the river. Taxes began to amount to large sums; so both Mrs. Tuttle and Brickell began to redouble their efforts to sell portions of their property.

Mrs. Tuttle was a very clever woman and possessed many good business qualifications. She had heard of Henry M. Flagler, since most of Florida was experiencing either directly or indirectly some benefit from his developments down the east coast. There is some possibility that Mrs. Tuttle knew Flagler before he left Cleveland, but at any rate she knew of his reputation in connection with the Standard Oil Company.

[3] Florida Press Association, *Bulletin*, March 22, 1901.
[4] E. V. Blackman, *Miami and Dade County, Florida*, 59.

She saw her opportunity, and decided to contact Flagler about Fort Dallas, hoping that he might be interested in extending his railroad there. At this time the road was not quite completed to West Palm Beach, but if Flagler should begin to buy land in Fort Dallas, reasoned Mrs. Tuttle, the activity would set off a land boom. She hoped it might come to pass.

Her first move was to visit Flagler in St. Augustine in 1893, but the trip was in vain. Flagler considered her just another salesman of land, and did not entertain any idea of building his railroad further than West Palm Beach. Mrs. Tuttle went back to south Florida very discouraged, but she did not let Flagler's refusal get the better of her. She then pestered him with letters offering to divide her large property holdings north of the river with him. But her persistent pleas continued to fall on deaf ears. Flagler's opinion of Mrs. Tuttle was lessened with his receipt of each letter. In the end, however, her continued efforts brought much success, but not until Providence favored her.[5]

Florida experienced her coldest weather in over a hundred years, some sources declare, during the winter of 1894–95. The first freeze occurred on December 24, 1894, and then on the night of December 28, 1894, the temperature fell to 19° in north and central Florida.[6] Oranges were ruined throughout central Florida. The cold spell lasted for several days. Again on February 6, 1895, another hard freeze hit the state.[7] The farmers were hardly over the first spell when the second crept down from the North Pole. These hard freezes of 1894–95 ruined not only the citrus crop but killed the vegetables and coconut palms as far south as Palm Beach. It damaged property to the extent of millions of dollars, and left hundreds of people without income from their crops. Many persons who had come to Florida to raise fruit and spend the winter packed

[5] Harry G. Cutler, *History of Florida*, I, 396.
[6] *Florida Times-Union*, December 29, 1894.
[7] *Ibid.*, February 8, 1895.

what they could carry of their earthly possessions and began their trek back North, leaving their houses to the bats, owls, or perhaps the Negro tramp.[8]

What the people of north and central Florida lost most in the freeze was their confidence in the state and its possibilities of becoming a great citrus-producing section. People with vision quickly saw what the disappointed people were experiencing. Mrs. Tuttle, taking advantage of the freeze, reminded Flagler of the fact that the Miami River region had been untouched by the cold weather. She reminded him that the settlement at the mouth of the river was in a tropical region and that it could easily become the center of a great citrus belt if Flagler would only lend a hand. Flagler began to think back over Mrs. Tuttle's propositions. He was in St. Augustine at the time, and instructed J. E. Ingraham, who was in Palm Beach, to make a trip to Biscayne Bay and investigate the conditions there. Ingraham immediately visited Mrs. Tuttle and was surprised but delighted to find that the freezing weather had not reached that far south. Flowers were in full bloom, and not a single orange tree had been killed. He concluded that the climate was ideal for the raising of citrus fruit. As evidence that the freeze had not hit the Miami River region Mrs. Tuttle and Ingraham picked some of the choice flowers and foliage in the little community, wrapped the stems in damp cotton, and sent the bouquet to Flagler in St. Augustine. The millionaire was amazed and impressed. He decided that it was at least worth a trip there himself. Flagler left St. Augustine a few days later in company with some of his lieutenants including Parrott, McDonald, McGuire, and in West Palm Beach they were joined by Ingraham. They were headed for Biscayne Bay to see Mrs. Tuttle.

Flagler had been there only once before. The sixty-six miles between Palm Beach and the Miami River was practically an unbroken wilderness. Mail was delivered to Fort Dallas only

[8] *In Memoriam, Henry Morrison Flagler,* 12.

once a week, carried by a man who walked the entire distance. The millionaire and his party covered the distance from Palm Beach to Ft. Lauderdale by launch and from there on they rode in a cart drawn by a mule. When they arrived at their destination they were all convinced that some better means of transportation south of West Palm Beach was necessary before any development could be made, but as yet Flagler did not feel that he was the one to provide the means. Upon arriving at Fort Dallas the party was entertained by Mrs. Tuttle. Flagler was soon convinced that the region had limitless possibilities. He conferred briefly with his associates and before he went to bed the first night, he had made up his mind to extend the railroad from West Palm Beach to the Miami River. Mrs. Tuttle, who had been most persuasive in her argument, backed up her talk with Florida's pioneer builder by giving Flagler one hundred acres of Tuttle land for a railroad terminal, railroad yards, and the hotel site. She kept for herself thirteen acres north of the Miami River, which today is the heart of the city of Miami. Another 527-acre lot was laid out in alternate strips, half of which she gave to Flagler and half of which she kept for herself. In return for this consideration, Flagler promised on June 12, 1895, to extend his railroad to Biscayne Bay, build a terminal station, lay out streets in the proposed town, and build a municipal water works.[9] Flagler also acquired other large holdings of land throughout the area. Mrs. Tuttle had finally succeeded in getting the millionaire interested in her section of Florida. All he needed was a little time.

The freeze of 1894-95 was responsible for further good work on the part of Flagler in Florida. He was very sympathetic with the people up and down the east coast who had lost their fortunes, and gave thousands of dollars to individual persons to help them replace what they lost. Through these benevolent deeds he restored confidence in the people of the

[9] Harry G. Cutler, *History of Florida*, I, 396.

state, because when money agencies, banks, and corporations realized that Flagler had faith in Florida, they, too, turned needed capital into the state.

There was one incident which involved a Captain Sharpe who had a large orange grove on the Indian River. Sharpe wrote Flagler a letter telling him that his crop was ruined and requested aid. Flagler had J. E. Ingraham visit Captain Sharpe at his home. Ingraham found him and his wife to be most worthy and deserving. Arrangements were made to rehabilitate the grove, and Sharpe was given money by Flagler to be repaid when the grove came into bearing again. The money was furnished without question. Captain Sharpe, however, insisted that Flagler take a mortgage on the property. Finally, the millionaire accepted the mortgage. Later, when the grove was again bearing fruit, Sharpe invited Flagler on one of his trips to stop and see the oranges. Flagler accepted and his special train was brought to a stop on the grove siding while the two men rode among the trees in the Captain's old buggy drawn by a mule. The Sharpes entertained Flagler royally. Sharpe never did pay the mortgage off because Flagler would not let him. The two men became fast friends, and as long as Sharpe lived he sent fruit to the Flaglers during the winter wherever they were.[10]

II

When Flagler contracted with Mrs. Tuttle to extend the railroad to the Miami River he realized that the undertaking was a big one. Mrs. Tuttle had insisted at the time that he complete his new hotel within eighteen months. Biscayne Bay was a long way from the more populous sections of Florida from which he had to draw most of his labor, but he had one of his assistants insert advertisements in the papers throughout the state proclaiming that laborers of all kinds could find em-

[10] J. D. Ingraham to author, February 14, 1946.

ployment in Miami, as the community was called by this time. The army of working men which descended on the little settlement was a large one. People came both by water and by land only to find no adequate living facilities. William B. Brickell, who had the only place of business in Miami, sold out his stock completely. He had to close his doors until new supplies could be shipped. Flagler began hasty preparations to bring more supplies and material to Miami. He was anxious to get started because he had promised Mrs. Tuttle that he would try to complete the road to Miami by February 1, 1896, and also to have the hotel ready for the winter season.[11]

Flagler began the surveys for the extension south of West Palm Beach in June, 1895. It took several weeks to complete the preliminary arrangements but full-scale construction was soon under way. Several steamers which had been running on the Indian River were transferred to the inland waters between West Palm Beach and Miami, giving service to the various railroad camps that were under construction between the two places. Portions of the inland waterway in south Florida were dredged so that larger steamers could make their way up and down the coast carrying materials and supplies to the scene of construction. The actual laying of the track south of West Palm Beach began in September, 1895. The distance of nearly seventy miles was covered in record time. As the rails were laid southward through the undeveloped stretch of country, several small towns were laid out. The workmen needed places to live; consequently Flagler aided them in establishing places where they might bring their families while they were employed on the railroad construction. The first town was Delray; then Deerfield, Fort Lauderdale, Dania, Hollandale, and Ojus were established. Fort Lauderdale was the first of the towns to grow to any considerable size. It was located on both sides of New River and consisted of good

[11] Charles E. Nash, *The Magic City of Miami Beach*, 82.

farm land. In 1897 Flagler built a railroad station there and it became the most prominent town on the road between West Palm Beach and Miami.[12]

Despite the level land over which the road was built, there was a considerable amount of grading which had to take place. Flagler contracted for this grading job in units, and it was one of the most expensive undertakings relative to the building of the railroad. But the expense did not bother the millionaire. His stock in the Standard Oil Company was becoming increasingly more valuable as the years went by and his fortune was steadily becoming larger.[13]

On April 15, 1896, the road was completed to Miami, and more people poured into the little town daily as a result. At last the Flagler railroad was anchored securely in south Florida. While Miami, on one end of the line, was just opening her eyes, Jacksonville on the other end of the line, 366 miles to the north, was already enjoying benefits of the railroad. Eighteen-ninety-six was a prosperous year for Jacksonville. The city set aside seven days in the spring as "Gala Week" to celebrate her growth and progress. The occasion almost reached proportions of a New Orleans Mardi Gras. The New York Giants held spring practice in the "Gateway City" to Florida, and Jacksonvillians were singing a brand-new song, "Take Me Out to the Ball Game." Huge crowds marvelled when George N. Adams set a world's bicycling record at Panama Park. Sports were becoming prominent everywhere. Miami was not to be denied very long.

In the meantime, September 7, 1895, it was decided to change the name of the railroad from the Jacksonville, St. Augustine and Indian River Railroad to the Florida East Coast Railway. This was necessitated by the accumulation of property which Flagler had bought and the continued developments which he contemplated. The new name of the

[12] *The Florida East Coast Homeseeker,* 9.
[13] Conversation with William R. Kenan, Jr.

FIRST TRAIN INTO DAYTONA BEACH

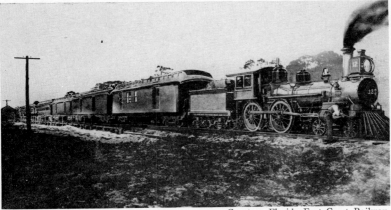

Courtesy Florida East Coast Railway.

FIRST TRAIN INTO MIAMI.

road was appropriate and suggestive of the territory which it served. The charter was granted on September 13, 1895, and was signed by Henry L. Mitchell, Governor of Florida.[14] Though trains were operated from New York to Miami, the Florida East Coast Railway was a Florida institution and escaped Interstate Commerce Commission regulations. This was especially beneficial to Flagler as he was able to charge a higher freight rate than most of the other roads could demand. Then, too, whenever the line crossed a bridge, he charged an extra freight rate. Such business methods earned for Flagler many a critic among his shippers, but in the long run he made very little money out of the Florida East Coast Railway.[15]

During the first few years of the Florida East Coast Railway, Flagler spent much more in operating his train than he made. The engines burned wood instead of coal, and within one year his trains consumed 15,305 cords of fuel, or an average of fifty-six miles per cord. The wood, which was chiefly fat pine, was cut and stacked at various places along the road. At these various intervals the train had to stop and get a new supply of wood. Flagler would not contract with a single lumberman for fuel, but bought from various ones all along the route. The engineer, after receiving his supply of wood left a "wood ticket" with the lumberman, and from time to time these tickets were presented to the railroad for payment. By 1900, the fat pine along the road was getting scarce and had to be brought long distances to the railroad; consequently the wood burners were changed to coal burners.[16]

[14] Charter of Florida East Coast Railway, Florida East Coast Files, Jacksonville. The charter was amended on September 14, 1899, June 12, 1909, July 23, 1909, June 28, 1911, February 10, 1914, September 12, 1920, and September 10, 1924.
[15] *Orlando Sentinel-Star*, November 26, 1933.
[16] Conversation with William R. Kenan, Jr. In 1915 the coal burners were changed to oil burners, and in 1939 the first Diesel-electric locomotive was acquired.

The coming of the railroad to Miami was the biggest single event in the city's history. The territory around Miami began to unfold rapidly, and a region which had been a veritable wilderness began to show signs of life. There was probably no section of the country which underwent so great a change in so short a time. The magic touch had been applied, and shortly a new city began to appear. Mrs. Tuttle and William B. Brickell did not have to wait long to see their dreams come true. Among the early arrivals in Miami was Joseph A. McDonald, who came there on February 15, 1896, to superintend all of Flagler's construction in the town. John B. Reilly came soon after as bookkeeper and cashier to McDonald, and John Sewell arrived from Kissimmee as foreman of the Flagler interests. Sewell said later, "I found Miami all woods. Mrs. Tuttle had done some developing but not much. She had started building a sort of hotel, but it was more like a barn where men slept." [17] Sewell spent his first night in Miami on a floating houseboat on the Miami River, but soon moved to Mrs. Tuttle's rooming house, where living conditions were crude and uncomfortable.

Other settlers who came to Miami in 1896 were G. E. Sewell, brother of John, who opened a clothing store and Frank Budge, who operated a hardware store. J. E. Lummas opened a general store; Isadore Cohen, a clothing store; John W. Watson, a hardware store; E. L. Brady, a grocery store; L. C. Oliver, a lumber yard; Salem Graham, a hotel; and William Burdine, a general store.[18] Flagler encouraged all these early inhabitants, and gave them what aid he could in making a success from their respective businesses. He also encouraged different people over the state to go to Miami by giving one free round trip ride on his railroad to any purchaser of lands in the area.[19]

[17] John Sewell, *Memoirs and History of Miami, Florida*, 10. John and George Sewell were born in Hartwell, Georgia, and went to Florida in 1886.
[18] E. V. Blackman, *Miami and Dade County, Florida*, 21.
[19] *The Florida East Coast Homeseeker*, 11.

Miami was incorporated on July 28, 1896, with only 502 voters, this action taking place about four months after the arrival of the first Florida East Coast train. The name Miami was appropriate and pretty and had been in use for some time though it was not official. There was a growing sentiment to call the town Flagler, but the millionaire himself expressed a desire that the old Indian word be retained. He did not desire the publicity which might result from having a town named for him. So Miami remained Miami, but the new town showed very little resemblance to the old community. John B. Reilly was chosen the first mayor on a compromise ticket. The town's two most prominent citizens were J. A. McDonald and John Sewell. McDonald, Fred S. Morse, Daniel Cosgrove, and Walter S. Graham were elected councilmen. Jack Graham was selected first city clerk.[20]

Perhaps the first building to be erected in Miami after the railroad was extended to that point was a home and office building for J. A. McDonald, Flagler's able assistant. McDonald had come to Florida as early as 1881, and had been associated with James A. McGuire. These two contractors worked almost exclusively for Flagler, but after McDonald went to Miami he liked the place so well he refused to leave. He became one of Miami's most loyal citizens, and later went into the lumber, ice, and transfer business. He built the Biscayne Bay Hotel in Miami, which was one of the city's first rooming houses.[21]

After Flagler paved a few of Miami's streets and laid out some new ones, his first big undertaking was the construction of a luxury hotel comparable to the Royal Poinciana and the Ponce de Leon. In his agreement with Mrs. Tuttle, this had been one of the things he had promised to do. Mrs. Tuttle

[20] E. V. Blackman, *Miami and Dade County, Florida,* 55. James E. Summers succeeded Reilly as mayor in 1900, and served until 1903. The other mayors of Miami during the Flagler era were John Sewell, Frank Wharton and R. B. Smith.
[21] Conversation with William R. Kenan, Jr.

reasoned that an adequate hotel in Miami would be a drawing card for wealthy people who might come there and purchase land. They decided to call the new hotel the Royal Palm because of the large quantity of royal palms found around Biscayne Bay. Work started on the new hotel two months before the railroad reached Miami. J. A. McDonald supervised the beginning of the work on February 15, 1896, but after a few days McDonald became ill and was unable to go on with his assignment. Therefore Flagler sent John Sewell to Miami to take charge of the construction until McDonald was well again. Sewell, who had been appointed foreman, remained in charge of construction for some time. George Sewell, his brother, also came down to work on the Royal Palm Hotel, and later opened a place of business of his own.[22] As in the case of all his developments, Flagler did not allow any phase of the construction to lag. He chose men to do the work in whom he had fullest confidence. One of the employees of the Royal Palm Hotel was J. J. Brinkerhoff, whom Flagler had known since his days in Cleveland. Flagler had been responsible for Brinkerhoff's investing in the Standard Oil Company, and since that time they had been good friends. J. F. Lewis was placed in charge of the plumbing and Dan Cosgrove had supervision of the steam and gas fittings. A. T. Best was the head electrician, Robert H. Horter the head painter, and E. W. Talmadge in charge of the brickmasons.[23]

The Royal Palm had the most nearly ideal location of all the seven Flagler hotels. Its grounds covered fifteen acres of beautiful land where the Miami River emptied into Biscayne Bay. The big frame structure opened its doors for the first time on January 16, 1897, but not in its completed state. Henry W. Merrill, the manager, was pestered with busy painters and plasterers for several months. The opening of the hotel was a significant date in Miami's history, because it was positive

[22] John Sewell, *Memoirs*, 8.
[23] *Miami Metropolis*, January 22, 1897.

proof of Flagler's faith in the future growth of the town. It was an occasion equally as great as the day the railroad was completed. People were present in large numbers to see the first guests register.[24]

The hotel was 680 feet long and 267 feet wide.[25] It was five stories high, and a large court was formed by wings running from the main building. From its verandas and from the upper floors, one could see in different directions a vast expanse of bay, ocean, keys, pine woodland, and marshy Everglades. Royal palms grew in profusion about the building, forming attractive walks and roads leading to the bay and the river. The sound made by the sway and rustle of the trees in the ocean breeze lulled the visitor throughout the day and night.[26]

The Royal Palm Hotel was only a small portion of Flagler's Miami developments. The one prevailing Flagler character-istic, that of seeing a project finished in record time, was evi-dent in all of his Miami undertakings. It took him some time to decide to spend any money in Miami but once he got started there was a strong urge to continue until a thriving city was built on Biscayne Bay. He was a real benefactor of the new town: he did more than build a hotel, and pave the streets and sidewalks. He made the new city livable and more attractive in many different ways. It was he who saw the need of an electric light plant, and built it. Electricity was a novelty to many of the residents, but its use was indicative of Flagler's advanced ideas. He also began a system of sewage and water-works of which few towns the size of Miami could boast.[27] With this start Flagler gave her, Miami grew with much rapidity. In fact, many have ventured to say that Miami was born a full-grown city.

[24] Agnew Welsh Scrapbook, #2, 26.
[25] *Miami Metropolis*, January 15, 1897.
[26] The Royal Palm was torn down in 1930 because the wooden structure was considered a fire trap. John Sewell, *Memoirs*, 188.
[27] J. E. Ingraham, "The Story of the East Coast," *Picturesque Florida*, I (January, 1910), 5.

Flagler very soon saw the need of public schools and churches, and worked to establish them. He donated the land on which the first public school was built and contributed most of the funds for its construction.[28] A short time later he was instrumental in the building of four churches, one each for the Baptist, Methodist, Episcopal, and Catholic congregations. He not only gave the land on which all of these churches were built but he contributed heavily to their support. His interest in the Episcopal Church was aroused through the efforts of Mrs. Tuttle, who was a member of that church. Joseph A. McDonald solicited his interest for the Catholic Church, John Sewell for the Baptist Church and E. V. Blackman for the Methodist Church.[29]

The church to which Flagler was most helpful was his own, the Presbyterian. This church was organized in Miami on April 1, 1896, with only four members by a Presbyterian missionary, the Reverend Henry Keigwin, who had been sent to south Florida to minister to the frontiersmen. At first the organization grew slowly, but in 1897 Flagler began to contribute heavily to its support. For the first few months services were held in a shack with a tent-like top, but Flagler soon built a handsome church edifice which he deeded to the congregation. Until his death in 1913 he donated generously to the First Presbyterian Church in Miami.[30]

To the City of Miami, Flagler gave several lots for municipal buildings in the center of the community. He also donated the location for a city market.[31] On March 20, 1896, as a result of his encouragement, a weekly newspaper was begun. He even gave it a name, the *Miami Metropolis*, which later became the *Miami Daily News*.[32]

The millionaire became interested very early in construct-

---

[28] Agnew Welsh Scrapbook, #35, 59.
[29] E. V. Blackman, *Miami*, 27.
[30] First Presbyterian Church, Miami, 2. Pamphlet in Kenan Collection.
[31] *Miami Metropolis*, September 5, 1902.
[32] *Miami Daily News*, May 12, 1946.

ing homes for his workmen. On one occasion he was visiting in Miami while the Royal Palm Hotel was being built, and expressed surprise to find that so few people had built permanent homes. John D. Reilly explained to him that most of the people who were employed in Miami were men who had lost heavily in the freeze. Flagler realized at once that it took all these men could earn to supply themselves and their families with the necessities of life. He hastily made an investigation to see where comfortable homes might be built. The bay front location was not chosen because he believed that wealthy people would buy lots and later erect homes there. Finally, he decided on reserving two streets, 13th and 14th, where he constructed dozens of modest but comfortable homes for all of his employees.[33]

Flagler was a lover of beauty and hoped in many instances to improve upon nature in trying to make Miami a place of charm. But he could not rush nature. He was growing old himself and was impatient when it took too long to create something he desired very much. He was advised by his friends that he could not expect trees to mature as rapidly as his plans for a hotel building. That explanation, however, did not satisfy him. He had a strong desire to see Australian pines growing in certain places around Biscayne Bay. Because of the fact that some of the soil in Miami was not conducive to the growth of these trees Flagler had certain sections dynamited and the soil cleared away. These places were then filled in with soil which was transported by rail from Palm Beach, where Australian pines grew in abundance. The trees were set out and hundreds of them grew to maturity before Flagler died.[34]

As Miami grew, she rapidly became a commercial center, and served as an outlet to many of the islands nearby. Flagler kept boats running to Key West and Nassau. When he started

[33] E. V. Blackman, *Miami*, 85.
[34] Unidentified Clipping, Flagler Collection.

his developments in Miami, the channel in Biscayne Bay was not safe for vessels which drew more than six feet of water. The millionaire again came forward and opened his pocket-book. He put dredges to work cutting a channel down the bay to Cape Florida. With a wider and deeper channel, ships were able to come into the mouth of the Miami River. In 1898 it was found that the entrance to the Miami River was impracticable for ocean going steamers; so Flagler decided to move the docks up the bay from the river. A new channel was dug to a point near Sixth Street where he built a large dock and wharves. For many years Flagler himself kept the channel dredged; however, later when the city took over the port, it also built municipal docks.[35]

As Miami rapidly became the biggest town in south Florida, there was increasing demand made for the county seat of Dade County to be moved there. Juno, a little town at the north end of Lake Worth, had been the county seat since 1889. Not only was Juno a small place, but it was at the extreme northern tip of Dade County which extended in the other direction all the way to the tip of Florida. But after Flagler's railroad had opened up most of the east coast, the voters in Miami outnumbered the voters in Juno. In 1889 the county seat was moved to Miami, and soon thereafter Palm Beach County was carved from the northern portion of old Dade County.[36]

Miami's growth was quickened by another disastrous freeze on February 7, 1897. It was the second of the great Florida freezes and vegetables which were nearly ready for shipment in central and northern Florida were completely killed. Again, as in 1894–95, Miami was spared from the cold weather and the news got around that Miami was totally frostproof. It was an invitation for more settlers to move to south Florida. Flagler, as before, came to the aid of the stricken farmers. He issued free seeds to those who had been hurt by the cold, and

[35] John Sewell, *Memoirs*, 165. In 1912 Flagler offered to expend $300,000 in port improvements, if the government would appropriate a like amount. The offer was promptly accepted. *Florida Times-Union*, January 23, 1912.
[36] John Sewell, *Memoirs*, 156, 157.

hauled fertilizer, and crate materials free of charge on his railroad. J. E. Ingraham was sent to the area hardest hit and instructed to use $200,000 as necessary to help the people. Flagler is quoted as saying, "I would rather lose it all, and more, than have one man, woman, or child starve." [37]

Miami's growth was arrested for a time in 1899 because of a yellow fever epidemic which broke out in the summer. It could have been disastrous to the thriving community had it been severe. The epidemic started as a result of ticks which were brought in by a cattle boat from Cuba. The fever became more and more severe and fourteen of 263 cases died. Miami was quarantined from the other states from October, 1899, to January 15, 1900. While the quarantine was on, Miami experienced some extremely hard times. Virtually every activity stopped. Flagler felt that he had to do something; so he began to pour money into Miami by giving work to hundreds of people who had been made idle by the restrictions. He financed the construction of new streets, sidewalks, and various other municipal improvements. Actually he kept many people from going hungry, especially the Negroes. He saw that all payroll funds were supplied. Anything that John B. Reilly or John Sewell wanted done for the city Flagler ordered carried through. Though the epidemic was deplored, in the long run it resulted in many new developments for the rapidly growing Miami.[38]

By 1902 Miami claimed a population of over 5,000, and construction was still going forward. By the time Flagler died in 1913 the little community into which he injected life in 1896 had a population of 10,875 and ranked fifth in size in Florida.[39] It had three banks, two elementary schools, one high school, six churches, and nine hotels. The city that Flagler

---

[37] H. G. Cutler, *Florida*, I, 65.
[38] Agnew Welsh Scrapbook, #8, 24; #6, 26; also see *Miami Herald*, July 8, 1945.
[39] George M. Chapin, *Official Program, Key West Extension of the Florida East Coast Railway*, 55. By 1948 Miami had grown to be Florida's largest city.

built was not only a prominent commercial center but was also a rapidly developing resort. From December, 1909, to May, 1910, more than 125,000 guests registered at Miami hotels. The magic spell of Flagler had not died out. In fact it was just beginning. Miami was still to see her period of greatest growth.

ELEVEN

Turbulent Years

DURING the years of Miami's infancy, Flagler was having domestic troubles which took much of his time and attention. His family had always been a great source of pleasure for him, but the death of his first wife left him sad and lonely. For a number of years after he tried to forget the past. He centered all of his affections on his second wife, Alice, and carried her with him on most of his business trips to Miami, Palm Beach, or New York. She liked yachting, boating, and entertaining, and Flagler tried to provide her with everything that might make her happy. At one time they owned two yachts, the sloop *Eclipse* and the schooner *Columbia*.[1] In addition Flagler belonged to two or three yacht clubs in order that Alice might enjoy the privileges.

Perhaps the finest yacht that the Flaglers ever owned was the *Alicia*. It was designed by Harlen and Hollingsworth, prominent New York builders, and cost $112,916.[2] It was a beautiful craft and very fast. Its length was 160 feet, yet it was easy to handle. Although seen often in Florida waters, the *Alicia* was used more during the summer when the Flaglers were at their Mamaroneck home. They often used it to visit friends in New London, Connecticut, fashionable summer resort.[3]

It seemed that Alice was happiest when she was doing

[1] William R. Kenan, Jr., to author, July 10, 1946.
[2] Flagler Yacht Ledger, Kenan Collection.
[3] Henry M. Flagler to Andrew Anderson, August 21, 1896.

169

something. She was nervously inclined, and had an abundance of energy. She was always a woman with marked characteristics and a somewhat eccentric nature. She was sensitive, emotional, and given to exaggerated forms of speech. She was self-centered and interested largely in matters that pertained to her own social standing and personal appearance. These tendencies seemed to increase; but her family and friends thought little about her idiosyncrasies. Dress and social position became more and more the subject of her thought and conversation, and the display of her husband's wealth was the dominant motive of her life. There would be sudden outbursts of emotion; and she would make uncomplimentary remarks about individuals, especially her family. At times her unkind remarks were directed at her husband.

The first time Flagler ever questioned his wife's conduct was on one occasion when she entertained a group of ladies with a yachting party off the coast of New England. On this particular cruise a storm arose, the wind reaching a velocity of sixty miles an hour. The storm lashed the yacht around in a high sea for six hours; and despite the pleas of the skipper, who was the only man on board, and many of her seasick friends, Alice refused to allow the boat to be put into port. They were six or eight hours overdue before they finally reached Mamaroneck safely. Flagler was worried, and he had right to be. Alice had acted foolishly, almost like an insane person. Several days later he expressed to a friend his fear for Alice's safety and his concern over her peculiar action.[4] Several years passed during which time she apparently lived a normal life except that occasionally her conduct would be a little out of the ordinary, especially when in the company of a large group of people. Although Flagler was often puzzled at her ways, he said little to anyone about it.

Mrs. Flagler's mental condition first attracted serious concern from her husband in 1894, though he still hoped it would

[4] *Ibid.*, August 4, 1885.

not call for widespread notice. She became erratic and impulsive and irritable in the presence of Flagler. The break came in the summer while the family was at Mamaroneck. Alice confided in several of her friends about the way her husband was mistreating her. She made a convincing story out of it and stressed the point that he was and had always been unfaithful to her. The friends, not suspecting any mental disorder, believed every word of her story and immediately changed their opinions of the millionaire. But the whole story was not to remain a secret very long. Her glib tongue and her nonsensical talk aroused the suspicion of Dr. George G. Shelton, a prominent New York physician and personal friend of the family. Shelton made it a point to place himself in her presence as much as possible; she was invited to his home and to his office for medical advice and attention. The unsuspecting Mrs. Flagler soon began to pour out her mind to the physician. She fell squarely into the trap he had laid for her.

At an appointed time Shelton made a personal call on the Flaglers at their Mamaroneck home. There were other guests in the home at the time, but the presence of her physician friend inspired her to confide in him about more "secrets." Stating that she had something important to tell him, she invited Dr. Shelton to go with her to a secluded corner of the porch. They walked down the long piazza of the home, and she began telling him about a prominent New York court case at that time being tried.[5] She spoke with so much freedom that the doctor got up from his seat and looked to see if anyone could be listening, fearing the servants would not understand why she should talk so openly and freely to him.

Dr. Shelton, embarrassed, tried to change the conversation; but Alice did not observe the caution. In fact, she increased her vehement talk. She referred to a well-known New York woman as the illegitimate daughter of a prominent nobleman of Europe, whose name at the time was before the public.

[5] A divorce case which involved two socially prominent New Yorkers.

171

Shelton was amazed at her statements. Excusing herself a minute, Mrs. Flagler hurriedly went to her room and came back with three little pebbles. She asked him if he could not see "certain marks" in the pebbles; and when he answered in the negative, she became infuriated. Finally she jerked the stones out of his hands and exclaimed, "Of course you cannot see them; there are only three people in the world who can, and only members of a secret society possess them and the power to interpret them; they are talismen; they are very, very old." Then picking the first one up in her two fingers she continued, "This one has cured many forms of paralysis, and this one," pointing to the second stone, "will produce pregnancy in a barren woman if she carries it with her for a month." The fact that she was childless had no doubt affected her mind, and Dr. Shelton realized it because he had been the one to tell her several months before that she would never be able to have children. He finally excused himself, thinking that his departure might snap her out of her nonsense; but before he left, she insisted that he take two of the stones and put them in his pocket for safekeeping. This he did. "The other one," she said gleefully, "I am going to send to the Czar of Russia." [6]

Dr. Shelton went back to his office in New York a stunned man. Henry M. Flagler was his personal friend, but should he tell him what he knew of his wife's mental state? He called Flagler in to receive the grim news, but the latter was not surprised. He had suspected long before that his wife's mental disorder was growing steadily worse. They talked freely about her condition, and the fact that Flagler knew now what he had for some months suspected about his wife's health opened the way for further action.

Flagler carried her from Mamaroneck to their Fifth Avenue

[6] Shelton Testimony, Flagler Divorce Proceedings, August 12, 1901, Seventh Judicial Circuit, Miami, Florida.

home because he felt that she could get better attention from Dr. Shelton there. She was encouraged to call the doctor when she felt ill; so she became nothing less than a nuisance to Shelton. Often she called to report a "slight headache"; but if he diverted her attention towards a new hat or some social matter, she would show no evidence of pain. He repeated such an experiment many times with the same results, spending a great deal of his time in the home. Flagler seemed to be more contented when Dr. Shelton was around.

Mrs. Flagler soon began to have delusions, one of which was in regard to her wealth. One day she gave her manicurist a check for a thousand dollars. The manicurist was naturally alarmed and reported the incident to Dr. Shelton. Shelton remonstrated with Alice but to no avail. She referred to the sum as a mere pittance of her vast wealth.

Mrs. Flagler's thoughts ran upon the general infidelity of men. Besides her husband, she accused many prominent New York people of all forms of immorality and crime. Scandal and gossip seemed to fill her mind. Such delusions increased, and one never knew when another was coming on. She carried on conversations with imaginary people, and laughed and joked with relatives who were nowhere near.[7]

During the first week in October, 1895, Mrs. Flagler began to speak of her great love for the Czar of Russia, explaining that she had just been informed by the Ouija board that the Czar was madly in love with her too. She divulged the information that she intended to marry the Czar immediately upon Flagler's death. She did not say when she expected her husband to die, but Dr. Shelton became fearful of Flagler's safety and took every precaution to prevent a tragedy. One day soon thereafter she visited one of New York's large jewelry stores and purchased a two-thousand-dollar cat's-eye diamond ring, which she sent to the Czar. However, the ring

[7] *Ibid.*

173

was intercepted by telegram and never reached its destination. Mrs. Flagler's mental illness became more critical every day.[8]

Henry M. Flagler grew more miserable as his wife's condition became worse. He did not seem to fear for his safety, but her illness was difficult for him to accept. At times his grief was hard to bear. There can be no doubt about his deep concern over her and he left undone nothing that would insure her comfort.[9]

On October 24, 1895, Dr. Shelton, acting upon the wishes of Flagler, called in for consultation Dr. Allan Starr and Dr. Frederick Peterson, specialists in the field of mental disorders. On that day, Mrs. Flagler became violent, and after a tantrum locked herself in her room and barricaded the door. Dr. Peterson, who, in addition to his private practice, was president of the Lunacy Commission of New York State, tried to force his way into the room; but she would not admit anyone except the maid. Peterson began a patient vigil in an adjoining room. Soon Mrs. Flagler sent her maid out of the room to call a detective. The maid related the story to Peterson, and he directed her to go back into Alice's room and report that a detective would be there shortly. In fifteen or twenty minutes Peterson went in, and the maid told Mrs. Flagler that he was a detective from the central office. With that the patient began to tell her own story. She said the house was full of Russian spies; that she was engaged to be married to the Czar of Russia; and that she constantly had communications with him through the Ouija board which she had on the table. She manifested certain delusions of persecution, one of which was an attempt on the part of her family to poison her. She made several homicidal threats during the course of conversation.

After the examination, Dr. Peterson told Mrs. Flagler that he would go get several more detectives to help clear the house of the spies, and that when he returned he would rap

[8] George G. Shelton to Andrew Anderson, October 25, 1895.
[9] *Ibid.*

three times on the door and that would be a sign for her to
open it. This she consented to do. Dr. Peterson retired to the
living room, where he consulted with Dr. Starr. The papers
for her committal to Choate's Sanitarium in Pleasantville, New
York, had already been drawn up by Dr. Shelton. The three
physicians pronounced the case as delusionary insanity and
recommended that she be sent to Choate's private asylum immediately.[10]

Dr. Peterson then went back to her room and gave the three
raps on the door as promised; and with one male attendant
and one female attendant, Mrs. Flagler was taken by force
down the stairs and put in a waiting carriage at the door. She
was carried to the station and transferred to a special railroad
car which sped her to Pleasantville, New York.[11]

After Alice's departure, Flagler was urged by Dr. Shelton
to go to Florida and remain there for the winter. Shelton felt
that Dr. Anderson in St. Augustine could do much to mend
his spirits. Said Dr. Shelton to Dr. Anderson in a letter written
the day after Mrs. Flagler was committed to the Pleasantville
asylum, "Mr. Flagler proposes to start for Florida next week.
I have advised very strongly that he do that because he is
almost prostrated with grief and anxiety. I have seen him in
deep trouble, but never has anything taken such a hold upon
him as this. I hope you will keep him in the South until the
edge of his grief wears off. . . . I believe you can cheer him
more than anyone." [12]

Flagler took Shelton's advice and went to St. Augustine,
but was restless and dissatisfied. He tried to forget his troubles
by prolonged work. He went to Palm Beach and Miami; he
tried working hard; he tried complete relaxation. When he
was in New York he yearned for Florida, and when he was in
Florida he longed to get back North. It was a long dreary

[10] Peterson Testimony, Flagler Divorce Proceedings, August 12, 1901,
Seventh Judicial Circuit, Miami, Florida.
[11] *Ibid.*
[12] George G. Shelton to Andrew Anderson, October 25, 1895.

winter for the man who was giving much of his money and interest to Florida. He kept in touch with Dr. Shelton, and at Flagler's request the doctor made two trips to Pleasantville to see Alice. At first she seemed to get no better. She continued to manifest delusions of grandeur and to speak of her love for the Czar of Russia. She despised seeing Shelton and threatened him for putting her in what she styled "that hole." Realizing that his visits did nothing but aggravate her condition, he discontinued his trips to the asylum.[13]

In the spring, 1896, Flagler returned to New York and talked personally with the doctors about his wife's mental disorder. Dr. Starr made an examination in May and found her much better than he expected. She talked freely with him about her delusions. In but one instance did she revert to the abnormal state and that was the incident about the ring for the Czar. She talked to Starr freely about that. She thought her husband was still in Florida; however, he had been in New York for several weeks. She told Dr. Starr to tell Flagler that she still loved him and that she was now clothed in her right mind. Dr. Starr reported to Flagler that it might be possible to bring her home within a short time but warned against overoptimism. He explained that she would most likely have a relapse in two to six months, though he would make no prediction beyond that. Flagler was happy to know that his wife was better but was disappointed because he was given no assurances that she would be permanently well. Said he in a letter to Dr. Anderson, "I shall try to keep up courage and make the best fight in her behalf that is possible."[14]

Flagler planned to open their Mamaroneck home in time for Mrs. Flagler's arrival, which he hoped would be before June 5, their wedding anniversary. Arrangements were made to bring from the institution one of her attendants as a com-

[13] Shelton Testimony, Flagler Divorce Proceedings, August 12, 1901, Seventh Judicial Circuit, Miami, Florida.
[14] Henry M. Flagler to Andrew Anderson, May 20, 1896.

176

panion, and only a few visitors were allowed inside the gates at Lawn Beach. Flagler hoped to continue Mrs. Flagler's rest cure there and planned to stay with her as much as possible himself. Dr. Starr warned against giving her the opportunity of meeting men acquaintances. She was to be given full liberty of action, to ride or go on the yacht, but her husband was always to be with her.[15]

On May 29, Flagler talked with Dr. Choate in New York about Alice. The owner of the asylum did not share Dr. Starr's fears concerning a relapse; so definite arrangements were made for Mrs. Flagler to rejoin her husband on June 5. Said Dr. Choate, "I regard Mrs. Flagler as entirely cured." [16] Flagler's enthusiasm and happiness knew no limits. He had been given a new lease on life.

Henry and Alice Flagler were happily reunited on June 5, 1896, in White Plains, New York. Dr. Choate accompanied her to this point, where she was met by her husband. The meeting was natural and without restraint. There was much to talk about, since their separation had been of nearly eight months' duration. Flagler was not able to detect the slightest flaw in her mental action. He discussed freely with her every phase of her former delusions and declared that he now believed in miracles because he thought her to be her normal self again. Joyfully he reported to Dr. Anderson several days after they reached Mamaroneck, "I am surprised and need not say delighted at the outcome—it seems too good to be true." [17]

The next few weeks were joyous ones; it was the first time Flagler had been happy since the preceding October when his wife was sent to Pleasantville for treatment. There were many amusements and diversions at Mamaroneck. Flagler had a number of fine trotting horses, which he purchased for the

[15] *Ibid.*
[16] *Ibid.*, May 30, 1896.
[17] *Ibid.*, June 8, 1896.

use of the family and their guests. He built a quarter-mile track, and this attracted much attention in the community.[18] Much time was spent in a new pleasure which had become popular in many parts of the country—bicycle riding. Mr. and Mrs. Flagler employed a tutor to instruct them in the art of mounting and dismounting. They rode seven to ten miles each day.[19] Flagler liked to read and at this particular time was enjoying *Ham and Dixie*, which Dr. Anderson had sent him from St. Augustine. While he read, Alice did handwork, busying herself with an afghan which she was making for the latest arrival at the Andersons' home, Baby Clarissa. She kept an album in which she had the pictures of many babies, with Clarissa's picture at the very front of her collection. "It seems an irony of fate," wrote Flagler to Dr. Anderson, "that Alice, who is so fond of babies, can't have one of her own." [20] This fact constantly preyed upon her mind, and she often spoke of her husband's vast wealth which he would leave to so few of his own.

Throughout the month of June, Alice's mental state was normal. Her happiness at Mamaroneck seemed complete. Consequently she asked her husband to sell their city home in order that they might divide their time between Mamaroneck and St. Augustine. Flagler thought it a wise course to pursue, since the memories of the Fifth Avenue home were none too pleasant. The house, however, was not sold immediately. Flagler spent one or two days each week at his office in the city but was away from Alice as little as possible.[21]

Most of the time the Flaglers were alone. None of the relatives were invited to Lawn Beach, except the Eugene M. Ashleys of Lockport, New York. Mrs. Ashley before her marriage was Eliza Adriance, a second cousin of Flagler on his mother's side. Of all of his cousins Eliza Ashley was his

[18] Conversation with Harry Harkness Flagler.
[19] Henry M. Flagler to Andrew Anderson, July 5, 1896.
[20] *Ibid.*, June 17, 1896.
[21] *Ibid.*, July 5, 1896.

favorite, and she was especially fond of him.[22] Eugene Ashley, a prominent lawyer, had much in common with Flagler and always enjoyed the hospitality of his home. The Ashleys arrived at Lawn Beach on July 1 for an indefinite stay. It was Flagler's hope that they would help divert Alice's attention to things which tended not to disturb her. They understood the case, and their presence was a great satisfaction to everyone concerned.[23]

Soon after the Ashleys arrived at Lawn Beach, Mrs. Flagler began to show signs of a relapse. She begged for a Ouija board and tried to bribe the servants to find one for her. She seemed perfectly well; but Flagler knew that he could expect the worst, for it was the Ouija board that threw her off balance the preceding year. After a week of apprehension, Eliza Ashley and the nurse began to notice Mrs. Flagler's queer actions. Mrs. Ashley confided to Flagler that his wife was as full of delusions as she was before she entered the institution at Pleasantville. Again Alice expressed her great love for the Czar of Russia; she also carried on in the same manner about her husband's lack of fidelity and her loss of respect for him. Though she talked in derogatory terms about him to Mrs. Ashley, she was very attentive and affectionate to him when they were alone. When not in her husband's presence, she talked glibly and nonsensically. Flagler tried to act normal around her, but his spirits began to ebb. In a letter to his friend, Dr. Anderson,[24] upon whom he leaned heavily for comfort and advice, Flagler said, "It almost breaks my heart to write this sad news. Please do not mention it to anyone. . . . Mr. MacGonigle [Presbyterian minister in St. Augustine] writes me occasionally expressing his joy over my happiness.

---

[22] Conversation with Harry Harkness Flagler.

[23] Henry M. Flagler to Andrew Anderson, July 5, 1896.

[24] Flagler always ended his letters to Dr. Anderson with this phrase, "With love to you and your good wife, I am, Affectionately yours, H. M. Flagler." See Dimick Collection for Flagler's correspondence with Dr. Anderson.

You may tell him about Alice's relapse, for I don't believe I can bear to receive any more congratulations, but don't say anything to others yet." [25]

Dr. Choate had died only a short time after Alice had returned from Pleasantville to Mamaroneck. Doctors Starr and Shelton were both vacationing in Europe, but Dr. Peterson was available and was consulted immediately. He warned Flagler of impending danger because he knew of the homicidal threats Mrs. Flagler had made the year before. When Flagler told him how critically his wife watched every move he made when he was near her, the doctor advised that he occupy another room at night. Flagler, however, did not think it wise to make any change, as it might excite her suspicions. In view of this fact, he decided to go on as usual, "depending," as he said, "upon God's mercy to keep me from harm." In his regular letter to Dr. Anderson, he continued, "I cannot tell you how this destruction of my hopes affects me." [26]

Through July and August, 1896, Alice's condition changed very little. At times she grew worse and her delusions became more pronounced, but after a day or two they would cease. Flagler was hopeful one day but filled with despair the next. He dreaded the thought of having to send Alice to an institution as he had done the fall before. In August Flagler consulted Dr. Seldon H. Talcott, superintendent of the asylum at Middleton, New York. On August 24, Talcott examined Mrs. Flagler and gave her husband encouragement. The doctor's words merely raised false hopes. Mrs. Flagler became worse; and in the absence of all other available doctors at that time, Flagler consulted Dr. Carlos F. MacDonald in an effort to find someone who might help her. Dr. MacDonald was the new owner of the sanitarium at Pleasantville, once run by the late Dr. Choate, and he had met Mrs. Flagler when she was

[25] Henry M. Flagler to Andrew Anderson, July 9, 1896.
[26] *Ibid.*

confined there in October, 1895. After a thorough examination he told Flagler that he doubted she was ever cured the
first time. He reminded Flagler that his wife was going
through a very trying time of life, and that this change, when
it was over, might easily cause her to get well or to get worse.
His advice was to give her time; a year or two might tell
whether she was to be permanently well or insane. He laid
quite as much stress as Dr. Peterson had done on the fact that
she might commit homicide. Flagler contended that it would
be impossible for him to occupy a separate bedroom without
exciting a suspicion in the direction he wanted to avoid. To
the casual observer Mrs. Flagler manifested no delusions. To
her husband she was the embodiment of affection and tender-
ness. The watching and waiting on the outcome was nerve-
wracking. The Ashleys were a great help. As best they could,
they tried to keep Flagler's mind on anything other than his
troubles. It was not an easy task.[27]

Friends advised Flagler to send his wife back to the asylum,
but he had made up his mind to do this only as a last resort.
He assured Dr. Anderson, "I shall not let her leave home until
it becomes absolutely necessary."[28] Dr. Talcott called occasionally and always left a ray of hope. After Dr. MacDonald's
visits, however, there was little but gloom. It was decided that
the family should not go back to the city, or to St. Augustine,
as was the custom in September, but that they should remain
at Mamaroneck to await the outcome of Mrs. Flagler's illness.

On October 10, the patient finally obtained a Ouija board
from a neighbor's wife and secluded herself in her room with
it. Within ten minutes her mental equilibrium was completely
destroyed. She played with the board constantly. Flagler's
first impulse was to take the board away from her by force,
but Eliza Ashley warned against this for fear that Alice might
hurt her husband. He consulted Dr. Shelton, who was back

[27] *Ibid.*, August 18, 1896.
[28] *Ibid.*, August 28, 1896.

from Europe, as well as Doctors Starr and Peterson; and it was decided to confine her at the Lawn Beach home. Four nurses, one male and three female, were secured and sent to Mamaroneck to be on constant guard. The exclusive services of an experienced physician, Dr. Roland du Jardins, of New York, were secured; and he, with his wife, went to live at the Flagler home. The doctor was to have charge of the patient and the nurses, and Mrs. du Jardins was to supervise the servants and the house. Flagler then left Mamaroneck and moved to the Manhattan Hotel in New York. "Mr. Flagler looked very bad," his secretary told Dr. Anderson. "The strain upon him was great indeed. However, now that the shock has come, he looks more composed. The feeling that he can now sleep without any apprehension must afford his mind some relief. It is indeed a sad case." [29]

Soon after he became settled at his hotel in New York, Flagler wrote to Dr. Anderson, "The year last past has taught me the truth of your remark, that, 'Living one's misfortunes down is a terribly slow and painful process.' I am learning this lesson by a slow and painful experience and I often feel that I should break down if it were not for the messages of love and comfort you so generously send me. I receive similar ones from others but none touch my heart as yours do." [30] Dr. Anderson, in replying, tried to reason with Flagler and insisted that he must quit worrying and become resigned to Alice's illness. To which Flagler responded, "I know that all you say is true, that having done everything for my poor wife that human skill can devise, my duty to myself and the enterprises upon which the welfare of so many depends, is to accept the situation and make the best of it—this I shall try to do. I realize that I am morbid, for sometimes I forget my sorrow for the moment and afterwards reproach myself that I could do so." [31]

[29] J. C. Salter to Andrew Anderson, October 24, 1896.
[30] Henry M. Flagler to Andrew Anderson, November 3, 1896.
[31] *Ibid.*, November 13, 1896.

The winter at Mamaroneck was a long one. Flagler went to Florida in November but was back in New York before the first of the year. He paid frequent visits to his summer home, but at no time was he allowed to see his wife. The doctors felt that it would not be for the good of either of them, since he was the object of most of her homicidal threats. The Ashleys remained with Flagler much of the time. The reports from Dr. du Jardins were anything but encouraging. Mrs. Flagler was in a violent state part of the time, and it was necessary to take away from her such articles as knives and forks. At one time she assaulted Dr. du Jardins with a pair of scissors she had hidden on her person. She bruised the doctor about the face and badly lacerated one of his hands before he could withdraw from the room.[32] She seemed to be a hopeless case. The crisis had passed, and she was left insane.

On March 20, 1897, Doctors Shelton and Peterson went to the Flagler summer home at Mamaroneck to examine Mrs. Flagler for commitment to the asylum again. She recognized them as the persons who had carried her to Pleasantville in October, 1895; so she was extremely difficult to handle.[33] Preparations were made to carry her to the sanitarium of Dr. MacDonald, successor to Dr. Choate, at Pleasantville, and she was committed there for the second time on March 23, 1897.[34]

Upon entering the sanitarium, Mrs. Flagler insisted that her name was Princess Ida Alice von Schotten Tech, and that she bore the evidences of her royal heritage. Concerning her husband, she said she had been married to Henry M. Flagler, but he was now dead and she proposed to marry the Czar of Russia at an early date. Her delusions of persecution continued. She insisted that Dr. Shelton had tried several times to poison her. She also had the idea that many of her friends had turned enemy to her and were trying to take all of her money. Throughout 1897 her mental aberration became more

[32] Shelton Testimony, *Ibid.*
[33] Peterson Testimony, Flagler Divorce Proceedings, August 12, 1901, Seventh Judicial Circuit, Miami, Florida.
[34] MacDonald Testimony, *Ibid.*

pronounced daily. She would sit at a window in an attitude of attention and smile and gesticulate in a way indicative of hearing voices. She painted her cheeks with red coloring matter extracted from woolen yarn, blacked her eyebrows with burnt cork, and rubbed the cream served with her coffee into her hair for a tonic.[35]

At times Mrs. Flagler was quiet and composed, and for weeks at a time the attendants had no trouble with her. Occasionally her brother, Charles F. Shourds, visited her; and during these visits she revealed to him a variety of delusions as to her age, her personality, her relations with the Czar of Russia, and as to her having been drugged and surgically operated on.

There was no change in Alice's condition during 1898. She filled numerous blank books with what she called poetry, and improvised music and lyrics, which were largely incoherent scribbling. She collected thousands of pebbles, which she called minerals, and on which she recognized faces and other mysterious characters. These pebbles she preserved with great care in a small bag which she had made of bits of silk. She ate and slept well, and, physically, kept well and healthy. Her husband was asked never to visit her; however, he had flowers sent to her twice each week. She spoke one day of her husband's being dead; the next, of his being alive. Visits made to her by Dr. Shelton and Dr. Talcott, at Flagler's requests, were never satisfactory. She disliked Shelton especially, and often refused to speak with him. Occasionally she upbraided him for unheard-of things.[36]

Advised by his physicians that Alice would never again be normal, Flagler decided to have the courts make an official declaration, so that a legal guardian could be appointed. He filed a petition with the New York Supreme Court on June 28, 1899, asking that Ida Alice Flagler be declared insane and incompetent. A commission composed of W. J. A. McKim,

[35] *Ibid.*
[36] *Ibid.*

Allan Fitch, and James Meng was appointed to hear the witnesses. Doctors Shelton, Talcott, and MacDonald, together with William H. Beardsley, appeared before the commission and swore that Mrs. Flagler was suffering from paranoia, a mental disease from which she would never recover. On August 4, 1899, the court ruled her insane, and appointed Eugene M. Ashley committee of her property, and Dr. Mac-Donald committee of her person. Flagler arranged for her to be provided for through channels set up by these two friends.[37]

By 1901, Mrs. Flagler's mental disease had progressed so far that it had reached what Dr. MacDonald termed the "third state." She was beginning to manifest evidences of enfeeblement of the mental faculties as shown by the impairment of memory, the loss of the power of attention, and the general lessening of the will power and affections and emotions. Flagler had watched her slowly reach that point, and with all of his might he made himself accept her illness. No one could doubt his love for Mrs. Flagler; but after she lost her mental equilibrium, there was no basis for companionship. The separation was final on March 23, 1897, when they carried her to Pleasantville. He never saw her again and his mind was gradually focused on other things. At times he even manifested signs of happiness, though he was lonely at heart. His developments in Florida helped to absorb his attention and to make life a little more pleasant.

Flagler had been pondering for some time the matter of a divorce from his insane wife. He knew the storm of criticism it would bring when once announced publicly. Many of his friends could see his side of the issue, but many advised against it. To him Alice Flagler existed no more. As time went on, he became more determined to free himself. It was impossible for him to secure a divorce in either New York or Florida, using

[37] Records from the Files of the New York Supreme Court, enclosed in Flagler Divorce Proceedings, August 12, 1901, Seventh Judicial Circuit, Miami, Florida.

insanity as the basis for the procedure; but he had accomplished things virtually impossible before, and he did not mean to fail in this attempt. Florida was the easier of the two states in which to gain his desired ends; so he moved his citizenship from New York to Palm Beach. His intentions were announced in the *Florida Times-Union* on April 23, 1899; and Editor Wilson commented favorably on "Florida's new citizen." The reason given for his change of residence was that his business interests in Florida could better be served. It was also stated that he wished to escape the excessive inheritance tax imposed by the state of New York. Business purposes were sound reasons for changing one's residence.[38] They were entirely legitimate; so far, the public suspected nothing.

In March, 1901, Flagler paid a visit to Dr. Anderson in St. Augustine, at which time he saw only a few of his intimate friends. Apparently a decision of importance was made in consultation with the doctor, for on April 9, 1901, a bill was introduced into the Florida State Senate "to be entitled an act making incurable insanity a ground for divorce for husband and wife, and regulating proceedings in such cases." On April 17, the bill passed the Senate with little opposition. Meeting a little opposition in the House, it passed this body by a vote of forty-two to nineteen on April 19. The way had been well cleared for its passage in both houses. Governor W. S. Jennings affixed his signature on April 25, 1901. The law declared that insanity in either husband or wife had to exist for four years prior to the filing of a bill of divorce. It also provided that the person accused must be judged insane by a competent court; that a committee or guardian must be appointed for the insane person; and that in case of a wife she was to be well provided for by her husband.[39] All of these provisions Flagler could meet.

[38] Exhibit No. I, Divorce Proceedings, Flagler Divorce Proceedings, August 12, 1901, Seventh Judicial Circuit, Miami, Florida.
[39] *Acts of Florida,* 119–120. The law was repealed in 1905.

It was apparent by this time that Flagler was the instigator of the law. He was accused of buying the legislature off, and many of his friends throughout the state were singled out for criticism.[40] The newspapers opened a double-barreled attack on him and the legislature. They dubbed the law the "Flagler Divorce Law." Very few of the newspapers took Flagler's side in the controversy. One, however, the *Ocala Banner*, edited by Frank Harris, upheld him and the new law. Harris argued, editorially, that all states should pass sensible divorce laws. He continued, "Man and woman were made one, and the two together were given dominion over the whole earth, but neither was given dominion over the other." [41] The *Palmetto News* accused Harris of getting some of the $20,000 which it believed Flagler spent in getting the law passed, and said that "Harris needs the prayers of the brethren of the press." [42] The *Bronson Times-Democrat* and the *Citrus County Chronicle* denounced the Ocala paper for its stand, as well as the *Pensacola Journal*. The latter paper accused Harris of "selling out" to Flagler, as well as the members of the legislature.[43]

The *Pensacola Journal* brought to light more evidence of what it called "Flagler's influence in state affairs." Soon after the law was passed, Flagler made a gift of $10,000 to the Florida Agricultural College at Lake City for a gymnasium, provided the State would appropriate $2,500 for equipment. In 1903, when the institution was renamed the University of Florida, he gave another $10,000.[44] Frank Harris was one of the trustees of the institution and may have been responsible for Flagler's liberal gift. At any rate, coming at the time it

[40] Conversation with Amy McMillan and A. B. Otwell.
[41] *Ocala Banner*, May 31, 1901.
[42] *Palmetto News*, May 27, 1901.
[43] *Pensacola Journal*, May 28, 1901.
[44] Florida Agricultural College was set up in 1884 in Lake City. The name was changed to the University of Florida in 1903, and it was moved to Gainesville, its present location, in the summer of 1906. See Bristol, MS., "The Buckman Act: Before and After," 2–25.

did, the gift took the form of a thank offering to the state for what it had done for him.[45]

The public mind was aroused over the divorce law. Few people thought Flagler would start divorce proceedings in the immediate future. He, however, tossed more timber on the fire on June 3, 1901, when he filed a bill of divorce against his wife with Judge Minor S. Jones in the Circuit Court, Seventh Judicial Circuit of Florida.[46] Flagler was now a citizen of the State, and incurable insanity was a ground for divorce. His wife had been declared incurably insane; so the way was clear for the final act.

No man could have made himself better known to the people of a state than Flagler had to the people of Florida. During the summer of 1901 his name was a household word. There were many critics; but, on the other hand, many stood by him. It was Flagler's nature to get what he wanted. He had been schooled in that philosophy. The case went through without any delay or hindrance.

Flagler had left no stones unturned; every angle of the case had been well prepared and reviewed. The law firm of Nicoll, Anable, and Lindsay of New York represented him; and DeLancey Nicoll personally attended the trial. Nicoll and George P. Raney acted as counsel for the complainant; Francis P. Fleming, guardian *ad litem* for the defendant; Eugene M. Ashley, committee of the property of the defendant; Carlos F. MacDonald, committee of the person of the defendant; and H. H. Buckman, solicitor for said committees.[47] The hearings took only one day, August 12, 1901. Those testifying in behalf of the complainant were Doctors Carlos F. MacDonald, George G. Shelton, Seldon H. Talcott,

[45] J. R. Parrott was also one of the trustees of the college, so it could have been that the gift came as a result of his friendship with Flagler. Flagler no doubt would have given $50,000 if the gymnasium had cost that much. See *Ibid*.

[46] Bill of Divorce, Flagler Divorce Proceedings, August 12, 1901, Seventh Judicial Circuit, Miami, Florida.

[47] Flagler Divorce Proceedings, August 12, 1901, Seventh Judicial Circuit, Miami, Florida.

and Frederick Peterson—all of whom were familiar with the case. Each testified in positive terms that Mrs. Flagler was suffering from paranoia, otherwise known as chronic delusional insanity, and that there was no possible chance of her ever being normal again. Declared Dr. MacDonald, "It invariably occurs in persons having what is known as a nervous or insane temperament, whether through heredity or inherited predisposition or whether acquired in early life. Such cases do not recover." He explained that this insane tendency lay dormant in Mrs. Flagler until she married. After that time she tried to live a life equal to the standing Flagler had given her but failed in the attempt, and the tendency became active.[48] Eugene M. Ashley, J. R. Parrott, and George Wilson also testified in Flagler's interest. Flagler's own testimony was interesting but pathetic. He reviewed the entire case. He stated that in the last four years, he had not seen his wife and that since he would not be permitted to see her again, it would be better for them both if they were entirely free. He reminded the court that during the last few years he had given her over two million dollars' worth of property and securities.[49] Eugene M. Ashley, who had charge of her property, reported to the court exactly what Mrs. Flagler had in the way of stocks, bonds, and money. She owned 2,420 shares, worth $795 each, in the Standard Oil Company; and 153 shares of Natural Gas Trust certificates, worth $200 each. She also possessed Natural Gas Trust bonds, worth $15,300; cash amounting to about $570,000; and small securities amounting to $68,322.03. She also had considerable property in St. Augustine, which did not contribute to her support. Ashley said the total in his hands was $2,373,137.42. All of these securities were in the state of New York and were annually accounted for by him to the Supreme Court of New York. Mrs. Flagler's annual income was about $120,000. Her expenses at the sani-

[48] MacDonald Testimony, Flagler Divorce Proceedings, August 12, 1901, Seventh Judicial Circuit, Miami, Florida.
[49] Flagler Testimony, *Ibid.*

tarium amounted to $15,600 per year; and additional com-
forts, to $5,000. The remainder of the income went into the
principal.[50]

There was no question about the adequacy of the income
which Flagler provided for her. This financial statement,
which was published in all the Florida newspapers, allayed
the fears and suspicions of some; still others could see nothing
good or pleasant coming out of the divorce case at all. There
was no effort on the part of Mrs. Flagler's family or friends
to interfere with the procedure. There were no testimonies
in her behalf. The divorce was officially granted in Miami on
August 13, 1901.[51] A long and turbulent chapter in Flagler's
life had come to an end.

The divorced Mrs. Flagler never realized what action the
court had taken. She continued to live in her world of delusions and hallucinations. She gave no thought to her enormous
income, her family, her friends, or her ex-husband. Many
years later she was moved by Eugene Ashley to a private
sanitarium at Central Valley, New York. There she was given
a special cottage on the grounds of the institution, and was
provided with an attendant and with all the comforts she
could enjoy. Physically, she continued to live in good health
until July 10, 1930, when she died of a cerebral hemorrhage,
at the age of eighty-two. She was buried in New York.[52]

II

On August 21, 1901, seven days after Flagler's divorce was
granted from his second wife, newspapers throughout the

[50] Ashley Testimony, *Ibid.*
[51] Final Decree, *Ibid.*
[52] *New York Times,* July 13, 1930.
Alice Flagler's wealth had increased rapidly from 1901 to 1930, largely
because of Standard Oil securities. She had no will and it was known that
the money was to be divided among her relatives. This fact attracted the
attention of persons, some of whom had an actual claim upon the money by
their relationship, while the kinship of others was so remote as sometimes to
be invisible to the eye of the law. A few of her distant cousins won awards

South and East carried an announcement of his engagement to Mary Lily Kenan. The news was received with mingled feelings. People who knew them both were expecting it, but yet were amazed when the information was actually released. Commented the *Atlanta Journal*, "The announcement caused no surprise, because the affair has been talked about and gossiped over for the past two years, although rumors concerning the engagement could never be confirmed." [53] Public opinion crystallized rapidly and was anything but favorable to the match between the twice-married seventy-one-year-old millionaire and the thirty-four-year-old North Carolina belle.

Mary Lily Kenan was a pleasing young woman who was born of an old North Carolina family on June 14, 1867. Wilmington was her home, but she had spent much time in other places in the state. She studied music at Peace Institute in Raleigh, and had become an accomplished pianist and vocalist.[54] There were three other children in her family, Jessie, Sarah, and William R. Kenan, Jr.[55]

---

from her estate before her death. The legal expense of defending the estate against the relatives was out of proportion to the actual expense of paying the claims allowed. A hearing in one case in which an annuity of $1,500 was recommended cost the estate $17,000. The fees of those who were administering the estate also were large. In 1925 Cornelius Sullivan and the Guaranty Trust Company, who had acted for years as the committee of Mrs. Flagler's estate, received allowances of $7,000 each as commissioners and a special allowance of $30,000 each for the year. In the same year the care of dependent relatives came to $61,000, while Mrs. Flagler's maintenance had increased to $132,211.

The exact amount of Alice Flagler's estate at the time of her death was $15,247,925. This sum was divided equally among her nearest of kin—two nephews and a grand niece.

This was a report made by the Guaranty Trust Company as of March 16, 1930. See *New York Times*, March 17, 1930. A few weeks later the *New York Herald-Tribune* said the tax appraisers had filed a report showing her net estate to be worth $13,277,814.

[53] *Atlanta Journal*, August 22, 1901.

[54] Her father was William Rand Kenan, and her mother Mary Hargrave, formerly of Chapel Hill, North Carolina. See W. R. Kenan, Jr., *Incidents By the Way*, 9–12.

[55] Jessie Hargrave Kenan married Clisby Wise; Sarah Graham Kenan married Graham Kenan (a cousin); and William Rand Kenan, Jr., married Alice Pomroy. See *Ibid.*, 10.

Flagler was first introduced to Miss Kenan in 1891 when she was visiting the Pembroke Jones family in St. Augustine. Pembroke Jones was also a North Carolinian, who, after making a fortune operating rice mills, retired and spent the winters in Florida and the summers in Newport, Rhode Island. Mrs. Jones and Miss Kenan were close friends and spent much of their time together.[56] Mary Lily was always popular with men, and in the resort towns she was never without an escort. Her suitors were struck with her grace and charm and her taste for beautiful clothes. Flagler was impressed with her from the start, and Alice Flagler, too, admired her for her pleasing personality and her elegant manners. The first winter she was in St. Augustine Alice Flagler entertained for her and the two became very friendly.[57]

The Flaglers saw Miss Kenan occasionally during the next few years in St. Augustine as well as in Newport, and it was always a pleasant meeting for them all. Then came Alice's mental breakdown, and after 1896 Flagler was without feminine company wherever he went. In the meantime Miss Kenan had become very intimate with Eliza Ashley, relative of Flagler, who spent much time in Florida at his invitation. By chance Flagler was thrown often in company with the two young women. They travelled to Palm Beach and Miami with him on business trips, and as Flagler was trying to make the best of his wife's insane condition, he escorted the young ladies to special places of interest. They liked the attention he paid them; that was nothing but natural. He enjoyed showing them a good time because it was the best way he had found to forget his troubles. Before he knew it his heavy heart had become lighter, his depressed feeling had all but vanished, and he was showing signs of becoming himself again.

[56] *New York Tribune,* August 25, 1901.
[57] *St. Augustine News,* March 22, 1891.

Turbulent Years

In 1897 Eliza Ashley and her husband were invited to spend the winter at Palm Beach as the guests of Flagler. They occupied a beach cottage, and the millionaire was there, too, a large part of the time. Miss Kenan spent most of the winter in Palm Beach as guest of the Ashleys. Mary Lily's charming personality became more pronounced, and she bubbled over with the kind of happiness which the elderly millionaire so much desired to share. Her musical talent was greatly admired by him, and he often requested that she sing his favorite songs. The friendship became warmer and more intimate, and Flagler and Miss Kenan were thrown together more each winter season. It was rumored that he lavished expensive gifts on her, none of which escaped the critical eye of the public. Palm Beach society began to gossip. The news spread to Miami, then to St. Augustine, and finally to all the fashionable places in the country. Flagler's intentions were honest. To him Alice Flagler existed no more, but what could he do about it? She did exist, but in an insane state.

It was not long before the public knew what Flagler planned to do. In 1899, he tried to get a divorce from Alice in New York, but the laws of that state would not permit it.[58] But the state of Florida did grant the divorce after his residence was established there. The couple lost little time after Flagler became a free man, and for that the public again watched critically. The wedding on August 24, 1901, was elaborate, but done in the presence of only a few friends and relatives. Liberty Hall, in Kenansville, North Carolina, a typical old ante-bellum home, where dozens of Kenans had been born and reared, was the scene of the affair. It was situated on the brow of a long rolling hill in the midst of a magnificent grove of oaks, sycamores, and elms. For this special event of August 24, it had been thoroughly renovated and repainted during the early summer. Peyton H. Hoge of Louis-

[58] *New York Tribune*, August 25, 1901.

ville, Kentucky, read the wedding vows in the spacious hallway which connected all of the rooms downstairs.[59] The
bride's wedding gown was of white chiffon over white satin,
trimmed with point appliqué with a veil of the same material,
adorned with orange blossoms. She wore no ornaments. Her
only attendant was a niece, Louise Clisby Wise. Flagler looked
dignified in a Prince Albert coat with light trousers. His advancing years were hidden behind a beaming countenance.[60]
He was a happy old man, and expressed his joy in the form of
expensive gifts to the bride, certain members of the family,
and the servants.

Soon after the wedding, the couple boarded Flagler's private train car at Magnolia, North Carolina, the nearest railroad point, and sped away to New York. The honeymoon
was spent at Mamaroneck, their summer home.[61] The many
messages of congratulation which greeted the Flaglers on
their arrival at Mamaroneck gladdened the aging man's heart.
Naturally he was interested in what his friends thought about
it. Perhaps some of the communications were not sent in any
degree of sincerity; at any rate, he was thankful for the
friends who had genuinely rejoiced with him in his good
fortune.[62] Not all of his own family accepted graciously the
new member of the Flagler clan, but that was to be expected.[63]
The general public had little mercy on either of them, and
contended that his fortune had entered strongly into the
match. Less critical persons accepted the marriage. There was
much to say in Mary Lily's behalf. She was far superior to his
second wife; she was cultured, well trained, and had an excellent background. She was Flagler's equal socially and intel-
lectually. She was a good wife to him, and during most of

[59] *Ibid.*
[60] *Palatka Times-Herald*, August 30, 1901.
[61] *Ibid.*
[62] Henry M. Flagler to Andrew Anderson, August 29, 1901.
[63] Conversation with Katherine S. Lawson.

their married years his interests came first with her. She was
socially inclined and loved excitement and a good time. Such
was afforded her whenever she desired it.[64]

If lavished wealth was what she craved, Mary Lily Flagler
had reason to be happy, for Flagler spared no expense to
give her anything that money could buy. She had always
wanted a marble palace for a home, so her aging husband
built a mansion costing $2,500,000 in Palm Beach which she
called Whitehall.[65] It was begun several months after they
were married and finished in a record time of eight months.
It was planned by the same architects and built by the same
contractors Flagler employed on the Ponce de Leon Hotel.
All of the interior work and furnishings were executed from
designs of Pottier and Stymus Company, under the personal
supervision of William P. Stymus, Jr. Flagler first conceived
the idea of reproducing a typical Cuban house. He had seen
the home of Dominquez Cerro, one of the most imposing
structures in Havana, and hoped to reproduce it; but as the
problem developed, it soon became apparent that the conditions which Flagler had established as to size, height, and
arrangement would interfere in a measure with his original
scheme. Beyond the general plan of the interior patio or court,
there was not much left of the original idea in Whitehall.
The Spanish court, typical of Cuban homes, contained rare
varieties of palms and shrubs of all kinds. In the center were
built a fountain and pool.[66]

From the outside, Whitehall was typical of great wealth
and beauty. It sat amidst grounds of flowers, shrubs, palms,
and graceful Australian pines. Broad marble steps led to the
colonnade which extended across the front of the building.[67]
Great bronze grille doors led into the grand hall occupying

[64] Conversation with Anna Fremd Hadley.
[65] *New York Herald*, March 30, 1902.
[66] *The Tatler*, March 21, 1903.
[67] *New York Herald*, March 30, 1902.

the center of the front, with its superb double staircase of white marble. The hall, 110 feet long and forty feet wide, was of white marble relieved by lines of black marble let in to form panels, and by heavily inwrought capitals that surmounted the columns separating the two flights of steps in the center of the hall and upholding the ceiling at either end of the passage.[68] The chairs and important pieces of heavier furniture in the hall were richly carved in Louis XIV design and were covered with tapestries and silk velvets. The clock, which was nine feet high, was made of rich bronze, and represented "Time" riding the world in a cloud. Across the room from the clock sat an antique Florentine chest, with a decorative panel representing the marriage of Boccaccio. Windows in the hall were draped in Spanish tapestry of green. Four slender pyramid trees, ten feet high, were placed near the windows to complete the color scheme. The interior of the house presented an atmosphere of the Old World. Agents searched France and Italy for superb furnishings and rare works of art. Rugs that usually required years were woven in months, and furniture was made in record time to fulfill the desires of the great builder.

Sharing the first floor with the grand hall were the salon, ballroom, library, music room, breakfast room, and grand dining room. Of these, the dining room was perhaps the most elaborately decorated. The room, forty-four by twenty-three feet, was treated in François I design and finished in satinwood, with the ceiling divided into panels and ornamented with papier-mâché in tones of green coloring, relieved by gold. The walls were hung in two shades of green tapestry, the windows being draped with plain green silk velours. Chairs in this room were covered with Aubusson tapestry, which was made especially for each. Window curtains were of rich Colbert lace; and the rug of Savonnerie, the center being plain green, with a rich border representing fruit and

[68] *The Tatler*, March 21, 1903.

game. Four bronze and crystal chandeliers lighted the room.[69]

The library occupied the southeast corner of the house with full views of Lake Worth from the broad arched windows. The spirit of the Italian Renaissance period prevailed in this room. The walls were hung in rich Spanish tapestry, and over the windows were Arabian laces. A large oil painting of Flagler hung over the mantel. Aubusson tapestry furniture, carved walnut chairs, and richly carved tables, and a Savonnerie rug in rich tones of red completed the furnishings of the library, which housed many rare and valuable paintings as well as books. One of its pieces was an old painting representing the landing of Ponce de Leon in Florida.

The music room was actually an art gallery because in it hung many fine paintings. It was sixty-four by twenty-four feet in size and was designed after the Louis XIV period. Its domed ceiling, treated with a decorative canvas panel of the aurora, was lighted by invisible electric bulbs. The pipe organ which graced one end of the room was reputed to be the largest ever placed in a private home in the United States.

For grandeur the ballroom had few equals, it being characteristic of the perfect type found in the time of Louis XV. Its dimensions were ninety-one by thirty-seven feet. Its color scheme was white and gold, the whole effect being soft in tone. A mezzanine for the orchestra was erected at one end of the room. Handsome mirrors, richly ornamented and divided into panels, were placed between the long windows. Introduced above the doors and windows were Boucher panels representing the four seasons and other interesting subjects, which gave the room a tone of the old masters. The window draperies were in two shades of rose de Berry silk damask. The jeweled chandeliers and brackets were the same as those used in grand salons in the fifteenth century.

Flagler had a private suite of rooms overlooking Lake

[69] "Whitehall, Mr. Flagler's residence at Palm Beach," *International Studio* (March, 1919), 11.

197

Worth, at the southwest corner of the house, which he used as offices for himself and his secretaries. The furnishings here were of mahogany, the walls and ceilings being treated to match, with floors of oak.[70]

On the second floor were sixteen guest chambers, nearly all of which had a different style and design, each representing an epoch in the world's history. Italy, France, Spain, England, the Orient, and American Colonial mansions were studied in order to carry out this distinctive plan. From each of these sixteen rooms there was a private hallway leading to the main hall. The average size of each of the rooms was twenty-five by eighteen feet. The beauty of the walls impressed the guest. The walls of one room had cream moiré panels; a second was in shades of cream and white stripes; another represented a green lattice on which pink roses appeared to be growing; a fourth was panelled in ecru moiré with red borders; while still another was covered with gold silk damask. The furniture in all the rooms varied, having been brought from France, Spain, and other European countries. Only one bedroom was in modern American style. This was noticeable by the twin beds, then being used widely by the more wealthy people in the United States. The floor coverings in the bedrooms ranged from small scatter rugs to large gold-colored Angora carpets. The window draperies, for the most part, were of silk tapestry. In passing from one room to another one was impressed with the perfect harmony in the color schemes. The fireplaces, andirons, locks, and fixtures for lighting were skillfully designed to be in keeping with the rooms for which they were selected.

Mrs. Flagler's bedchamber was the most beautiful of all the bedrooms. The walls were done of silk damask, the window draperies were of the same material; and the curtains, of silk lace. The furniture, in two tones of pearl gray, represented the period of Louis XV. The bed was draped with a gold

[70] *Palm Beach Daily News* (Annual Historical Number), 1903, 6.

damask canopy. Each corner of the bed was ornamented with a woman's head and shoulders in bronze. The maple floor was covered with an Axminster rug. The bath, which opened from Mrs. Flagler's bedroom, was seventeen by eleven feet, and contained a sunken tub. The floor was laid with marble tile. From this room opened a clothes closet fitted with armoires having glass doors to show the gowns, and compartments for jewelry, laces, and lingerie. In this suite also was a dressing-room for Flagler.[71]

Whitehall was too elaborate and formal to be a livable place. It lacked the feeling of warmth that characterizes a home. The foreign atmosphere never wore off. The structure became a show place, and only when large crowds assembled at banquets and parties did there seem to be much happiness within the marble walls.[72] Mrs. Flagler enjoyed entertaining, and her husband entered as gracefully as he could into the pastime though he was getting old and wished many times to be away from crowds and excitement. A certain amount of entertaining had to be done, however, in keeping with their standing in the community. Their common pleasure was music, and each winter some prominent organist was employed to give regular weekly programs at their home. The musician who filled most of the engagements was Russell Joy, who had been organist for a while at Memorial Presbyterian Church in St. Augustine. He not only presided at the console at Whitehall but also played at the Royal Poinciana Chapel. Organ music was a feature of all the social functions given by the Flaglers regardless of the formality.

Perhaps the most brilliant social season for the Flaglers was the winter of 1901–1902. They had been married only a few months when they arrived in Palm Beach, and it did not take

[71] *Ibid.*
[72] Whitehall was sold by the Flagler estate a few years ago, and a large wing was added to the original structure. It is now an exclusive hotel-apartment building. From the front entrance it still resembles the Whitehall of the Flagler era.

Mrs. Flagler long to create a place in the social register for herself. All the affairs given by her were in keeping with the vast wealth of her husband. She entertained at elaborate bridge parties, teas, and banquets throughout January, February, and March at the Royal Poinciana Hotel, since Whitehall was not completed. At one of the bridge parties she gave as prizes a cut glass scent bottle set with an amethyst stone in a gold top, a gold buckle set with pearls, and a bouquet of lilies of the valley in which was hidden a hat pin set with pearls and turquoise.[73]

Whitehall was completed before the 1902–1903 season and became a mecca for socially prominent visitors. Flagler gave several stag dinners, and his wife entertained at several elaborate affairs; her guests always represented the wealth and fashion of the nation. Among the notables who were entertained by the Flaglers at Whitehall were Sir Gilbert Carter, Governor of the Bahama Islands;[74] Admiral George Dewey, hero of Manila Bay;[75] Elihu Root, cabinet member of Theodore Roosevelt;[76] John Astor; Henry T. Sloane; Lyman J. Gage; and P. C. Knox. Their friends were many and their interests always varied.

One of the most welcomed winter visitors at Whitehall was the famous English actor, Joseph Jefferson. He was a lovable character, and was always witty and funny, but very sensible. Flagler liked his companionship and grew to rely heavily upon him as a source of pleasure. Others who frequented the Flagler mansion from time to time were Eliza and Eugene Ashley, of New York; Jessie Wise, of Georgia, sister of Mrs. Flagler; Senator Camden of West Virginia; William R. Kenan, Jr., of North Carolina, brother of Mrs.

[73] *Palm Beach Daily News*, March 21, 1902.
[74] *The Tatler*, March 20, 1897.
[75] *Ibid.*, February 1, 1902.
[76] Flagler was generous to Hamilton College in his will, perhaps because of the influence of Root, who was a loyal benefactor of that institution. Conversation with William R. Kenan, Jr.

Flagler; and the Andrew Andersons of St. Augustine. Whitehall was seldom without visitors.

Mary Lily Flagler was a charming hostess, and the art of
entertaining became second nature with her. Her parties were
well planned and always enjoyed by those attending. She was
especially fond of Christmas Eve and New Year's Eve parties
because of the gaiety engendered by the holiday season. She
served expensive wines of which she was especially fond.
However, her husband never touched strong drink, and was
always much opposed to it.[77] She was a graceful dancer, too,
but in this form of entertainment her aging husband usually
defaulted in favor of some younger partner. Her clothes were
beautiful, without exception, especially her party frocks. Most
people liked her tastes in other matters as well as clothes. She
was respected by her contemporaries in Palm Beach, and
though there were a few critics among her so-called friends,
she mixed freely with the best of society in Palm Beach and
also at their summer home in Mamaroneck.[78]

After several years very little entertaining was done at
Whitehall. Flagler's age kept him from entering actively into
any social life while Mrs. Flagler found social attractions elsewhere. House guests were not as frequent as they had been,
and the mammoth marble structure seemed more like a tomb
than a home.[79] Flagler deserved a place for rest and relaxation
during his latter years, for his domestic life had long been
anything but settled.

[77] Conversation with Anna Fremd Hadley and Belle Dimick Enos.
[78] *Ibid.*
[79] *Palm Beach Daily News*, February 3, 1909.

201

🏛 TWELVE 🏛

Flagler's Folly

THE last phase of Flagler's railroad construction in Florida was his most expensive and most daring undertaking, the overseas extension from Miami to Key West. The project cost about $20,000,000, and though it was in operation for twenty-odd years, it was never a paying proposition. Many of Flagler's friends advised him against building the extension, and his critics rebuked him for sinking so much money along the Florida Keys, but his great desire for building something great and magnanimous got the better of him. Flagler was growing old when he started the extension; he was seventy-five and had already spent $30,000,000 in Florida. It was unusual for a man of his age to begin such a task, and as the road neared completion he became more and more interested in seeing it completed. His faithful lieutenants were spurred on by his enthusiasm, at times doing things against tremendous odds in order to please their aging boss.

A railroad connecting Key West with the mainland of Florida had been talked about for a long time. Years before Flagler's era in Florida certain interested people had urged, and some had even prophesied, the building of an overseas extension to Key West. From both a commercial and military standpoint it was practicable. As early as 1831, a Key West newspaper advocated, in a report to the upper House of Congress, the building of a railroad to the island town. The editor explained the great advantage the nation would derive from the railroad. He argued that Key West was in a strategic location and was in position to serve as a great naval base, but nothing was done for a long period of time. In 1883, General John B. Gordon, of Georgia, secured a franchise to build a railroad to Key West. Actually fifty or sixty miles of railroad were completed on the Florida mainland by the General, but the work was abandoned before the Florida coast was ever reached.[1]

During the 1890's there was much speculation as to the possibilities of such a road's being built. Early in this decade the Trustees of the Internal Improvement Fund in Florida engaged an engineer, H. S. Duval, to inspect the railroad south of Daytona and to make recommendations as to the advisability of building further railroads in South Florida, and if so, how far south. Duval made the following report:

> It does not appear where the final terminus of this road [Flagler's road] is to be, but no doubt when the great capitalist [Flagler] learns that the Florida Keys are islands enclosed in a harbor made by natural submerged breakwater called the Florida reefs and are therefore not really exposed to the violence of the outer sea, and may be connected with ordinary creosoted trestle work as now existing across Escambia Bay, he may rise in a culminating spirit of enterprise and moor Key West to the mainland.[2]

This was the first time that anyone had even mildly predicted that Flagler would extend his road to Key West. However, this report began to center public attention on him and from this time on, there was a feeling among those who knew Flagler best that someday, if he lived long enough, he would undertake the tremendous task. After the Florida East Coast Railroad was completed to Miami, speculation increased over Flagler's next move. The *Bartow Courier-Informant* on

[1] H. G. Cutler, *History of Florida*, I, 60.
[2] Minutes of Trustees of the Internal Improvement Fund, Vol. IX, 295.

Florida's Flagler

April 3, 1895, predicted that a railroad would be built at an early day from some point, "on the lower east coast of Florida across the many keys which skirt the mainland, to the city of Key West." The paper made known the fact that competent engineers had announced the project a practicable one, and that Flagler had agents working out details for the building of the road. The *Courier-Informant* also revealed that he had purchased about one-half of Key Largo, which was the first important island off the mainland at the southern end of Biscayne Bay. In the county clerk's office at Key West there had been filed deeds for small tracts of lands on sixty-three different keys, all in the name of one purchaser, whom the Bartow paper believed to be an agent of Flagler. It was also reported that Flagler would build an immense hotel on Key Largo at once.[3] Most of the information divulged at this time came from certain of Flagler's associates. It was unofficial and somewhat premature, but it was made in the light of how Flagler had accepted other great challenges in the field of development.

People in Key West were more anxious for the extension than anyone else. In 1894, Jefferson Browne wrote: "The hopes of the people of Key West are centered in Henry M. Flagler, whose financial genius and public spirit have opened up three hundred miles of the beautiful east coast of the state. The building of a railroad to Key West would be a fitting consummation of Mr. Flagler's remarkable career." There were between 15,000 and 20,000 people in Key West by 1895, and most of them had become thoroughly aroused over the hope of their town's being connected to the mainland by railroad. In September, 1895, two of Key West's leading citizens, George L. Babcock and George Lowe, were sent to St. Augustine and Jacksonville to solicit interest in those towns. Citizens of both cities talked encouragingly to the Key West delegates.[4]

[3] *Bartow Courier-Informant*, April 3, 1895.
[4] *Daily* (Key West) *Florida Citizen*, September 11, 1895.

204

Flagler did not hurry in making his final decision to build the extension. He wanted to know more about the possibilities and the practicability of building such a road. For several years his agents made surveys, produced figures, and estimated costs. He gave himself plenty of time to appraise these reports. Another thing, too, which perhaps delayed him in making a final decision, was the mental illness of his second wife and his subsequent divorce from her. His domestic troubles were not cleared up until after 1901, and then with a free mind, a new wife, and at a ripe old age, he plunged forth into the greatest undertaking of his career.

There were several reasons for Flagler's decision. First of all he had a flair for doing great things, and the Key West extension was a grand climax to all his other developments. He realized that such an undertaking would cost a tremendous amount of money, and he knew full well that it would take long years for the extension to pay for itself. But, as in the case of all his other developments, he felt sure that it would be a good investment and it would be the means of linking Florida and the United States with Central and South America. He felt that Key West would become a sort of "American Gibraltar." The Spanish-American War, in 1898, had virtually placed Cuba in our hands, and Key West would easily serve as an outlet to the former Spanish island. Flagler realized that as the years went by the American government would be compelled to maintain closer relations with Cuba.[5] He himself was particularly interested in Cuban trade. He had made a number of visits there and had expressed a desire to invest in cultivation of Cuban oranges. In addition he had bought some shares in several Cuban railroads. All this made him vitally interested in the economic future of the island.

The decision by the federal government to build a canal across the Isthmus of Panama also helped to influence Flagler in his decision. America had for a number of years anticipated the building of a canal across some narrow portion of

[5] *San Mateo Item,* June 12, 1909.

Central America. When the way was finally made clear for
the construction of the Panama Canal, Flagler soon began to
think in actual terms of connecting Key West with the mainland. During this time, Flagler was in touch with Elihu Root,
Secretary of War and a friend for many years, concerning
the proposed extension. It was Root's feeling that our interest in the Caribbean would be strengthened considerably
with the building of the canal.[6] Flagler perhaps was influenced
to no small degree by Root's predictions as to our future in
that section of the world. Flagler and his agents began to study
the preliminary surveys and engineers' reports in a new light.
The assurance that the Panama Canal would be built made
the Florida Keys, and Key West in particular, a most promising area. Key West was almost 300 miles nearer the point
where the eastern terminus of the canal was to be located than
any of the other Gulf ports. It was a natural base for guarding
and protecting the canal on the east.

By fall, 1904, it was certain that Flagler would build the
extension to Key West, but no official announcement had
been made to that effect. Railroadmen, businessmen, and
newsmen hounded the life out of Flagler to see what he was
going to do. Newspapers everywhere announced prematurely
the decision. All the while surveyors and engineers were still
at work furnishing Flagler with data and information.[7] On
January 30, 1905, Flagler and a group of his associates left
Miami by steamer for a tour of the proposed route of the
Florida East Coast Railway extension. They went all the way
to Key West, where Flagler spent several hours in conference
with the leading citizens of the town. He promised the people
there that the construction would begin within a short time.
Key West buzzed with excitement over Flagler's proposed
program, which meant so much to the tiny water-bound city.[8]

[6] Philip Jessup, *Elihu Root*, I, 47.
[7] *St. Augustine Record*, October 13, 1904.
[8] *Miami Metropolis*, February 2, 1905.

Flagler's Folly

On July 31, 1905, the *Miami Metropolis*, official mouth-piece for Flagler and his associates, announced, in a special Key West edition, the plans and unfolded the entire scheme. The *Metropolis* told, for the first time, all about the unique and daring scheme. Flagler's plans included not only the over-seas extension but he hoped to construct in Key West twelve piers each 800 feet long and two hundred feet wide. These piers were to be covered by sheds with basins two hundred feet in width, each basin affording berths for four large ships. The paper also announced that Flagler expected the road to be in operation by January 1, 1908,[9] but this ambitious pro-gram was actually not completed until about four years after that date.

Several years prior to Flagler's decision to build the over-seas extension, he had started extending his railroad south of Miami on the mainland. The vast unsettled lowlands were tapped by the invasion of a twelve-mile extension south of Miami in 1903. This short line was known as the Cutler Ex-tension, and was used primarily for shipping fruits and vege-tables out of the region. In 1904 the line was extended into what was known as the homestead country, twenty-eight miles south of Miami. At the point where the road termi-nated, a small community group grew up and became known as Homestead. As in the case of many of the other small towns which Flagler had built, it derived its existence primarily from the railroad. The road went no farther until Flagler made up his mind to span the keys. Construction was idle and the terminus of the road remained unchanged until the final jump was made to Key West.[10]

For a time, Flagler was undecided as to what route he should take to Key West. One possibility was to extend his road only a few miles south to the eastern tip of Florida, taking off from the mainland at Jewfish and from there across

[9] *Ibid.*, July 31, 1905.
[10] *St. Augustine Record*, May 30, 1913.

the keys to Key West. The other was to construct an extension from Homestead to Cape Sable at the southwestern tip of Florida and from there take off over open seas to Key West. Cape Sable was closer to Key West than Jewfish, but if he chose the latter route he would not have the advantage of all the keys. Engineers advised strongly against this route; consequently Flagler soon abandoned any idea of extending his road across the swamps and jungle through the Everglades to Cape Sable.[11]

Preliminary surveys, mappings of channels and water courses, observations of winds and storms, and the charting of the route over the keys from Jewfish were completed early in 1905. Actual construction began in the summer on this undertaking which many financiers had termed as "unthinkable" and scores of engineers thought "impossible." When Flagler announced to his friend, George M. Ward, that he had decided definitely to build a railroad over the keys to Key West, the elderly churchman, thinking of what a preposterous idea it was, remarked, "Flagler, you need a guardian." [12]

The Florida Keys over which Flagler built his railroad were small patches of land completely surrounded by water, and numbering in the hundreds. They extended like a long finger, pointing about one hundred and twenty-eight miles from the mainland to Key West. They were composed of coral and lime rock formations and were a part of an extensive reef. Many of them were in lonely places, uninhabited, and unexplored. The intricate network of channels among these keys had for a long time formed an ideal retreat for the pirates who preyed upon the rich commerce of the Spanish Main. It was also along this route that the Florida wreckers hid like vultures to pounce on stricken ships that had been

[11] *Florida Times-Union*, January 23, 1913.
[12] J. W. Travers, *History of Palm Beach*, 7.

grounded by storm and winds. Smugglers and renegade sailors used the keys as a haven of refuge.[13]

Native vegetation on the keys was distinctly subtropical in character and was of much interest to the naturalist. Most of the trees were stunted in growth and included a variety of mahogany, dogwood, wild rubber, and bay. The chief commercial products were limes, fish, and sponges. The shoals and channels, and the Gulf Stream, whose course lay only a short distance from these islands, abounded in all sorts of marine life. Between five hundred and one thousand varieties of fish were found there, some of which rivaled the rainbow in coloring and resembled the ever-changing water. Big game fishermen looked upon the keys as one of the most productive spots on the Florida coast. The difficulties which confronted Flagler and his associates when they began the extension were many and complex. One of the first things they did was to advertise for bids on the construction in all of the leading newspapers in the United States. After giving ample time for those who desired to have the job to send in their bids, Flagler was astonished to find that only one contractor was willing to talk about the task, and he wanted a cost-plus contract to do the job. Flagler refused to sign such a contract, and decided to have his own lieutenants, headed by Joseph R. Parrott, undertake the task themselves.[14] No other person would have worked more diligently and more faithfully than he did. No one except one of his faithful, long-time associates would have undertaken the job.

Labor was a problem throughout the seven years of construction. It was hard to get a man to work under the existing conditions; yet the force at one time reached a maximum of 4,000 men, with an average of nearly 3,000 working all the

[13] J. M. Rockwell, "Opening of the Over Sea Railway," *Collier's*, January 20, 1912.
[14] E. V. Blackman, *Miami and Dade County*, 54.

time. The intense heat and the vicious mosquitoes were two of the biggest hindrances. Flagler's rule that there should be no whiskey in the camps was not too enticing for many who felt that they could not work without their weekly drunken spree. The only available places for the laborers to get liquor were Miami and Key West, and they were so far away it was not hard for this rule to be enforced. Occasionally a "booze boat," as they were called, shuttled about among the keys leaving its intoxicants with the laborers in the water-bound camps, but the operators of these boats ran a great risk of being caught and handled with as little ceremony as actual pirates.[15]

Recruiting of labor was done wherever it could be found. A few Spaniards from Cuba were used, as well as a few blacks from the Cayman Islands. Now and then a Norwegian showed up, although he generally would not stay long unless made a foreman. The bulk of the laborers were secured through agencies in New York and Philadelphia, many of them being only derelicts and hoboes who were looking for adventure. Many of them skipped camp as soon as they were paid, and went to Miami to drink up their earnings. About eighty per cent of the workmen came from cities in the North. Native Negro labor was found to be both insufficient and inefficient, though a large number of Negroes were used on the construction the last three years. One of Flagler's associates commented, "One of our most trying problems has been to take a big body of low-grade men, take care of them, and build them into a capacity for performing high-class work."[16] Among the highly skilled was a group of Greek divers who worked faithfully throughout the project. There was some loss of life among the workmen, but very little in comparison with the size of the undertaking. There were no epidemics nor prevailing sickness among the laborers.

The camps where the men lived were located at various

[15] J. M. Rockwell, "Opening of the Over Sea Railway," *loc. cit.*
[16] G. M. Chapin, *Official Program Key West Extension,* 13.

places along the keys, depending upon the location of the work at any given time. Each camp was under the entire supervision of the engineer in charge, and regular discipline was maintained. Each man got his board and lodging in addition to a salary. Flagler's officials maintained close supervision over these camps, and saw to it that no lowering of fixed standards took place. The diet was substantial, wholesome, and bountiful, and the occasional visitor found it decidedly appetizing. The steward in charge of the dining rooms ordered all of his supplies from the chief steward at Marathon where the depot was located. Supply boats were dispatched three times each week from that place.[17]

Flagler provided his men with proper hospitalization for all emergencies. In each camp there was a first-aid station, manned by two trained persons. Here emergencies and ordinary illnesses were cared for. In case the patient needed more specialized treatment, he was sent immediately to the company's hospitals at Key West or Miami, where he received service free of charge. The Miami hospital was especially well fitted to care for sicknesses and injured patients. Flagler realized this would be an attraction in trying to secure workmen. Dr. J. M. Jackson, Jr., was selected as the chief physician in charge of the extension work, and Dr. J. A. Heitlinger, of Bellevue Hospital, assisted him.[18]

The matter of drinking water was one of importance which had to be solved satisfactorily. Fresh-water wells could not be dug on the keys. Several diggings were made as deep as two thousand feet without any success. To solve this problem two special trains of flatcars carrying large tanks of water operated daily from the little station of Everglades, not far from Homestead, to the various camps down the keys. The water in most instances was transported over a hundred miles. At one time experts thought they could cut down on this

[17] *St. Augustine Record*, January 22, 1912.
[18] *Miami Metropolis*, March 9, 1906.

distance by hauling it from Manatee Creek, only about fifty miles from the main camp. A water station was located there but before it was put in operation along came a northwest wind and blew all the water out of the bay, so that it was impossible for boats to get within two miles of it. Therefore it was necessary to abandon the station until the water regained its natural level. Three weeks later the wind came from the opposite direction and piled the water up in the bay in such quantities as to drive them out again.[19]

Among the interesting features connected with the overseas construction was the various equipment which had to be used. Some of it was lost in storms, and some sank at times for lack of repairs, since most of the machinery had to be put on floating units. Before he began work Flagler purchased the following equipment: twenty-seven launches, ranging from five to fifty horsepower; eight stern-wheel Mississippi River steamers; three tugs; twelve dredges; eight concrete mixers for work over water; two concrete mixers for work on land; nine pile drivers for water work; two track pile drivers; one skid pile driver; ten power excavators; one catamaran for handling coffer dams; eight derrick barges; 150 lighters; two steel barges; six locomotive cranes; and two sea-going steamers. All of the floating equipment was fitted with dynamos for generating electric light because a great deal of the concrete work could not be interrupted by the coming of night. Part of the crew worked almost regularly at night.[20] All of the equipment was expensive, and at the end of the eight-year period was of little value to any other engineer.

Flagler thought he had made all the necessary preparations before the work started, but as the construction progressed many problems arose which had to be worked out. For one thing, nature's resistance had to be reckoned with, the known factors of her force computed, and the unknown factors pro-

[19] *Palm Beach News,* May 17, 1907.
[20] G. M. Chapin, *Official Program Key West Extension,* 17.

vided against. Another riddle was the growth of the average wave over miles of sea. This had to be measured, and the wind force had to be taken into consideration. New methods of construction had to be devised to meet the needs in various places, and special materials, answering special purposes, were brought from long distances.[21] Special permission had to be obtained from the federal government to build certain draws and also to close the spaces between the different keys. With the help of his faithful associates, Flagler was able to meet all of the requirements necessary to the completion of the work.[22]

Flagler and Parrott chose Joseph C. Meredith as the constructing engineer on the project, and his selection proved to be an excellent one. Meredith was from Kansas City, and had attracted considerable attention for his work at various places over the country. Just prior to accepting the job with Flagler, Meredith had been employed by the Mexican government to build a pier at Tampico. When he was offered the job with Flagler he accepted immediately, indicating that he liked to undertake daring tasks which other engineers tended to shun. Meredith took over and worked for several years with skill and determination, facing every danger and meeting every difficulty without any hesitation. He was always on the job, flitting in and out of the various construction camps in a launch, giving orders here and there. He was usually standing, with binoculars to his eyes, like a military leader observing the movement of his troops on parade. The exhaustive pace at which he travelled brought him to an early death on April 20, 1909, several years before the great task had been completed.[23] There was no associate of Flagler who worked harder on his assigned task than Meredith. His great desire was to see the extension completed before Flagler's death; but the engineer himself did not live to see the job finished.

[21] *Announcement of Key West Extension*, 3.
[22] Conversation with William R. Kenan, Jr.
[23] *Announcement of Key West Extension*, 2.

William J. Krome, a young, muscular giant, was assigned to finish the task which Meredith had begun. He had attended the University of Illinois, but left there to study engineering at Cornell University, where he had made an outstanding record. He went to Florida in 1902 and worked for several years helping make the preliminary surveys in preparation for the construction of the extension. He had been one of the engineers who for two years had toiled and sweated through the jungles and swamps of the Everglades to Cape Sable. He had been chiefly responsible for the Cape Sable plan's being abandoned. When Meredith died, Krome, who was already serving as first assistant, was made engineer-in-chief. He grasped the meaning of the great undertaking before him and set about to finish Meredith's work. Possibly even more responsibility rested on Krome's shoulders than on Meredith's because the latter phases of the work were more difficult. It was the happiest moment of his life, he declared, when Flagler's special train reached Key West on its first run.[24]

Engineer Krome was backed by a capable group of assistants whose loyalty was equaled only by their ability to meet constantly recurring emergencies. They were young men, most of them, who had not passed their mental prime of life. The work evoked so much interest among them that each man all along the line gave the project his unqualified effort and support. These able assistants included P. L. Wilson, C. S. Coe, R. G. Smiley, and Ernest Cotton, division engineers; R. W. Carter, bridge engineer; E. H. Sheeran, general foreman; and B. A. Deal, auditor of construction. Work on the extension lasted seven years and nine months, and most of the assistants remained on the project throughout the time.[25]

Construction over the first twenty-eight miles south of Miami to Homestead was comparatively easy, but the next twenty miles to Jewfish Creek, the jumping-off place, was

[24] *Florida Times-Union*, January 23, 1912.
[25] H. G. Cutler, *History of Florida*, I, 69.

through the marshy Everglades and heavy mangrove swamps. There was not sufficient water to float dredges, and not enough solid ground for wheelbarrow work; so it was necessary for the engineers to make channels to accommodate dredges, so that a roadbed could be built up. Two excavations were made wide enough to contain dredges with a depth of two and one-half feet of water; then two machines made their way down the two sides of an embankment, digging their own channels, using the material excavated for rearing the embankment. The work was hampered and delayed at many points by rocks and solid formations which came so near the surface that it was necessary to float the dredges over them. Six dredges were used in this particular phase of the construction. Some worked northward and others southward, meeting at a mid-way point between Jewfish Creek and Homestead.[26]

From this point on, the work became even more difficult, because the railroad left the mainland and began hopping islands. More than thirty islands were used for stretches of construction, some as long as fifteen or twenty miles, some less than a mile. The first concrete bridge off the mainland crossed Cards Sound at the south end of Biscayne Bay to Key Largo, the first key touched by the sea-going railroad. Key Largo, the largest of all the keys, was twenty-seven miles at its longest point, but the construction was not so difficult as in many other places. However, here, as on all the keys, the work was a web-footed proposition, and the engineers expected marshy swampy earth on each key which the railroad crossed.[27]

Below Key Largo there was Tavernier Creek, less than a mile in width, before another low key was reached. Across the low keys the roadbed was built of natural coral reef; and where it was exposed to the destruction of the winds and water of the sea during storms, a heavy application of marine

[26] *Palm Beach Daily News*, May 17, 1907.
[27] *St. Augustine Record*, January 22, 1912.

marl was made. This marl, which is of a calcareous nature and soft in consistency, flows out, forming a smooth leathery slope that hardens soon after exposure to the air and is able to withstand the heaviest seas. Matecumbe Key was the next formation of earth of much size, being fourteen miles in length; however, six of those miles were creeks and swamps. It was eight miles south of Key Largo, and adjacent to Long Key on the south.[28]

Southwest of Long Key the first of the three great viaducts on the extension began. It was called Long Key viaduct and was 2.68 miles long. It was built of concrete in water from ten to thirty feet deep, and in most places exposed to the full gales of the Atlantic. At times the concrete had to be mixed on barges and placed in position by powerful boom derricks. At other places molds were formed by driving piling which held watertight framework in place. This bridge, which was one of the most expensive, had a series of 180 arches, eighty feet long, built of reinforced concrete. The spans, which gave the appearance of a Roman aqueduct, rested on piers set into solid rock. From the water to the crown of the arch was a distance of about twenty-five feet. This distance was usually determined by the depth of the water. The engineers had to determine the size of the waves in rough weather, so as to build the viaduct out of reach of the watery spray.[29]

From the Long Key viaduct the railroad ran to Grassy Key, a strip of land about fifteen miles long, and from there to Knights Key, less than a mile long. Four years were required to finish the road to this point. On January 22, 1908, the first train on this lap of the overseas extension reached Knights Key, a distance of eighty-three miles south of Homestead, 112 miles south of Miami and 477 miles south of Jacksonville.

[28] S. W. Martin, "The Second Discovery of Florida," (Master's Thesis, University of Georgia, 1935), 45.
[29] Pan-American *Bulletin* (February, 1912), 216.

Flagler's Folly

After the road was opened to Knights Key, steamships from Havana and Key West transferred passengers and freight there, thus saving 112 miles of water route north to Miami.[30]

The work was halted for only a short time at Knights Key while more materials and supplies were gathered, and more men were recruited, for some of the hardest and most tedious work on the extension was yet to be done. Between Knights Key and Bahia Honda Key, the next strip of land of any size, there were seven miles of almost unbroken open water. The viaduct over these seven miles was the second of the great bridges built on the extension. Roughly speaking, it was one long bridge, 35,815 feet in length; however, it was divided into four sections—the original Knights Key bridge; Pigeon Key bridge; Moser Channel bridge, or Little Duck viaduct; and Pacet Channel viaduct. The first three short bridges actually constituted one long bridge made of concrete piers with steel girder spans laid on top to carry the track. The Moser Channel section was the longest portion of the bridge, being 13,947 feet or well over two miles in length.[31] The last section, the Pacet Channel viaduct, which was two miles long, was constructed on steel arches. The rails were laid twenty-nine feet above the mean low tide.

There were ten other gaps of ocean, some large and some small, after the railroad passed the Pacet Channel viaduct. The greatest problem of construction presented itself when the Bahia Honda bridge, which connected Bahia Honda Key and Big Pine Key, a distance of about a mile, was built. This bridge, constructed in the deepest water the engineers encountered on the entire project, was 5,056 feet in length. The engineers not only had to support the concrete piers on solid rock, but they were determined to anchor each one there

[30] E. S. Luther, "The Transformation of the Florida East Coast," *Banker's Magazine* (February, 1909), 262.
[31] J. M. Rockwell, "Opening of the Over Sea Railway," *loc. cit.*

217

immovably. As in the case of the other bridges, the location
of the pier was first determined, after which a coffer dam was
floated into place on a catamaran. After the coffer dam was
made to rest on the bottom, the soft mud was pumped out.
Then a steel punch was driven into the rock to make places
for the wooden piles which followed. These piles driven into
the rock as far as they could be forced were used as anchors
for each pier. Twenty-four piles were driven for each pier.
The next step was to sink a large quantity of cement through
specially prepared pipes to the rock bed. It was a cement imported from Germany which had a special quality for harden-
ing under water. It formed a solid union with the underlying
rock, and also made the coffer dam virtually watertight. This
was then pumped dry, and the piling, which was already en-
cased in the cement foundation, was sawed off below the ordinary low tide level. Then the form or mold for the pier base
was put in place, and was filled with the same specially treated
cement. It took seven days to dry completely; then the coffer
dam was removed. It was upon this foundation the pier was
built. Alternate arches were constructed and allowed to
harden for four weeks, then the missing arches were filled in
and joined to those already in place by an interlocking device
which held each firmly in position and closely bound to its
neighbor. Since each alternate arch was a separate piece of
concrete and was constructed at different times, its shrinkage
and wear cannot affect that of any other. In this bridge there
were thirteen spans, each one 128 feet long; thirteen other
spans, each 186 feet long; and nine arches of concrete, each
eighty feet long.[32]

The Bahia Honda bridge connected Big Pine Key, another
larger body of land. This key was connected to Key West by
the Boca Chica viaduct, the last bridge of any length before
the terminus was reached. The total distance from Miami
to the Key West station was 155.84 miles; from Homestead it

[32] G. M. Chapin, *Official Program Key West Extension*, 15.

was 127.84 miles.[33] Of this distance seventy-five miles was built over water or extremely marshy land. Across some of the keys the ocean was far enough away so that construction here closely resembled that of ordinary road building. Occasionally, there were dense jungles to be penetrated, but such terrain did not present the problems equivalent to those of the open sea.

Flagler built the overseas extension with the full encouragement of the federal government. However, the Navy department at one time protested vigorously against the taking of mud from Key West harbor; the Navy Secretary contended that the mud would be needed someday to fill in one of the nearby keys for a torpedo station. One of Flagler's associates replied rather sarcastically that he would put the mud "right back where he found it." The federal government made one other requirement, and that was the construction of a draw in the Knights Key bridge, a direct passage connecting the Atlantic Ocean with the Gulf of Mexico. This draw was originally planned for the Bahia Honda bridge, but Flagler was glad to comply with the government's request. Three other

[33] *Ibid.*, Appendix I. The exact distance from Miami to Key West over the keys is as follows:

Miami to Homestead	28.00	miles
Homestead to Jewfish Creek	21.39	"
Jewfish Creek	.02	"
Key Largo	16.64	"
Tavernier Creek	.06	"
Long Island	4.88	"
Windley's Island Creek	2.01	"
Matecumbe Key	14.05	"
Long Key	4.05	"
Long Key Viaduct	2.68	"
Grassy Key	15.57	"
Knights Key to Little Duck Viaduct	8.95	"
Bahia Honda Key	2.22	"
Bahia Honda Viaduct	1.04	"
Big Pine Key	28.41	"
Boca Chica Viaduct	1.68	"
Key West	4.19	"
Total	155.84	"

219

draws besides this one were built between Homestead and Key West: one at Jewfish Creek, one at Indian Key, and one at Key West.[34]

During the construction of the overseas road, there were several hurricanes which hampered the work considerably. One came in 1904 during the surveys, two in 1906, one in 1909, and one in 1910. The October storm of 1906 was by far the most destructive. The facilities were far too inadequate to resist such a strong blow and at that particular time there were more men working on the extension than perhaps at any other time. Most of the floating camps and houseboats were destroyed. These floating camps broke loose from their anchors, and in one case more than seventy men were blown out to sea and never heard of again. The Italian steamer *Jenny* and the British steamer *Alten* picked up many others, and for days and even weeks after the storm, news of other rescued workers kept coming from distant ports such as London and Buenos Aires. During this particular hurricane the wind reached a velocity of 125 miles per hour; however, the concrete trestles that were being pushed out in the sea from coral island to coral island, stood, and Flagler became more convinced than ever of the ultimate success of his theretofore untried railroad.[35] As soon as the sea was calm again, the engineers began to hurry the completion of the extension with more determination than ever before. The hurricane of 1909 was even more severe than the previous storm; however, it was not as destructive as the one in October, 1906, because more care had been taken to guard the lives of the men and secure safety for the company's property. By this time most of the workmen were living in large stormproof dormitories, which were a decided improvement over the floating camps. The storm of 1909 taught Flagler's engineers a valuable lesson. They had calculated on the allowance that had to be made only for the

[34] *Ibid.*, 15.
[35] Unidentified clipping, Kenan Collection.

ebb and flow of the ocean tides, and had not taken into consideration the great amount of water that would pass under the open arches and piers of the bridges in times of great winds. Most of the winds from these Caribbean hurricanes forced the ocean water through the Gulf of Florida. The Gulf of Florida stretches out a hundred miles wide between Cape Sable and Key West, but farther northward, along the southeastern coast of the mainland, it narrows gradually until the keys meet the southern tip of the state. Naturally this great force of water had to be reckoned with, and the engineers solved the problem by building stronger bridges where the force of the water was greatest.

Before the work was finished the engineers believed they had mastered the threat of the storms. They kept in close touch with the Weather Bureau at Washington, and watched their barometers more frequently than they did their watches. During the months of August, September, and October, when the tropical hurricanes were most likely to occur, the inquiry most often passing over the telephone wires connecting their various offices and stations was, "How does your barometer read?" During the "hurricane season" no women were allowed to remain in the camps. Even the engineers who frequently had their wives and daughters in their quarters were cautioned against letting them stay after the first day of August each year.[36]

Flagler encouraged families of the workmen to visit the scene of construction at certain desirable times throughout the year. He provided them with comfortable places to stay, and realized that in many cases his employees would be much happier with their loved ones near. Fishing camps with good accommodations were built at logical points along the extension, attracting many sportsmen as well as sightseers and relatives of workmen.[37] Flagler acquired the new Russell

[36] G. M. Chapin, *Official Program Key West Extension,* 12.
[37] *Palm Beach Daily News,* February 4, 1909.

House in Key West, which for a number of years had been a third-rate hotel, and renamed it the Key West Hotel. It was practically rebuilt and entirely refurnished and was used by many persons from the mainland, many of whom were indirectly connected with the construction.

As the work on the extension neared its end, Flagler was noticeably becoming more and more inactive, but his interest was as keen as ever. In February, 1911, the question of finishing the road for traffic in the shortest possible time came up. Engineer Krome was asked by J. R. Parrott if he could complete the work so that Flagler could ride into Key West in his private car over his own rails on his next birthday, January 2, 1912. He would be eighty-two on that day, and he was most anxious to see the extension completed by that time. Krome promised to do the job if no great storm or other unforeseen delay should overtake him. He kept his promise with twenty-four hours to spare; however, the first train did not arrive in Key West for several weeks. Flagler's twenty-million-dollar construction job across the keys had been finished.

On the afternoon of January 21, 1912, the bridge foreman closed the cross-over span at Knights Key trestle, the last link in the line of rails connecting the overseas road with the main line of the Florida East Coast Railway, and soon thereafter the pilot train from Knights Key left for Key West. It gave the road a thorough testing and found it in prime condition for the opening. Engineers J. F. Norton and Ed Goehring, Pilot William Nichols and Fireman Jack Basskopp had the distinction of having carried the first train into the island city.[38]

There was one specific regulation which these first trainmen, and all others who piloted trains over the extension, understood and that was concerning the cancellation of schedules in time of high wind. No train was allowed to travel over the road during times of strong wind because such pressure might sweep a moving train from the tracks, though the

[38] *Savannah* (Georgia) *Morning News*, January 22, 1912.

222

road itself was built to stand extremely strong wind. The viaducts were fitted with wind gauges which measured the velocity of the wind on every part of the great stretch of masonry and steel, and by electricity registered it at each end. This register was attached to a block system which automatically set the switch against the approaching train when the recorded wind velocity reached fifty miles per hour on any section of the bridge. There were many other safety precautions, one of which was the speed limit. No train was permitted to run over the bridges of the extension faster than fifteen miles per hour. Engineers said that the strength of the greatest viaducts would warrant speed of seventy miles per hour, but the possibility of an accident from a broken rail or imperfect car equipment demanded extraordinary precautions for safety of life and property. Normal train speed was resumed after the viaducts were passed. With the prescribed limit of speed, half an hour was required to cross the Knights Key bridge, and almost fifteen minutes to traverse the length of the Long Key viaduct and its approaches.

The first official train to cross the extension arrived at Key West on January 22, 1912, at 10:43 A.M. Ten thousand people were present to see the first section of a number of specials arrive. Many of the natives saw a passenger train for the first time, as many were born either in Key West or the Bahamas. They yelled and cheered themselves hoarse, and added to all the noise was the babel of several tongues, including Spanish and French. On the train with Henry M. Flagler were several of his close associates and many dignitaries. The most notable personage was Robert Shaw Oliver, assistant Secretary of War, representing President William Howard Taft. In the throngs that cheered the arrival of the two sections of the train were also representatives of numerous foreign embassies and legations, including Italy, Mexico, Portugal, Costa Rica, Ecuador, Guatemala, San Salvador, and Uruguay. General Jose Marti, representative of President Gomez, of Cuba, accompanied by a Cuban band, arrived at Key West on board a Cuban gunboat and was followed soon thereafter by a delegation of residents of Havana and other Cuban cities.[39]

As soon as the Flagler train arrived, Mayor J. N. Fogarty went aboard with the celebration committee. Brief ceremonies were held on the observation platform of the rear car. Flagler made his way to the edge of the platform and briefly surveyed the throng of people. He was rapidly becoming a feeble old man. His once keen eyes were weak and blurry. The years had mellowed him, and there was a kind smile on his face. His shoulders were slightly stooped, and he wore his ever-present gray cap. The mayor welcomed him to the island city in a fitting speech. Then George W. Allen presented the railroad builder with a tablet of silver and gold, containing a likeness of himself, as a gift from the residents of the city. Another tablet was presented him, which was also of gold, in behalf of the men who did the actual work of constructing the railroad over the sea. Flagler replied to each with a brief speech. One of the other features of the welcome to Flagler was a children's chorus, composed of a thousand school children, who sang patriotic songs. After the capitalist left the platform he was escorted to the front of the children's bandstand where he greeted the boys and girls individually. The aging man was overcome with emotion by the demonstration given him.

Several other sections of the "first train" arrived in Key West at various intervals all during the day. On one, a solid Pullman train, came a congressional delegation, foreign diplomats, high army officers and other distinguished guests. Another section of the train bore officials from various cities in the South, particularly Florida. One of the sections was a through train from "New York to Havana" and had been advertised as such. The passengers were carried close to the dock in the train, and there they transferred to the American steamer, the *Governor Cobb*, which sailed about four o'clock in the afternoon. Many Floridians made the trip. The

[39] Unidentified clipping, Kenan Collection.

Miami and Jacksonville specials were the last trains to arrive in Key West, and thousands of people remained at the station to welcome the throngs of visitors who came for the celebration.[40] Governor Gilchrist of Florida arrived on the last train.

The celebration, which lasted for several days, included balls, receptions, and other social events. Perhaps the most brilliant affair was the military ball which was given in honor of Flagler on the evening of the first day. Governor Gilchrist spoke and a message was read from President Taft. When Flagler was introduced he was given a thunderous ovation.[41] One of the receptions given in honor of Flagler was preceded by a political rally, the affair being well planned and arranged. Florida was experiencing a hotly contested race for the governorship, and the two leading candidates, Park Trammell and J. W. Watson, were on hand to take part in the rally. Each, in his turn, tore into his opponent with the vigor of a frontier preacher admonishing the devil.

Key West and her twenty thousand inhabitants had never experienced such a celebration. The streets were gaily dressed with American flags and bunting, and the homes were arranged with evergreens, palms, coconuts, and tropical foliage hanging around the verandas, making picturesque scenes. In the show windows there were miniature trains going over the viaducts and bridges, all of which received much favorable comment from the visitors. The amusement features were many. A circus from Cuba performed stunts equal to those of the great Barnum shows. A Spanish opera, moving pictures, and a carnival on the terminal grounds in sight of the tracks where the trains were stopped performed to capacity crowds. In the harbor were seven warships, including the fifth division of the North Atlantic squadron, commanded by Rear Admiral Bradden A. Fiske.[42]

The *Miami Herald* enthusiastically called the extension the

---

[40] *Florida Times-Union*, January 23, 1912.
[41] *Miami Herald*, January 26, 1912.
[42] *Florida Times-Union*, January 23, 1912.

"Eighth Wonder of the World," [43] and spoke in glowing terms about what it would mean for Key West. Said the *Florida Times-Union,* "Today marks the dawn of a new era. The Old Key West—one of the most unique of the world's historic little cities—is shaking off its lethargy and from today the spirit of progress and development will be greater than ever." [44] Other newspapers throughout the nation were also enthusiastic in their predictions for the future of Key West. Key West had come a long way since its charter of incorporation was issued on January 8, 1828. Its history had shown a slow but steady growth. It was built on a coral island standing boldly between the Atlantic Ocean and the Gulf of Mexico. About seven miles long and one mile in breadth, Key West was possessed originally by the Spanish; however, it was transferred to the United States when Florida was purchased from Spain in 1821. In its early days Key West was merely a fishing and wrecking hamlet, but the establishment of several large cigar factories changed it completely, and developed it into a city of some importance, though it continued backward and old-fashioned in its ways.

But Key West did not grow into the great metropolis most people expected, and it did not become "America's Gibraltar" as was so often predicted. The overseas extension never enjoyed the volume of business Flagler hoped it would, because very little freight came out of Cuba and other South American countries. Flagler did not live to realize the folly of his great undertaking; he died believing his road would be the very making of Key West. Key West's population remained in the twenty thousands for some time. In 1945 it had less than 15,000 population, a population far beneath the dreams of those who lived during the Flagler era.

The overseas extension was not destined to last forever. It served Key West and Florida for twenty-two years, but on

[43] *Miami Herald,* January 22, 1912.
[44] *Florida Times-Union,* January 23, 1912.

Labor Day, 1935, an unusually strong hurricane lashed the Florida Keys. Miles of embankment were washed away, and the track over part of the route was left a torn and twisted wreckage. In some places it was washed a great distance from the roadbed. The large bridges, however, survived the storm with only minor damages. The efforts of many years had been laid waste in a short period of a few hours. The Florida East Coast Railway had not survived the depression too well anyway, and the expense of repairing the damages to the extension after the storm was one the company could not undertake. Was it worth another try? The state of Florida thought it was. The State Road Department acquired the partially wrecked extension and built a modern highway where once the railroad had been. The overseas highway was completed in 1938. Much of the road was constructed on the sturdy viaducts and bridges which were built by Flagler and his associates many years earlier.[45] Key West was again connected to the mainland.

[45] *Miami Daily News,* March 6, 1938.

THIRTEEN

The Flagler System

THE combination of all of Flagler's enterprises in Florida was known as the Flagler System. Each enterprise was incorporated and functioned as a separate unit though administered by the same group of officers. Flagler remained actively in charge of all his various incorporated units until April 9, 1909. At that time the presidency was given to James R. Parrott, the most prominent man in the organization besides Flagler himself. He became a vital part of the Flagler System.

Parrott was born in Oxford, Maine, and spent his early years in the East. He graduated from Yale University with an A.B. degree and also an LL.B. degree. "Polly" Parrott, as he was affectionately known by his classmates, was an all-round good fellow. He was a member of his college varsity crew team and won considerable recognition as an athlete. He had broad shoulders, square jaws, and a muscular build. While at Yale, Parrott was thrown with several young men from the South, one of them being S. Price Gilbert, of Columbus, Georgia. From Gilbert's accounts of his native state, Parrott became interested in moving to Georgia. He liked Atlanta especially, and wanted to open an office there but the necessary arrangements could not be made. His second choice was Jacksonville, though he had never been there. Gilbert assured him that it offered many opportunities for a young lawyer, and wrote in his behalf to a friend of long standing, Duncan U. Fletcher, who had just begun to practice law there. Fletcher spoke encouragingly about Jacksonville and the legal profession in that city; so on the day after he graduated from Yale Law School in 1885, Parrott set out on the long journey to Florida. Quite by coincidence Henry M. Flagler had just begun his program of development in Florida.[1]

Duncan U. Fletcher gave the young lawyer a warm reception to Jacksonville. Parrott got off to a good start and with Fletcher's aid was soon doing fairly well in his profession. He became acquainted with the more influential citizens of the town, and it was due to these connections that he was made attorney for the small Jacksonville, Tampa and Key West Railroad. The railroad undertook a tremendous program of expansion, found it impossible to carry through, and consequently fell into the hands of the receivers. Parrott was appointed by the court as a receiver less than five years after he arrived in Jacksonville. He did a good job and made the road do more than pay expenses. About 1890 Flagler heard of Parrott, and decided he was just the man for his organization. The millionaire's great building program was well under way but it needed brilliant young men with a passion for work and advancement. Parrott was hired as a legal adviser to the Flagler enterprises, and thus began a long and valuable period of service. Parrott made good in every respect. He launched out in the work, inspired by that optimism which characterized the spirit of the undertaking. He gathered about him a corps of competent workers and entered into every enterprise with as much zeal and enthusiasm as the capitalist himself did. Like Flagler, he did not recognize the word failure; therefore the two men made a fine working team.[2]

In 1892 Parrott was made vice-president of Flagler's short line, but after a period of growth, in 1899, he was made vice-president and general manager of the Florida East Coast Railway. At the same time he was made president of the Florida East Coast Hotel Company. Then three years before Flagler's

[1] S. Price Gilbert to author, October 2, 1945.
[2] *Florida Times-Union*, January 23, 1912.

229

death, he accepted the presidency of all the corporations.[3] Through all of his services with Flagler, he never gave up his duties as head of the legal department. The fact that Flagler virtually turned over all his enterprises to Parrott is proof enough of his confidence in him. When Flagler died in May, 1913, he directed in his will the continuance of Parrott as president of the Florida East Coast Railway. Parrott was also made one of the three trustees to carry out Flagler's plans as stated in the will.[4] However, he lived only five months after Flagler died. The year 1913 was a tragic one for the Flagler System, because its two strongest leaders were taken from active roles in its development.[5]

Another valuable young man connected with the Flagler enterprises was William R. Kenan, Jr., who later served as president of the Flagler System. His dealings with Flagler were somewhat more intimate than those of Parrott, because of the fact that his sister, Mary Lily Kenan, became Flagler's third wife in 1901. Kenan, who was a North Carolinian by birth, was the youngest of the Flagler lieutenants, but that was no handicap. He graduated from the University of North Carolina in 1893, after making an impressive record.[6] Very little of his formal training was done in the engineering field, but he had great possibilities in this particular line of work.

[3] Conversation with William R. Kenan, Jr.

[4] *St. Augustine Record*, May 30, 1913.

[5] W. H. Beardsley was made vice-president and treasurer when Flagler died, and then succeeded Parrott as president when the latter died. Beardsley was perhaps with Flagler longer than any of his other associates. Throughout most of the time he handled financial affairs for Flagler. Beardsley and Kenan picked William A. Blount to succeed Parrott as legal adviser in the firm, and Blount chose Scott M. Loftin as his assistant. Loftin is still connected with the Florida East Coast. J. P. Beckwith was another vice-president, and was active manager of traffic and operations.

[6] On November 13, 1926, William R. Kenan, Jr., gave to the University of North Carolina $275,000 with which to construct a football stadium as a memorial to his mother and father. Mrs. Mary Lily Kenan Flagler left an endowment which annually produces $75,000 to be used for Kenan Professorships at the University of North Carolina. Conversation with William R. Kenan, Jr.

One of his early jobs was with the Carbide Manufacturing Company at Niagara Falls, New York. While with this firm Kenan was sent to Australia for the business of constructing a carbide plant in one of the larger cities. On this trip he returned by way of Berlin, and though only twenty-six, he remained there for several months as a consulting engineer to the German Acetylene Company. After returning to this country William R. Kenan was located in Wisconsin and Michigan, but on June 1, 1900, he became associated with the Traders People Company, Lockport, New York, as assistant manager. While employed by this firm he made a number of trips to New York, and on one occasion became acquainted with Henry M. Flagler.[7]

Flagler was impressed with the young engineer from the outset, and shortly thereafter invited him to help with certain construction projects in connection with his Florida developments. His first assignment was to build the power plant at the Breakers Hotel in Palm Beach. After considerable study, Kenan made an estimate of the cost of the plant which was cheaper than the one Flagler himself had figured. The thrifty Flagler was pleased with Kenan's first assignment, because it saved more money than he had expected. From this time on the elderly capitalist depended strongly on the opinion and judgment of his younger associate.

Kenan had no official title in the Flagler System at first because he gave only part of his time to the organization. However, in 1904 he resigned his job with the paper concern in Lockport, New York, and became a full-time officer, serving directly under Flagler. In addition to building the power plant he also installed the ice machinery and laundry. Kenan directed the work of the power plant at several other of the hotels, and served as a consultant in connection with the vapor heating, electric lighting, water, and laundry plant at Whitehall. His official position was that of a consulting engineer.

[7] William R. Kenan, *Incidents By the Way*, 30–50.

In March, 1904, he was made a director of all the Flagler corporations, and also a vice-president. He became influential in the Flagler enterprises and was given the authority by Flagler to sign papers or checks at any time, and to do anything which he thought was for the best interest of the Florida developments. He made important decisions for Flagler without even consulting his boss; this fact alone attested the confidence which Flagler had in him.[8]

The two oldest corporations within the Flagler System, ones in which Flagler, Parrott, and Kenan were more closely concerned, were the Florida East Coast Hotel Company and the Florida East Coast Railway Company. These were the parent organizations, but as various schemes were undertaken other corporations were formed.

The Florida East Coast Hotel Company was the first of the corporations. The great chain of hotels that stretched along the east coast of Florida created one of the most popular resort areas in the United States. It was evidently the purpose and ambition of Flagler to make his hotels collectively and separately the finest in the world. He chose the most beautiful spots in Florida on which to construct the buildings, and he summoned as his advisers the foremost landscape artists and architects, and urged them to employ their highest skill. His hostelries offered wide variety and catered to various tastes. Some were the winter gathering places of wealth and fashion from the North. At the Ponce de Leon, the Royal Poinciana, and the Royal Palm visitors moved in exclusive circles. No more fastidious groups could have been found at any other place in the world than at these three hotels. Some people preferred sporting activities along with their social interests, so they chose the Ormond Beach Hotel or the Breakers or maybe the Alcazar. Later Flagler built the Hotel Continental at Atlantic Beach, which was about twenty miles from Jack-

[8] At present he is President of the Florida East Coast Railway and Hotel Companies.

sonville. It was open to the public in 1902 and its construction made the only digression in Flagler's hotel building, aside from the one in the Bahamas. Instead of opening each year on various dates between the middle of December and January 10, and closing between April 1 and 15, the Continental opened late in March as the others were closing, and remained open through August, taking care of all summer visitors who might have come to that vicinity. The reason for the summer opening of the Continental lay in the fact that Atlantic Beach got the full benefit of the breezes from the north and of cooling ocean currents.[9]

In 1898, Flagler left his pursuit of the Florida coast line and the sands of the beach long enough to jump nearly two hundred miles over the ocean to Nassau in the Bahama Islands where he purchased the Royal Victoria Hotel, and soon thereafter established a steamship line between Nassau and Miami. When Flagler first thought of the plan to buy the property at Nassau he made an offer to the British authorities to purchase the hotel building at their own price. The authorities first of all wanted to know what Flagler would do with the hotel if it were sold to him. When he made it known that he would rebuild a larger hotel on the site, the plan was so startling to Sir William Haynes-Smith, the governor, that he refused at first to entertain any such idea. However, after corresponding with his government in England, Sir William changed his mind. It was thought that the Standard Oil magnate had two motives in mind when he invaded the Bahamas: one, to prove to the American people that it was not necessary for them to go to Europe if they felt determined to get out of the United States for a vacation; and second, to establish a steamship line which made direct connections with his railroad running down the east coast of Florida.[10]

[9] E. S. Luther, "The Transformation of the Florida East Coast," *Banker's Magazine* (February, 1909), 263.
[10] *Miami Metropolis*, February 11, 1898.

Flagler paid $50,000 for the Royal Victoria Hotel and there resulted much rumor and speculation as to what he might do with the building. This move was not one that many people had anticipated. In fact, Flagler himself had thought very little of adding foreign property to the already growing list of interests which he was acquiring in Florida. He was on a visit to the Bahamas to expedite the flow of building material from the British Islands to the scene of his construction in Florida when he got interested in making the purchase. After he got control of the hotel, Flagler spent an additional $50,000 in rebuilding the structure. It was renamed the Colonial Hotel and was opened for business in 1899, attracting vacationists from all over the world.[11] Over a thousand workmen were sent to the Bahamas to hasten its completion. The five-hundred-room structure, built on a hillside, was made of stone quarried both in America and in the Bahamas. It was only two stories high but was equipped with elevators and electric lights, luxuries known to few people in the islands at this time.[12] Though one of the last of the Flagler hotels, the Colonial brought as much satisfaction to its owner as any of the group of the Florida East Coast Hotel Company.

Just prior to his purchase of the hotel in the Bahamas, Flagler inaugurated steamship service from Nassau, which was the central part of the British Islands, to Miami. The distance was 175 miles, and the line gave excellent service after the Colonial Hotel was opened. Flagler extended his steamship service by opening a line from Miami to Havana, which was extended on to Savannah. Prior to this time Henry B. Plant had proved himself a developer also. He came to Florida from the North soon after the Civil War, and in 1877 he reorganized the Atlantic and Gulf Railroad of Georgia under the name of the Savannah, Florida and Western Railroad,

[11] *The Tatler*, January 14, 1899.
[12] *Miami Metropolis*, February 11, 1898.

serving northern Florida. The road was completely remade and new equipment and steel rails installed. He next got interested in the St. Johns River, and soon began operating steamers from Jacksonville to Sanford. From this his attention was turned to railroad construction on the west coast of Florida, resulting in the building of the Plant system of roads.[13] In 1902 Flagler's East Coast Steamship Company was consolidated with the Plant Steamship Company forming the Peninsula and Occidental Steamship Company in which Flagler held equal interest with Plant. The newly-organized company put on added schedules, and largely because of Flagler's efforts expanded their services even more.[14]

Flagler's second corporation, the Florida East Coast Railway, included more than the main line which ran from Jacksonville to Key West, a distance of 522 miles. Several short branch lines were purchased and were immediately rebuilt and more adequately equipped. Some of the branch lines reached inland and tapped rich agricultural lands or commercial points on the St. Johns River; however, none of them extended very far out of the east Florida area. Flagler had no desire to go west of the St. Johns River and Lake Okeechobee. The Plant System extended throughout West Florida, and Flagler respected the monopoly of his fellow developer in that section of the state.

In 1899, Flagler bought a small narrow-gauge railroad running from Jacksonville to Pablo Beach at the mouth of the St. Johns River. Several years later, he rebuilt the short line and renamed it the Jacksonville and Atlantic Railway, and extended it to connect Jacksonville Beach, Atlantic Beach, and Mayport with the city of Jacksonville. At Mayport, the Standard Oil magnate constructed large coal and lumber

---

[13] Conversation with William R. Kenan, Jr.
[14] *Ibid.* The steamship line is currently run by the Atlantic Coast Line Railroad, which bought out the Plant System.

docks, hoping that his road would serve as a vital link between the beach town and Jacksonville.[15] Many of Flagler's friends thought that he would build a large hotel at Pablo, but he moved down the coast a few miles and erected the Continental Hotel at Atlantic Beach.

Another branch of the Florida East Coast Railway system was completed in March, 1893, when Flagler acquired the Atlantic and Western Railway, extending from Blue Springs, a point on the upper St. Johns River, to connect the main line of his road at New Smyrna.[16] Six years later Flagler absorbed another short line, the Atlantic Coast, St. Johns and Indian River Railway, running forty-seven miles in length from Enterprise on the St. Johns to Titusville on the Indian River.[17] This was an important acquisition to his system of railroads because it brought to five the total number of points where Flagler's railroad touched the St. Johns River; namely, South Jacksonville, Tocoi, East Palatka, Blue Springs, and Enterprise. A traveller could easily reach the coast from the St. Johns at any of these places.

Perhaps the most important of all the branch lines of the Florida East Coast Railway was the extension from New Smyrna through Maytown southward into the interior of Florida. This was known as the Okeechobee division and was begun in 1911, only two years before Flagler's death. The line reached the little town of Okeechobee, on the Nosohatchee River, two miles northeast of Lake Okeechobee, in 1915. It was thought best to put the terminus on the river, where shipping could be protected, rather than in the open waters of Lake Okeechobee. At the time of Flagler's death in 1913, the road had been built no farther than Kenansville, a small settlement which Flagler named in honor of his wife's family. The great builder would have been extremely happy to have

[15] *St. Augustine Record*, May 30, 1913.
[16] *Florida Times-Union*, April 24, 1893.
[17] H. G. Cutler, *History of Florida*, I, 67.

lived to see this division reach its destination, but death cut short his hopes.[18]

Several years after the Okeechobee division was completed, the road was extended around the eastern shores of the Lake as far south as Lake Harbor, opening to rail perhaps the richest agricultural section in the state. This region is known as the Florida Everglades, the soil of which is composed of a rich peat-muck and is almost a solid decomposed vegetation. Before the new extension was built, there was comparatively little farming done in the region because of inadequate transportation and drainage. The establishment of this line, combined with the extensive work done in drainage and flood control, has made the Everglades area a tremendously productive region. From that section the Florida East Coast Railway soon began to haul hundreds of cars of vegetables each year, more than fifty per cent of which were beans, the balance being made up of cabbage, peas, tomatoes, and miscellaneous produce. The Everglades also became an important sugar-producing area, and many tons of sugar and molasses were shipped each year over the Florida East Coast.[19]

Besides vegetables, the Florida East Coast Railway handled a large volume of the citrus freight in Florida. From the start, oranges were its biggest item of freight, but another money crop was coming into existence in the 1890's along the southern banks of the Indian River. Pineapples were being grown successfully, and the producers were finding a ready market at profitable prices. The crop expanded satisfactorily and spread farther down the coast. For a number of years pineapples proved so important as a source of freight that a picture

[18] Conversation with William R. Kenan, Jr.
[19] *History of the Florida East Coast*, 25. Currently, the Florida East Coast Railway has plans for the construction of a new cutoff which would connect the main line at Fort Pierce with the Okeechobee division at a point ten miles north of Port Mayaca. The distance would be only 30 miles and would cost over a million dollars but would shorten the distance considerably from the Everglades area to Jacksonville. Conversation with William R. Kenan, Jr.

of a pineapple was carried as a sort of trademark on the company's letterhead. Soon after the Spanish-American War, however, the low wage competition and the improved transportation from Cuba and Hawaii caused a serious setback to the production of Florida pineapples. From Delray to Stuart there were 5,000 acres of rich pineapple land which soon went almost untended. Many people accused Flagler of helping kill pineapple production in Florida because they believed he was allowing Cuban pineapples to be shipped over his road at a cheaper rate than the Florida pineapples. This was partially true, because large pineapple producers in Cuba were using Flagler's steamship line from Havana to Miami and from that point they shipped by the Florida East Coast Railway. He catered to the Cuban producers because of the longer distance which they had to ship. Flagler never felt that Florida would excel in the production of pineapples, competing with Cuba. Furthermore it was simply a business matter with Flagler, but his critics did not see it that way.[20]

The Florida East Coast Railway when finally completed consisted of 765 miles of tracks and represented a building project carried on by one individual. Flagler tied up a large portion of his fortune in the railroad, advancing the funds throughout the period of construction. It was estimated that he spent upwards of $35,000,000 on the building of his railroad system.[21] Of all this capital which was spent on the railroad, $12,000,000 was funded into a first mortgage dated June 1, 1909. The railroad was not bonded until the extension was built, and then only the railroad company was affected. These bonds were sold to brokers in the North and East as the builder needed the money. Because of the immense cost of building the Key West extension, the Florida East Coast

[20] Conversation with E. D. Anthony.
[21] E. S. Luther, "The Transformation of the Florida East Coast," *loc. cit.*, 264.

The Flagler System

Railway represented an extremely large outlay of capital, and though the road did a fair volume of business its earning power remained low throughout Flagler's lifetime.[22] All the other corporations remained free of any debt. Flagler set up the capital structure for his railroad in such a way that his investments were adequately safeguarded against loss which might result from any temporary setback. During Flagler's lifetime, however, the road was still in the stage of promotion, construction, and development. The value of the properties rose from five and one-half million dollars in 1894 to fifteen million dollars in 1914, though the gross revenues rose very slowly and passed the million dollar mark in 1899 for the first time. In 1908, it reached three million dollars, and the year Flagler died, 1913, it went as high as five million dollars. The total net income from 1892 to 1914 was only $9,531.[23] Every indication points to the fact that he received very little compensation during his lifetime as a promoter of the railroad. His many other Florida interests proved more productive.

Perhaps one of Flagler's most profitable pursuits was the acquisition and subsequent sale of large tracts of land throughout the east coast area. The state of Florida, under an act passed by the legislature, gave to railroad builders a certain number of acres of land for each mile of track laid. By May, 1889, the state had given through the Trustees of the Internal Improvement Fund, between eight and ten million acres to the various railroad companies.[24] Thousands of acres of land had been granted to the various small railroads between Jacksonville and Daytona which Flagler bought prior to 1890.[25] After Flagler began his railroad building in 1892, he claimed from the state, under a law passed in 1893, eight thousand acres per mile of railroad. His total claims amounted to 2,040,-

[22] Milton S. Heath, "Analysis of the Florida East Coast Railway," MS., 2.
[23] *Ibid.*, 3.
[24] R. H. Rerick, *Memoirs of Florida*, II, 188.
[25] *Minutes of the Trustees of the Internal Improvement Fund*, V, 265.

007 acres, this being in addition to the alternate sections of land previously granted by the state.[26] It was estimated that a grand total of between 1,500,000 and 2,000,000 acres of land were granted to the company while the road was under construction.[27]

Flagler established a special department of the Florida East Coast Railway Company to handle the sales and management of his land acquisitions. However, on February 6, 1896, this unit was incorporated as the Model Land Company, a separate organization of its own. Other subsidiary land companies were the Fort Dallas Land Company, chartered March 17, 1896; the Perrine Grant Land Company, chartered on May 6, 1899; and the Chuluota Land Company, chartered in 1912. The Model Land Company, and its associated organizations, controlled land from Jacksonville to Key West, and contributed in a large measure to the agricultural and industrial growth of the east coast of Florida. The company and its group of experts gave liberally of time, money, and experience in assisting the development of the soil areas. Expert agriculturalists, horticulturalists, and stockmen were employed to give years of attention to the practical development of the east coast country.[28]

Serving as president of the Model Land Company was James E. Ingraham, who had worked previously as the land commissioner of the railroad system. Ingraham was a native of Wisconsin, and spent his early years there. For a short time he lived in St. Louis, but in 1874 he moved to Florida and was employed by Henry S. Sanford. As a young engineer, his early work in Florida consisted of building the South Florida Railroad from a point near Sanford to Kissimmee. Ingraham became president of this road in 1879 and continued in that capacity until 1892. For a while he was associated with

[26] *Twenty-seventh Biennial Report of the Department of Agriculture of the State of Florida, Land and Field Note Divisions,* July 1, 1942, 21.
[27] Conversation with E. D. Anthony.
[28] *The Tatler,* January 18, 1896.

Henry B. Plant, helping to plan the construction of a road through the Florida Everglades. He was entrusted with the important job of making a survey through the Everglades from Fort Myers to Miami but found that a railroad in that area was impracticable. His report, though not favorable to the building of a railroad, did point out the possibilities of a road on the east coast. Flagler heard of Ingraham's survey and conferred with him about it. As a result, Ingraham was offered a responsible position with the Flagler enterprises.[29] He undertook all of the pioneering work for the construction of the railroad, and was responsible for the establishment of towns along the proposed route and the accumulation of technical data. His greatest contribution to the developments was in his position as land commissioner for the railroad.[30] Ingraham had complete charge of the Florida East Coast land department, and later the Model Land Company. More than anyone else, Ingraham was credited with advertising Flagler and his developments all over the nation through his official position. Ingraham published booklets, pamphlets, and a magazine called the *Homeseeker*, in which he told about the advantages of the east coast and described the lands which were for sale at most of the points. These lands were sold at relatively low prices, ranging from $1.50 to five dollars per acre. The terms were in three to four yearly payments at eight per cent interest. Special prices were given on large tracts of land, also for land paid for in cash, or for groups of people wanting to colonize.[31]

Ingraham, who made his headquarters in St. Augustine, had a splendid corps of assistants working for him all along the east coast. In some cases the railroad agents at various stations would serve as representatives for the Model Land Company in addition to their other duties. Most of them were fairly well

[29] H. G. Cutler, *History of Florida*, III, 370.
[30] *The Tatler*, January 18, 1896.
[31] *Florida East Coast Homeseeker*, 1897, 12.

versed on soils, crops, and production. They usually gave out reliable information to persons in their vicinity. Flagler realized the importance of bringing people to the east coast, because the freight and passenger traffic which they produced would help his railroad. He once said that every new settler along his railroad was worth $300 to him, since an inhabitant along the Florida east coast had to bring in everything he used and send out everything he produced over the Flagler railroad.[32]

Many of the settlements along the Flagler railroad grew out of the efforts of small groups to plant colonies at various points. In 1895, the settlements at Linton and Boynton were established by pioneers who purchased land from the railroad. Two years later Boynton had seventy settlers, thirteen of whom had located there with their families. Over one hundred acres of land were being cultivated. At Linton there were 177 settlers, only forty of whom did not own any land. There were 130 acres planted in vegetables and sixty acres in fruit. Another small colony called Modelo had been established in the same vicinity. It was a Danish colony and newcomers were mostly from Illinois, Michigan, Wisconsin, and Iowa. Holland was another colony in lower Florida which was settled in 1897. It was composed mainly of Swedes, and after the first few arrived, drainage ditches were put in, lands staked out, and sales begun. Other settlements were also under consideration, and the following Florida towns grew up as a result of colonization: Delray, Deerfield, Fort Lauderdale, Dania, Ojus, Perrine, Homestead, Chuluota, Kenansville, and Okeechobee, in addition to the two principal towns of Miami and West Palm Beach.[33]

Flagler made many concessions to people who came to colonize. In order to encourage and stimulate the planting of lemon, grapefruit, and orange groves in Brevard and Dade

[32] *Miami Herald*, November 16, 1941.
[33] H. G. Cutler, *History of Florida*, I, 67.

counties, the railroad magnate made a temporary reduction of 50% in freight rates on nursery stock shipped over his lines to points south of Titusville. The Model Land Company frequently gave a variety of seeds to people in the area. At one time it was believed that tobacco could be raised with some ease in Florida, and in 1895, Sims W. Rowley, of San Mateo, raised 2,800 pounds of leaf per acre with plants donated by Flagler and Ingraham. Rowley, who planted it between rows of young orange trees, argued that tobacco was as easily grown as a crop of tomatoes and predicted that if the orange grower combined the two industries, "he will make this [Florida] one of the wealthiest agricultural sections in the Union." [34] At Hastings, New Smyrna, Rockledge, and Titusville, people were given tobacco seed, and many of them raised the weed with some degree of success, but all of the growers lacked experience. Before long, the production of this crop was abandoned for fruit and vegetables which were more promising to many and which entailed less risk. Flagler himself undertook farming on a large scale in Florida at various points. He established a model farm at Hastings, and the result was that he gave that little town a good lead in the production of potatoes. In the year 1909 the products of Hastings' farms realized nearly a million dollars to their owners chiefly from Irish potatoes. At San Mateo Flagler owned a large orange grove in which he took much pride and interest, and just south of West Palm Beach he had a large plantation on which he raised pineapples. Flagler was not an expert farmer, but he employed men who were; hence his achievements in this endeavor are significant. Through Flagler's and Ingraham's efforts the Model Land Company probably contributed as much to the building of Florida's east coast as the railroad or the hotel corporations.

Flagler's interests in Florida were expanded into many other fields, but none of them ever rivaled the organizations of

[34] *Florida East Coast Homeseeker*, 1895, 6.

the railroads, the hotels, and the land. These other corporations in the Flagler System were: the Miami Electric Light Company, the West Palm Beach Water Company, the Fort Dallas Land Company, the Okeechobee Land Company, the Perrine Land Company, and later the Florida East Coast Car Ferry Company; however, Flagler did not live to see this last corporation in existence. It was put into operation soon after the overseas extension was completed in 1913, operating three ferries each day from Key West to Havana.[35] Flagler also purchased controlling interests in various Florida newspapers during his lifetime, including the *Miami Herald*, the *St. Augustine Record*, and the (Jacksonville) *Florida Times-Union*.

The results of Flagler's efforts in east Florida showed great returns for that state over a period of years. The gross valuation of the seven east coast counties in which Flagler's developments were centered amounted to $12,166,137 in 1884. By 1908 that figure had jumped to $37,603,724. At the same time the total valuation of the entire state had increased from $60,000,000 in 1884 to $159,000,000 in 1908.[36] Florida's east coast had definitely taken the leadership in growth and development. Flagler's hotels accommodated 40,000 guests and his railroad served adequately a wide range of persons and places. Towns sprang up all along the Atlantic coast line in Florida; they were not mere villages and backwoods hamlets but places that were a credit to the state. Flagler's System left a great imprint on the state of Florida.

[35] After the storm in 1935 the overseas extension was badly wrecked, and the Key West base was moved to Port Everglades on the Florida mainland, from which point the same schedule was operated to Havana. With the coming of World War II the Navy Department took over the ferries as mine sweepers for the duration. Conversation with William R. Kenan, Jr.

[36] Florida East Coast Files, St. Augustine.

🏰 FOURTEEN 🏰

A Full Life

FLAGLER began to show increasing effects of old age soon after he began construction on the overseas extension. He participated less and less in any of the affairs pertaining to his program of development, and left most of the work in the hands of his trusted lieutenants. As he grew more feeble, his eyesight became bad, and it was hard for him to recognize people except by their voices. He was sensitive about his condition; so his friends always spoke to him in a way which enabled him to detect who they were. Later he became hard of hearing. Old age, however, never took from him his dignified appearance. He was moderately tall, fairly erect, and handsome. He had an excellently shaped head, short white hair parted in the center, a straight classic nose, and a closely trimmed mustache. His mind remained clear and alert.[1]

His last years were spent in Palm Beach among his faithful friends, some of whom were his employees. His advancing years made him more friendly than he had ever been. His disposition continued pleasant and he was always an optimist. His personal valet, George Conway, an English lad in his early twenties, was his constant companion.[2] Conway read many hours each day to him; he rolled him along the lake front in his wheel chair; he pushed him over the grounds at Whitehall to inspect his flower beds of Marèchal Niel roses;

---

[1] Conversation with Mrs. L. A. Bradstreet.
[2] George Conway now resides in White Sulphur Springs, Montana, where he is proprietor of a ranch. Conversation with George Conway.

and he carried him occasionally into town when he desired to go. The aging millionaire was especially fond of children, and when he was feeling well, no better storyteller lived anywhere. The children in his neighborhood learned to watch for him and Conway each afternoon as they wheeled down the lake front at the same hour. It was a common scene to see several children walking alongside his wheel chair. Usually a little white spitz dog belonging to Mrs. Flagler followed close behind.

Besides Conway, there were many others employed at Whitehall who did everything in their power to make life more pleasant for the old man, including George Cooper, George Holland, Jim Weeks, Lila Cooper, Bernard O'Brien, Sidney Capon, Ida Scheiffer, Carl Fremd, and William Fremd.[3] Some of these persons Flagler brought from New York with him and they remained lifelong friends. Such was the case of William Fremd, a German immigrant, who came to America in 1879. He first lived at Rye, New York, later moving to Mamaroneck, where he worked as keeper of the grounds and gardens. After Flagler transferred his interests to Florida, Fremd moved to St. Augustine and helped to lay out the grounds for the Ponce de Leon Hotel. He was next made superintendent of the grounds at the Royal Poinciana and the Breakers hotels.[4] He loved Flagler perhaps as much as anyone, yet worked most of his life as an humble servant for the millionaire.[5]

Flagler's personal secretary, J. C. Salter, was another employee who helped to bring comfort to the old man during his last years. He lived at Whitehall with Flagler, and shouldered many of the responsibilities which otherwise would have fallen heavily on the capitalist. His pastor, George Morgan Ward, was also faithful. He paid regular visits to Whitehall

[3] Conversation with the Carl Fremds and the George Conways, all of whom were personal servants of the Flaglers.
[4] Fremd died in 1943. Conversation with Anna Fremd Hadley.
[5] J. W. Travers, *History of Palm Beach*, 6.

for long chats with Flagler. Ward, who was ordained a Congregational minister in 1896, was President of Rollins College in Winter Park, Florida, for a time, and did not go into the ministry until Flagler carried him to Palm Beach in 1903 as pastor of the Royal Poinciana Chapel. The chapel of the Royal Poinciana was non-sectarian, having been built for the guests of the Flagler hotels in Palm Beach. Though Flagler and Ward seldom agreed on anything, there was much understanding and friendship between them.[6]

Whitehall in some respects was not much of a home, and it never meant much to Flagler, other than the joy of building it. During his last years when entertainment of all sorts was foregone, the huge structure appeared drab and colorless. It took crowds of people, gaiety, and laughter to make the place warm and friendly. It served its purpose for only a few years after it was built. A friend commented one day on the size and beauty of his home, and Flagler jokingly answered, "I wish I could swap it for a little shack." He continued to live there mainly because Mrs. Flagler liked it. Despite his wife and friends, he gave every appearance of being a lonely old man.[7] His life had been so full of activity it was extremely difficult for him to give over to his feebleness.

Feebleness was the cause of an accident which he suffered on January 15, 1913, as he was descending the long flight of white marble stairs in Whitehall, which led from the second to the first floor. On the third step from the bottom, his leg gave way; and he plunged the remaining distance to the grand hall. He was badly bruised and shaken up, and his right hip was broken. He suffered much pain but seemed to rally after several days. Improvement thereafter was slight, and his friends realized that he would never again leave his bed. Many expected his death in early April. His condition grew much worse at that time, and J. R. Parrott and J. E. Ingraham

[6] Conversation with George Conway.
[7] Conversation with Mrs. L. A. Bradstreet.

of the Florida East Coast Railway were summoned.[8] Warm spring weather came early in 1913, and the invalid man seemed to suffer from the heat; so he was moved to Nautilus cottage which he owned on the beach, about two miles from Whitehall. He rested better there, but his condition grew more and more serious. By May 10, he was taking so little nourishment that his immediate friends and business associates were called again.[9] The only son, Harry Flagler, who had not seen his father since his marriage to Mary Lily Kenan in 1901, was informed of Flagler's critical illness. The son was invited to the Palm Beach mansion for the first time. The younger Flagler came promptly to his father's bedside, but the dying man had lapsed into a state of unconsciousness and did not recognize his son. George M. Ward; Dr. Owen Kenan, his physician; George Conway and Jim Weeks, personal servants; and Mrs. Flagler were the only persons who saw Flagler frequently after he became critically ill. Henry M. Flagler died at ten o'clock on the morning of May 20, 1913, at the age of eighty-three. The end came peacefully, as though he were sinking into slumber.[10] His death was attributed to old age and sheer exhaustion.

It was his wish that he be buried in St. Augustine where his Florida developments had begun. He always loved that city and had spent many happy hours there. The body was carried from Palm Beach to St. Augustine, on May 23, where it lay in state at the Ponce de Leon Hotel for several hours before the funeral services. At three o'clock in the afternoon the funeral procession made its way from the Ponce de Leon Hotel to the Memorial Presbyterian Church, where the funeral rites were conducted. The church overflowed with friends and admirers. Among the active pallbearers were his close personal friends, including J. R. Parrott, J. E. Ingraham, J. A. McGuire, J. A. McDonald, J. C. Salter, T. V. Pomar,

[8] *New York Times*, April 2, 1913.
[9] *Savannah Morning News*, May 10, 1913.
[10] *St. Augustine Record*, May 30, 1913.

Leland Sterry, and A. J. Krome. Honorary pallbearers numbered fifty or sixty. A large group of people from Jacksonville attended the funeral, including the members of the Board of Trade. The Reverend J. N. MacGonigle, former pastor of Memorial Presbyterian Church, and close friend of Flagler, read the selections from the Scripture of which his deceased friend was especially fond. His tribute to Flagler was brief but sincere. Others who assisted MacGonigle were Dr. George M. Ward, Flagler's friend from Palm Beach, and the Reverend Alfred S. Badger, pastor of the Memorial Presbyterian Church. The services were simple, in keeping with Flagler's wishes.

The committal service, which followed the funeral, was private; only the members of the family and immediate friends remained for it. Flagler's body was placed in the mausoleum adjoining the church, very near the vault containing his daughter, Jenny Louise, and her infant daughter.[11] This service was conducted by Dr. Ward and the Reverend Peyton Hoge, of Louisville, Kentucky. Organ music and the reading of a poem completed the last rites for Henry M. Flagler.[12]

No period of mourning was declared in Florida for its benefactor. Mrs. Flagler requested that it not be done, despite the fact that several towns expressed a wish for it. She thought that Flagler himself would not have approved of it.[13] Thousands of telegrams of sympathy, however, were sent to his widow; and hundreds of floral wreaths were placed around his vault in the mausoleum, attesting the love and admiration people held for him throughout the nation.

Four days after his burial, on May 27, 1913, Flagler's will was made public for the first time. It brought to light an estate worth nearly $100,000,000. The will spoke in endearing terms of his wife, and the bulk of his fortune was left for her under

[11] The body of his first wife, Mary Harkness Flagler, has since been placed in the mausoleum.

[12] *St. Augustine Record,* May 23, 1913.

[13] *Atlanta Journal,* May 23, 1913.

a trusteeship. J. R. Parrott of Jacksonville, W. H. Beardsley of New York, and William R. Kenan, Jr. of Lockport, New York, were named as trustees.[14] The trusteeship was to continue for five years from Flagler's death. At the end of that time if the condition of the Florida East Coast Railway and the hotel companies called for financial assistance, then the trusteeship would continue. It was stipulated, however, that the trusteeships should terminate after two five-year periods.[15] Under the trusteeship, Mrs. Flagler was given $100,000 a year and the residence Whitehall at Palm Beach and Flagler's New York City realty. After the trust expired and all other bequests were made, she was to inherit the balance of the vast estate. Harry Flagler, the only son, received 5,000 shares of stock of the Standard Oil Company; and the children of Harry Flagler, 8,000 shares each. Horace Flagler, a cousin, was left $2,000 a year until the trusteeship ended. Memorial Presbyterian Church, where Flagler was buried, received $3,000 during the trust and also $75,000 as an endowment.[16] The following bequests were to be made at the expiration of the trust: J. R. Parrott, $100,000; Hamilton College, $100,000; W. H. Beardsley, $50,000; J. E. Ingraham, $20,000; J. A. McGuire, the contractor who built the Ponce de Leon Hotel, $10,000; J. C. Salter, his private secretary, $10,000; Robert Murray, manager of the Ponce de Leon Hotel, $10,000; J. G. Greaves, manager of the Royal Palm, $10,000; Leland Sterry, $10,000; J. P. Beckwith, vice-president of the Florida East Coast Railway and Mrs. Ella Green of Palm Beach, $5,000 each.[17] The will did not list the properties which included the

[14] "Last Will and Testament of Henry M. Flagler," Florida Historical Society Collections.
[15] The trusteeship ended after Mrs. Flagler's death.
[16] The will stated that Stetson University was to receive $60,000 and Florida Agricultural College (later the University of Florida) was to receive $20,000 at his death, unless it was paid prior to that time. The University of Florida got her $20,000 in 1903, and Stetson received her grant several years later.
[17] *New York Times,* May 28, 1913.

A Full Life

entire East Coast Railway system, the hotels Ponce de Leon, Alcazar, Cordova, Continental, Royal Palm, and other stock in the Peninsula and Occidental Steamship Company, Standard Oil, and other corporations, vast tracts of valuable Florida lands, many small manufacturing plants, and other enterprises.[18]

Flagler, like all men with money, power, and ability was a controversial figure. His critics at the time of his death might be classified into several groups. People opposed to big corporations naturally thought of him as one of the leaders of the Standard Oil Company. But his enemies did not stop there because many Floridians were opposed to his efforts in that state. He was made aware of that fact on every turn. Every move he made was closely watched by the public and certain antagonistic groups were soon formed. There was one group who disliked him and distrusted him because of his divorce from Alice Flagler and his subsequent marriage to Mary Lily Kenan. He never quite lived it down, though people who understood sympathized with him in his predicament. Persons who knew Flagler only through reputation remembered the divorce and ignored or discounted everything else he did. Another group which opposed Flagler was made up of those who, for no good reason at all, kept fresh the memory of the Civil War and Reconstruction in Florida. To them Flagler was a carpetbagger from the North, and nothing more. They believed his only purpose in coming to Florida was to choke from them what profits he could.[19] They belittled him whenever possible; they made his work in the state extremely diffi-

[18] Mary Lily Flagler did not live long to enjoy the vast fortune which was left her. She died suddenly on July 27, 1917, after having married, during the preceding December, Robert Worth Bingham, Louisville, Kentucky, publisher, an acquaintance of long standing. Only six weeks before her death, she added a codicil to her will leaving $5,000,000 to her husband. The bulk of her fortune, however, went back into a trust fund from which payments were made to the various enterprises. Bingham contributed a great deal of money to the Democratic campaign in 1918, and was later sent to England as ambassador. Conversation with William R. Kenan, Jr.

[19] Unidentified clipping, June 23, 1893, Marcotte Scrapbook.

251

cult at times by not extending ordinary courtesies he was due.
It is believed that in several cases citizens refused to sell him
land on which to construct certain buildings because they
thought his motive was not for their best interest.[20]

Still another group opposed to Flagler were those who were
jealous of his money. These citizens made Flagler the target
of their condemnation and persistently persecuted him.[21] They
were would-be developers themselves, but never had the
ability, ingenuity, aggressiveness, and, most of all, the money
to put into operation any large program of improvement.
Because of their clamor the state was placed in an ungenerous
position which, in the end, wrought much damage. As
Flagler's program of development was pushed toward completion, there was a subsidence of this malicious agitation, and
he was permitted to work out his plans in comparative peace.
Concerning these critics, Flagler said to his friend T. T.
Reese, President of the Farmers Bank and Trust Company,
Palm Beach,

> I have lived too long and have been a target too often to
> allow myself to be disturbed by the jealousy of others who
> have been less fortunate. I don't know of anyone who has
> been successful, but that he has been compelled to pay some
> price for success. Some get it at the loss of their health; oth-
> ers forego the pleasures of home and spend their years in the
> forests or mines; some acquire success at the loss of their
> reputation; others at loss of character, and so it goes; many
> prices paid, but there is one universal price that I have never
> known any successful man to escape, and that is the jealousy
> of many of the community in which he moves.[22]

Though the hostility to Flagler centered in Palm Beach, men
like Reese upheld him and encouraged him to go forward with
his plans.

[20] Conversation with the late Sims W. Rowley.
[21] *St. Augustine Record*, May 30, 1913.
[22] Henry M. Flagler to T. T. Reese, April 19, 1906, Kenan Collection.

Most of Flagler's employees liked him, but those who were not ambitious were never given much consideration. They saw him at his worst, for he had no patience with one who loafed or wasted his time. On one occasion while the Ponce de Leon was under construction, Flagler was inspecting the work in the lower part of the structure. In one remote portion of the building he came upon four or five employees who were idle, with seemingly nothing to do. "Well," said Flagler, "can't you men find something to do?" Not recognizing his employer, and certainly not expecting to find him supervising the details of construction, one of them answered, "Yes, we've got plenty to do, but old man Flagler will never miss the money he is paying us just to do a little loafing." Indignant but collected, Flagler replied, "Go straight to the office; get the portion of 'old man Flagler's money' that is due you and don't ever come back to me for employment." Embarrassed and subdued the men went hastily for their last pay envelope.[23] Other employees who were not punctual and efficient found very little about Flagler which they liked.

In the South generally Flagler was well received except in extreme anti-corporation circles. At one time, Governor Hogg of Texas, desiring to keep himself before the public, became active in a crusade to uphold the Sherman Anti-Trust law. Since Flagler had received much acclaim in Florida, Hogg centered his Standard Oil attack upon the railroad builder. Expressing a desire to arrest every official of the Standard Oil Company, the Texas Governor sent requisition papers to Governor Mitchell of Florida for the arrest of Flagler on the grounds of violation of the anti-trust law. Hogg had reason to dislike railroad builders too, for the railroads in Texas had fought him in a recent election.[24]

Governor Mitchell honored the request, since it was sent through regular channels, and it appeared for a time as if Hogg

[23] Conversation with T. V. Pomar.
[24] *Florida Times-Union,* December 26, 1894.

might take Flagler to Texas for trial. The Florida Governor was besieged by Flagler's friends to revoke his decision. Letters and telegrams flooded the Governor's office, each asking for mercy in Flagler's behalf. But Mitchell was a stubborn man, and held out for several days. He declared that he knew no difference in a pauper and a millionaire where the law was concerned. However, he quickly changed his decision when he was reminded that his political life in Florida would last considerably longer if he were not so hard on Flagler. It was too much public pressure for the Governor. He explained his action to the press by declaring that Governor Hogg could not establish his claim to Flagler as a fugitive from Texas.[25]

From time to time, Flagler's foes tried to drag him into politics, but he refused to become involved, either in local or national affairs. Nationally, he was a Republican, but he never manifested much zeal or enthusiasm over any of the big issues. Like all good citizens, he followed with considerable interest each national campaign, but when he was in Florida he said little about it because he knew how solidly Democratic the South had been since the Civil War. In one or two campaigns he manifested a little more interest than usual. For instance, in the campaign of 1884 he was particularly anxious for the Republicans to win because their candidate, James G. Blaine, represented the capitalist element of the nation. Flagler supported Blaine with a substantial contribution, and was disappointed when Grover Cleveland was elected.[26] Another election in which Flagler became concerned was the McKinley-Bryan campaign in 1896. The Republicans, more than ever before, espoused the cause of men like Flagler. A victory for McKinley meant a victory for the moneyed class. Mark Hanna, McKinley's campaign manager, called on Flagler to exert his influence in Florida on the party's behalf, but there was almost nothing a Republican

[25] *Ibid.*, January 4, 1895.
[26] Conversation with Harry Harkness Flagler.

could do in St. Augustine for his party. Flagler knew that Florida would vote a Democratic ticket, but he expressed faith in an overwhelming victory for McKinley in the East.[27]

Flagler was acquainted with many of the Republican leaders, but he probably knew Theòdore Roosevelt better than any of the others. He never admired Teddy to any great extent. Flagler was a guest of Roosevelt at a White House dinner on one occasion, but the affair was purely social.[28] The railroad builder never received patronage of any sort from Roosevelt, and very little from any of his other Republican connections. To him, politics was for the politician and not for the businessman; however, in the summer of 1901 he was boomed by several newspapers in Florida for a post in the United States Senate. At this particular time, Flagler was in the limelight anyway. The state legislature had just passed the much discussed Flagler divorce law under which he secured freedom from his mentally ill wife. He was accused of having encouraged the legislative body by making liberal gifts of money. Despite his enemies, persistent rumors connected him with the senatorial job. But Flagler was a Republican, and many doubted if he would ever be appointed by a Democratic legislature.[29] The *Ocala Banner* argued that it would not be a breach in party policy for him to be selected. The editor reminded his readers that "under the very flexible definition given to democracy it is a very easy matter for Mr. Flagler to be styled a Democrat, though, really if at heart he be not one." [30] The *Pensacola Journal* voiced an opinion that Flagler would be a good choice for the Senate, "as the senate has many rich men in it, and could at this time be called a convocation of millionaires." [31]

[27] Henry M. Flagler to Andrew Anderson, August 18, 1896, Dimick Collection.
[28] Henry M. Flagler Diary, December 12, 1904.
[29] At the time United States senators were elected by the various state legislatures.
[30] *Ocala Banner*, June 7, 1901.
[31] *Pensacola Journal*, June 1, 1901.

Despite the backing Flagler got for the high post, he refused to give any thought to a political career. He had never entertained political ambitions, and when he became a citizen of Florida he specifically said so. He reminded the people that "as far as political ambitions are concerned, I do not now, nor have I ever entertained them. There is no office in the gift of the American people that I could be induced to accept, and I hope my Florida friends will not fall into error of thinking otherwise." [32] He perhaps could have held any of the better political jobs in Florida had he desired to do so. One of his contemporaries, William Dudley Chipley, builder of the Pensacola and Atlantic Railroad in western Florida, became prominent in the public life of the state and threw his influence behind the forces opposing Wilkinson Call, United States Senator from Florida. Chipley fought Call, a progressive Democrat, to a finish because the latter had given much opposition to the railroads. Chipley came out of the fray with many political scars and a defeat in the senatorial race of 1897.[33] It is safe to say Flagler was the wiser of the two.

Though Flagler refused to become involved in state politics, there was nevertheless a faction which organized within the state to oppose him. It was short-lived, however, since it had only the one objective. It was appropriately called the anti-corporation party and was headed by Guy Metcalf, editor of the West Palm Beach *Tropical Sun*. The faction spread throughout east Florida, but was strongest in the Palm Beach area. Metcalf and Flagler had not always been enemies; in fact, at one time the two men had been very friendly. The break came when Metcalf defaulted in the payment of a debt amounting to $3750, which Flagler felt he was fully able to pay. The railroad builder hated a debt. In the first place he hated to lend money to his friends because he realized the

[32] *Miami Metropolis*, June 16, 1899.
[33] Edward C. Williamson, MS., Wilkinson Call, A Pioneer in Progressive Democracy, 191.

strained feelings which might result. After the break with Metcalf over the debt, Flagler made it a rule never to lend money to a friend, though often he made money gifts to people close to him. Several years later, the people of West Palm Beach elected Judge William Metcalf, father of Guy Metcalf, to the mayorship of the city. Flagler was much opposed to their selection and ceased to take any interest in public affairs of West Palm Beach. Flagler had always expressed a love for West Palm Beach, but after the Metcalf episode, he requested that he not be buried there.[34]

No one, not even his enemies, doubted his modesty and his sincerity. He was known generally for kindness and his slow deliberate manner. He never had a flair for words but every statement he made was sound. He neither swore nor used indecent language. "Thunder" was his strongest word. When he became provoked with anyone, he usually stamped his cane on the floor, frowned, and exclaimed, "Now wouldn't you think a man would have more sense than that!" [35] He was careful to control his feelings concerning his work, accepting the bitter with the sweet. His business affairs were taken in stride; however, his domestic affairs preyed on his mind and kept him upset for a long while. On one occasion in Palm Beach an associate broke the news to him that the Standard Oil Company had just been fined over twenty million dollars by the federal court. Flagler felt strongly about the matter because he was a part of that organization although he was inactive. For a moment he looked as if he were going to say something but merely nodded and said casually. "Do you happen to have those Whitehall plumbing bills handy?" [36] Many stories were told concerning his kindness. It was not uncommon for him to give a faithful helper a home, a sum of money, or a farm. There was one case of an employee who had done

[34] Conversation with E. D. Anthony.
[35] Edwin Lefèvre, "Flagler in Florida," *Everybody's Magazine* (February, 1910), 178.
[36] *Ibid.*, 179.

his best to hamper the building operation at Palm Beach. Later, the disgruntled worker was incapacitated by a serious accident, and during his period of forced inactivity his wife and children suffered from insufficient care. When approached about the need of the man's family, Flagler paid all the expenses until the wage earner was able to take his place again on the road.

As to his views on intoxicating liquors, Flagler reflected his strict Presbyterian training. He made it a condition in his land contracts and deeds at Miami that no intoxicating liquors should ever be manufactured or sold on the premises, under penalty of forfeiture. The liquor dealers of the state combined and bought a lot, erected a store and commenced selling liquor. They proposed to test the legality of the restriction and engaged Major Alexander Abrams to represent them. Determined not to be outdone, Flagler obtained an injunction and closed the store.[37] As long as he lived he did his best to discourage the use of liquor by his friends and employees.

Outwardly, he was faithful to his church and to all for which it stood. His enemies contended that he had no deep religious convictions, but after a careful study of his private life, one finds that he had definite religious beliefs.[38] He was reared in a Puritan home by Presbyterian parents, and he never forgot his early training. He was active in religious circles wherever he lived. In New York, St. Augustine, or Palm Beach he took a keen interest in the church. He was never narrow in his denominational beliefs. During his lifetime he subsidized several churches, either by endowment, building new plants, or donating lots on which to build new structures.[39]

Despite the enemies he made in getting ahead, Henry M. Flagler was a man who was genuinely admired by a majority

[37] *Bartow Courier-Informant*, December 16, 1896.
[38] Conversation with E. D. Anthony.
[39] Conversation with Harry Harkness Flagler.

of the people. Measured by the importance to humanity of his achievements, he may justly be regarded as an important historical figure. The evil to which his critics like to point was so far outweighed by his virtues that it would be unfair to designate him as other than a good man. If he took advantage of the conditions which made it possible for him to accumulate great wealth, it should be remembered that he employed that wealth to far greater advantage to his fellow men than have some of our much-vaunted philanthropists. When men asked for bread he did not give them a promise, but his great enterprises opened the way for thousands to secure support while maintaining their self-respect.

His influence upon the development of Florida will never be fully recognized except by the thoughtful few. It is not only in the immediate section where his activities took shape that this influence was operative. That section, indeed, owes to him its transformation from a barren, desolate waste to a fair and fruitful country; but the effect of the enterprises inaugurated there was to turn the eyes of the nation upon a state which before had been but slightly regarded, and the impetus to immigration thus given has affected every portion of Florida, and will be felt in cumulative effect perpetually.

Henry M. Flagler lived a long life, a full life, and a successful life. He had very little else for which to wish. He drank the sweetest draught from the cup of undertaking—the joy of accomplishment. It was given to him to finish the great task of remaking Florida which had so long been his dream, to look upon his completed work and to pronounce it abundant and successful.

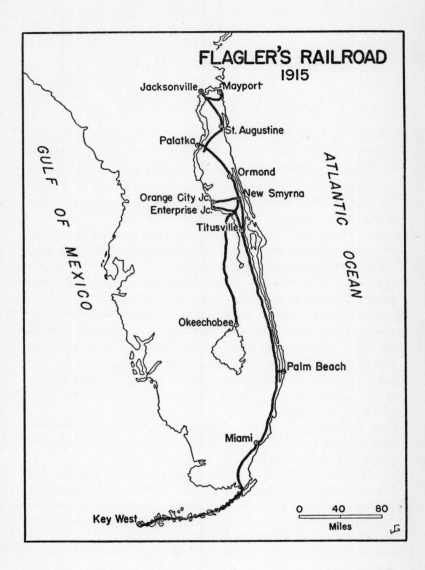

FLAGLER'S RAILROAD
1915

Jacksonville   Mayport

St. Augustine

Palatka

Ormond

Orange City Jc.   New Smyrna
Enterprise Jc.

Titusville

GULF

OF

MEXICO

ATLANTIC

OCEAN

Okeechobee

Palm Beach

Miami

Key West

0   40   80
Miles

BIBLIOGRAPHY

MANUSCRIPT COLLECTIONS

Anderson Collection. Contains nearly a hundred letters, mostly personal; Henry M. Flagler to Andrew Anderson; J. C. Salter to Andrew Anderson; George G. Shelton to Andrew Anderson. Sworn statement about facts concerning Henry M. Flagler by Andrew Anderson in 1923. Collection owned by Mrs. Clarissa Anderson Dimick.

Camden Collection. Contains several dozen letters from J. N. Camden to Henry M. Flagler; in library of West Virginia University, Morgantown, West Virginia.

Flagler Collection. Consists chiefly of family records and newspaper clippings; in possession of Harry H. Flagler.

Florida East Coast Railway Collection, Jacksonville, Florida. Includes: Corporate History, Florida East Coast Railway; Charter of the Florida East Coast; and newspaper clippings, pamphlets, etc.

Florida Historical Society Library Collection, St. Augustine. Contains: Letters, clippings, manuscripts, and last will and testament of Henry M. Flagler.

Kenan Collection. Includes: Newspapers, magazines, pictures, two ledgers (one on Yacht *Alicia* and one on Mamaroneck property), owned by William R. Kenan, Jr.

Martin Collection. Private correspondence of the author from the following persons: Philip C. Jessup, S. Price Gilbert, Harry Harkness Flagler, James P. Martin, Mrs. Katherine S. Lawson, William R. Kenan, Jr., James D. Ingraham, Paul H. Giddens, and Mrs. Clarissa Anderson Dimick.

Smith Collection, Duke University, Durham, North Carolina. Several letters written by Flagler to E. C. Smith in Raleigh, North Carolina.

St. Augustine Historical Society Library Collection. Contains diaries kept by Henry M. Flagler for the years 1880, 1885, and 1904. Also contains newspaper scrapbook kept by Captain Marcotte, *Florida Times-Union* correspondent, 1892–1894.

DOCUMENTS

Acts and Resolutions Adopted by the Legislature of Florida at its Fourth Regular Session Under the Constitution of A. D. 1885. Tallahassee: Privately Printed, 1893.

Acts and Resolutions Adopted by the Legislature of Florida at its Eighth Regular Session, April 2 to May 31, 1901, Under the Constitution of A. D. 1885. Tallahassee, Florida: Privately Printed, 1901.

Divorce Proceedings of the Henry M. Flagler Complainant *vs.* Ida A. Flagler Defendant, Divorce Case. In the Circuit Court, 7th Judicial Circuit of Florida, in and for Dade County. At Titusville, Florida, August 12, 1901 (unpublished).

House Journal, Florida, 1901.

Minutes of the Board of Trustees Internal Improvement Fund of the State of Florida. 24 vols. Tallahassee: Privately Printed, 1904. IV, V, VI.

Poor's Manual, Railroads of the United States. New York: Privately Printed, Vol. 22, 1889; Vol. 23, 1890; Vol. 25, 1892; Vol. 28, 1895; Vol. 33, 1900; Vol. 46, 1913.

Senate Journal, Florida, 1901.

The Reports of Committees of the House of Representatives for the First Session of the Fiftieth Congress. 1887–1888. 11 volumes. Washington: Government Printing Office, 1888. IX.

Twenty-seventh Biennial Report of the Department of Agriculture of the State of Florida. Land and Field Note Division. Tallahassee: July 1, 1942.

NEWSPAPERS

The *Atlanta Journal.* Scattered copies of 1901, 1913, and 1914.
The *Courier-Informant* (Bartow). Files 1893 through 1912.
Bellevue Gazette, May 22, 1913.
The *Cleveland Herald.* Scattered copies of 1872 and 1873.

Bibliography

Cleveland Leader. Complete files 1866 through 1913.

Cleveland Plain Dealer. Broken files of 1913.

Daily (Key West) *Florida Citizen,* September 11, 1895.

The *Everglades News* (Canal Point, Florida), June 1, 1945.

Florida Times-Union (Jacksonville). Complete files of 1885 through 1896. Also broken files of 1906, 1910, 1912, and 1941.

Fostoria (Ohio) *Daily News.* Scattered copies of 1913 and 1941.

Lake Worth News. Broken files of 1896, 1897, 1898, 1900, 1901, 1902, and 1903.

Marine Journal, December 26, 1914.

Miami Daily News. Scattered copies of 1938 and 1945.

Miami Herald. Scattered copies of 1911, 1912, 1944, and 1945.

The *Miami Metropolis.* Complete files from 1896 through 1906, 1913.

New York Herald-Tribune. Broken files of 1872, 1884, 1885, 1894, 1901, 1902, 1906, 1913, and 1930.

New York Times. Scattered copies of 1883, 1913, 1924, and 1930.

The *Observer* (Daytona Beach), January 4, 1936.

Ocala Banner, 1901, 1913.

Oil City Daily Derrick. Complete files of 1877 through 1879.

Orlando Sentinel-Star, January 2, 1938.

Palatka Times-Herald. Broken files of 1901, 1902, and 1904.

Palm Beach Daily News. This was a seasonal newspaper. Files of 1898–1910. Also the Historical Edition for 1936 and a souvenir number for 1903.

Palm Beach Post-Times, November 17, 1940.

Pensacola Journal, 1901, 1902.

Pittsburgh Daily Post, 1879.

San Mateo Item, June 12, 1909.

Savannah (Georgia) *Morning News.* Scattered copies of 1912 and 1913.

St. Augustine Evening Record. Scattered copies of 1899, 1900, and 1913. The *Daily Herald* became the *Evening Record* on September 1, 1899. Later became the *Record.*

St. Augustine Record, March 17, 1940.

St. Augustine Weekly News. Scattered copies of 1889 and 1890.

The *Tatler of Society in Florida* (St. Augustine), January 9, 1892, through March 30, 1901. This publication, edited by

Anna M. Marcotte, was a society sheet published twelve weeks during each winter season.

Tropical Sun, (West Palm Beach). Scattered copies of 1896, March 5, 1937.

Weekly Floridian (Tallahassee). Broken files of 1888, 1891, 1892, and 1893.

PAMPHLETS AND BOOKLETS

A Brief History of the Florida East Coast Railway and Associated Enterprises. St. Augustine: The Record Company, 1936.

Announcement of Key West Extension, opened January 22, 1912. Privately printed pamphlet, 1912.

Chapin, George M., *Official Program, Key West Extension of the Florida East Coast Railway.* St. Augustine: The Record Company, 1912.

Cleveland City Directory (Privately printed), 1880, 1881.

Florida East Coast Homeseeker. St. Augustine: January, 1897.

Florida Press Association Bulletin. Miami: March 22, 1901.

In Memoriam Henry Morrison Flagler. The Matthews-Northup Works: New York, 1914.

Official Program, Centennial of Fostoria. (Privately printed), 1941.

Reynolds, Charles B., *Architecture of the Hotel Ponce de Leon.* (Privately printed), no date given.

Western Reserve Historical Society Publication. Cleveland, Ohio. October, 1920. (No. 102).

UNPUBLISHED WORKS

Anonymous, "Life of Stephen V. Harkness" (A short manuscript in Western Reserve Historical Society Library, Cleveland, Ohio).

Bristol, L. M., "The Buckman Act: Before and After" (Unpublished manuscript: University of Florida), 1946.

Frohman, L. C., "From the Florida East Coast Files." (Unpublished manuscript: St. Augustine), 1928.

Heath, Milton S., "Analysis of the Florida East Coast Railway." (Unpublished manuscript: privately owned), 1933.

Bibliography

McGuire, Robert E., "My Family" (Unpublished manuscript: Florida Historical Society Library), 1940.

Martin, S. Walter, "The Second Discovery of Florida." (Unpublished thesis, University of Georgia), 1935.

Williamson, Edward C., "Wilkinson Call: A Pioneer in Progressive Democracy." Gainesville, Florida (Unpublished thesis: University of Florida), 1946.

PERIODICALS

Destler, Chester McArthur, "The Standard Oil, Child of the Erie Ring, 1868–1872. Six contracts and a Letter," in *Mississippi Valley Historical Review*. XXXIII, No. 1 (June, 1946), 89–114.

Firelands Pioneer, Firelands Historical Society, Norwalk: American Publishing Co., Vol. XIII, June, 1916; XXII, June, 1921; Vol. XX, Jan., 1920.

"Florida East Coast," *Locomotive Engineers Journal*, Vol. 69 (October, 1935), 726, 727.

"He Made Florida," *Literary Digest*, XLVI (May 31, 1913), 1240–1242.

Ingraham, J. E., "The Story of the East Coast," *Picturesque Florida*, I (January, 1910), 3–7.

Kellogg, Frank B., "Results of the Standard Oil Decision," *Review of Reviews*, XLV (June, 1912), 728–730.

Kennedy, James H., "Stephen Vanderburg Harkness," *Magazine of Western History*, IX (November, 1888), 288–292.

"Key West and Cuba," *Bulletin of the Pan American Union*, XXXIV (February, 1912), 212–222.

King, Edward, "The Great South," *Scribner's Monthly*, IX (November, 1874), 1–31.

Latham, Thomas W., "Revelations of an Old Account Book," *Firelands Pioneer*, XXII (January, 1921), 133–138.

Lefèvre, Edwin, "Flagler and Florida," *Everybody's Magazine*, XXII (February, 1910), 168–186.

Luther, E. S., "The Transformation of the Florida East Coast," *Banker's Magazine* (February, 1909), 259–264.

Moffett, Samuel E., "Henry Morrison Flagler," *The Cosmopolitan*, XXXIII (August, 1902), 416–419.

Montague, Gilbert H., "The Rise and Supremacy of the Standard

Oil Company," *The Quarterly Journal of Economics,* XVI (February, 1902), 265–292.

——, "The Later History of the Standard Oil Company," *The Quarterly Journal of Economics,* XVII (February, 1903), 291–325.

Moody, John and Turner, George K., "The Masters of Capital in America," *McClure's Magazine,* XXXVI (March, 1911), 564–577.

Nichols, George Ward, "Six Weeks in Florida," in *Harper's Magazine,* XLI (October, 1870), 655–667.

"No One-man Ownership in Standard Oil," *The Literary Digest,* LXXVI (January 13, 1923), 73.

Rockefeller, John D., "Some Random Reminiscences of Men and Events," *The World's Work,* XVII (November, 1908), 10878–10894. (March, 1909), 11340–11355.

Rockwell, J. M., "Opening of the Over Sea Railway to Key West," *Collier's,* XLVIII (January 20, 1912), 16, 17.

"Sketch of Henry M. Flagler," *The Outlook,* (May 31, 1913), 231–232.

Tarbell, Ida M., "The Rise of the Standard Oil Company," *McClure's Magazine,* XX, (December, 1902), 115–128.

——, "The Oil War of 1872," *loc. cit.,* (January, 1903), 248–260.

——, "An Unholy Alliance," *loc. cit.,* (February, 1903), 390–403.

——, "The Price of Trust Building," *loc. cit.,* (March, 1903), 493–508.

——, "Defeat of the Pennsylvania," *loc. cit.,* (April, 1903), 606–621.

"The Standard Oil Decision," *The Nation,* Vol. 89 (November 25, 1909), 502–503.

"The Standard Oil Melons," *The Literary Digest,* LXXV (October 28, 1922), 5–6.

"Whitehall, Mr. Flagler's Residence at Palm Beach," *International Studio,* XL (March, 1919), 11–12.

BOOKS

Abbey, Kathryn Trimmer, *Florida, Land of Change.* Chapel Hill: The University of North Carolina Press, 1941.

Bibliography

Aldrick, Lewis Cass, *History of Erie County*. Syracuse, New York: D. Mason and Company, 1889.

Allen, William H., *Rockefeller, Giant, Dwarf, Symbol*. New York: Institute for Public Service, 1930.

Asbury, Herbert, *The Golden Flood*, New York: Alfred A. Knopf, 1942.

Blackman, E. V., *Miami and Dade County, Florida*. Washington: Victor Rainbolt Publisher, 1921.

Browne, Jefferson B., *Key West, the Old and the New*. St. Augustine: The Record Company, 1912.

Burns, Arthur Robert, *Trusts and Economic Control*. New York: McGraw-Hill Company, 1936.

Burton, Theodore E., *John Sherman*. New York: Houghton, Mifflin and Company, 1906.

Butterfield, C. W., *History of Seneca County*. Sandusky: D. Campbell and Sons, 1848.

Cabell, Branch, and Hanna, A. J., *The St. Johns, A Parade of Diversities*. New York: Farrar and Rinehart, Incorporated, 1943.

Cutler, Harry Gardiner, *History of Florida, Past and Present*. 3 vols. Chicago: Lewis Publishing Company, 1923.

Dau, Frederick W., *Florida, Old and New*. New York: G. P. Putnam's Sons, 1934.

Davis, Thomas Frederick, *History of Jacksonville, Florida and Vicinity, 1513 to 1924*. Jacksonville: Florida Historical Society, 1925.

Dodd, Dorothy, ed., *Florida Becomes a State*. Tallahassee: Florida Centennial Commission, 1945.

Faris, W. W., *First Presbyterian Church, Miami: Some Memorials of Early Days*, 1918.

Faulkner, Harold Underwood, *American Economic History*, Fifth Edition. New York: Harper and Brothers, 1943.

Flynn, John T., *God's Gold, The Story of Rockefeller and His Times*. New York: Harcourt, Brace and Company, 1932.

Giddens, Paul H., *The Birth of the Oil Industry*. New York: The Macmillan Company, 1938.

Gilbert, S. Price, *A Georgia Lawyer, His Observations and Public Service*. Athens: University of Georgia Press, 1946.

Hacker, Louis M., and Kendrick, Benjamin B., *The United States*

Since 1865. Third Edition. New York: F. S. Crofts and Co., 1939.

Hargis, Harry, *Miami in Your Pocket*. Miami: Pan American Printing Corporation, 1945.

Jessup, Philip C., *Elihu Root*. 2 vols. New York: Dodd, Mead, and Company, 1938.

Johnson, Allen, and Malone, Dumas, editors, *Dictionary of American Biography*. I, New York: Charles Scribner's Sons, 1928–1937. 20 vols.

Josephson, Matthew, *The Robber Barons, The Great American Capitalists, 1861–1901*. New York: Harcourt, Brace and Company, 1934.

Kenan, William R., Jr., *Incidents by the Way, Lifetime Recollections and Reflections*. Lockport, New York: Privately Printed, 1946.

Lawson, Thomas W., *Frenzied Finance*, Vol. I. New York: Ridgeway-Thayer Company, 1906.

Leonard, John W., ed., *Men of America*. A Biographical Dictionary of Contemporaries. New York: Lewis R. Hamersly and Company, 1908.

Lloyd, Henry Demarest, *Wealth Against Commonwealth*. New York: Harper and Brothers Publishers, 1894.

Martin, Frederick T., *The Passing of the Idle Rich*. Doubleday, Page and Company, 1912.

Martin, Sidney Walter, *Florida During the Territorial Days*. Athens: The University of Georgia Press, 1944.

Mills, James Cooke, *History of Saginaw County, Michigan*, Vol. I. Saginaw: Seemann and Peters, 1918.

Montague, Gilbert Holland, *The Rise and Progress of the Standard Oil Company*. New York and London: Harper and Brothers, 1903.

Moody, John, *Truth About the Trusts*. New York: Moody Publishing Company, 1904.

Nash, Charles Edgar, *The Magic of Miami Beach*. Philadelphia: David McKay Company, 1938.

Nevins, Allan, *The Emergence of Modern America*. New York: The Macmillan Company, 1927.

Nevins, Allan, *John D. Rockefeller; the Heroic Age of American Enterprise*. 2 vols. New York: Charles Scribner's Sons, 1940.

Bibliography

Patrick, Rembert W., *Florida Under Five Flags*. Gainesville: University of Florida Press, 1945.

Pieke, H. L., *History of Erie County, Ohio*, 2 vols. Cleveland: Penton Press Company, 1925.

Post, Charles Asa, *Doans Corners and the City Four Miles West. With a Glance at Cuyohoga County and the Western Reserve*. Cleveland: Caxton Company, 1930.

Randall and Ryans, *History of Ohio*, 4 vols. New York: Century History Company, 1912.

Rerick, Rowland H., *Memoirs of Florida*, 2 vols. Atlanta, Georgia: Southern Historical Association, 1902.

Ryan, Daniel J., *History of Ohio*, 4 vols. New York: Century History Company, 1912.

Sewell, John, *Memoirs and History of Miami, Florida*. Miami: The Franklin Press, 1933.

Tarbell, Ida M., *The History of the Standard Oil Company*, 2 vols. New York: McClure, Phillips and Company, 1904.

Travers, J. Wadsworth, *History of Palm Beach*. Palm Beach: Privately Printed, 1927.

Tuttle, Charles Richard, *General History of the State of Michigan*. Detroit: Tyler and Company, 1873.

Upton, Harriett Taylor, *History of the Western Reserve*, 3 vols. New York: Lewis Publishing Company, 1910.

Van Tassil, C. S., *Book of Ohio*, 2 vols. Toledo, Ohio: B. F. Wade Printing Company, 1901.

Wilkins, Carl, *History of the State of Ohio*, 5 vols. Ohio State Archeological Society, 1843.

Williams, W. W., *History of the Firelands*, comprising Huron and Erie counties, Ohio. Cleveland: Leader Printing Company, 1879.

Williams, W. W., *History of Huron County*, 2 vols. Chicago: S. J. Clarke Publishing Company, 1909.

Wilson, Ella Grant, *Famous Old Euclid Avenue*, 2 vols. Privately Printed, 1937.

Winkleman, B. F., *John D. Rockefeller*. Philadelphia: Universal Book and Bible House, 1937.

Winkler, John K., *John D., A Portrait in Oils*. New York: The Vanguard Press, 1929.

INDEX

A

Acme Oil Company, organized by John D. Archbold, 80; subsidiary of Standard Oil Company, 72.

Agricultural region, 136; of Florida, 237.

Allegheny River, 37; in oil region, 40; traffic along, 40.

Alcazar Hotel, description of, 121, 122.

Alexander, Scofield and Company, 58.

Alicia, hospital, 129.

Alicia, private railroad car, 123.

Anderson, Andrew, 107, 113.

Anderson, John, 135.

Andrews, Samuel, 35, 42, 45, 47, 57, 88.

Archbold, John Dustin, leader of Petroleum Producers Union, 66; member of Standard Oil Company, 80; member of Standard Oil Trust, 82.

Armour, Philip, 24.

Arter, Frank, Cleveland refiner, 60.

Ashley, Eliza Adriance, 178, 192.

Ashley, Eugene, 178, 179, 185.

Astor, William B., 76, 105; bought St. Johns River Railroad, 94.

Atlanta Journal, 191.

Atlantic and Great Western, 30, 49, 62, 67.

Atlantic Refining Company of Philadelphia, subsidiary of Standard Oil Company, 72.

Australian Pines, planted in Miami, 165.

Automobile racing, 135.

B

Babcock, G. L., 204.

Bacon, Henry, 84.

Bahia Honda Key, 217.

Baltimore United Oil Company, subsidiary of Standard Oil Company, 72.

Bananas, production of, 151.

Banking, 20.

Barnsdall, William, drilled oil well, 40.

Barrel industry, 31.

Bartow *Courier-Informant*, 203, 204.

Beekman, Henry, 3.

Benedict, Frederick Hart, son-in-law of Flagler, 127.

Bellevue, 4, 6, 11, 14, 15, 18, 19, 23, 24, 25, 27, 28, 29, 32.

Big Pine Key, 218.

Biscayne Bay, 215.

Biscayne Bay Company, 151, 152.

Biscayne Bay Hotel, 161.

Bissell, George H., developer of petroleum, 38.

Black gold, discovery of, 41.

Blackman, E. V., 164.

Bloxham, William D., elected Governor of Florida, 101.

Bostwick, Jabez A., died in 1892, 88; member of Standard Oil Trust, 82; stockholder in Standard Oil Company, 60.

Bostwick and Company, J. A., subsidiary of Standard Oil Company, 72.

Brady, E. L., early merchant of Miami, 160.

Breakers, The, 148.

Brewer, Francis Beattie, 38.

Brewster, Benjamin, 60, 82, 107.

Brickell, William B., early pioneer at Fort Dallas, 151, 157.

Bridges, need of, 132; built by Flagler, 133; on the Extension, 216, 217, 218, 219.

Buckingham Hotel, Flaglers moved to, 77.

271

Index

Index

Crosby, Dr. Dixi, professor at Dartmouth, 38.
Crude oil, 36, 49.
Cuban trade, 205.
Cutler, Extension, 207.

D

Dania, established, 157.
Daytona, Florida, 99, 136, 203.
Deeming, Charles C., secretary of railroad, 137.
Deerfield, established, 157.
DeLand, H. H., laid out town of DeLand, 101.
Delray, established, 157.
Devereux, J. H., vice-president and general manager of Lake Shore, 50.
Dimick, E. H., alderman of West Palm Beach, 144.
Dimick, Captain E. M., early merchant of West Palm Beach, 144.
Discrimination by railroads, 41.
Disston, Hamilton, 101.
Distillery business, 18, 19, 20.
Divorce granted, 188, 190.
Divorce law, 186.
Domestic troubles of Flagler, 169.
Drake, Edwin L., drilled for oil, 39, 40.
Dutchess County, 3, 4.
du Jardins, Dr. Roland, New York physician, 181.
Duval, H. S., 203.

E

Earman, John S., first mayor of West Palm Beach, 144.
East Palatka, 131, 132, 133.
East Saginaw Salt Manufacturing Company, 27.
Eau Gallie, 139, 142.
Eclipse, Flagler's yacht, 169.
Egan, John, land granted to, 150.
Equipment used on Extension construction, 212.
Erie and the New York Central Railroad, 30.
Erie Canal, 9.
Erie, Lake, 10, 30, 41, 47.

Erie Railroad, 62, 64.
Erie System, Atlantic and Great Western Railroad absorbed in, 49.
Estate of Henry M. Flagler, 250.
Euclid Avenue, 32, 46, 47.
Everglades area, 237.

F

Flagler, Alice, 91, 125, 126, 169, 170; death of, 190; declared insane, 185; financial status of, 189–190; mental condition, 171, 173–179, 181–184.
Flagler, Ann Caroline, 4, 25, 79.
Flagler, Carrie, 24; died at age of three, 24.
Flagler, Harry Harkness, 24, 32, 126, 248.
Flagler, Henry M., 1, 2, 5, 43, 44; church work, 28; critics of, 251, 254; death of, 248; divorce, 188–190; education, 6; Florida, becomes citizen of, 186; Florida, first trip to, 77; funeral, 248, 249; grain business, participation in, 30; Harkness, Dan, relations with, 12; Harkness, L. G., Company, employed by, 12; Harkness, Mary, marriage to, 16; House Committee hearing, 84; Investigating Committee hearing, 83; Kenan, Mary Lily, marriage to, 193; lieutenants of, 228; liquor, views on, 258; Mamaroneck summer home, 79, 80; Miami building program, 150, 164; New York, moved to, 76; New York Senate Committee hearing, 87; Palm Beach building program, 145, 146; parentage, 3, 5; petroleum industry, figure in, 53, 54, 56, 57, 62; religious activity, 258; resigns directorship Standard Oil Company, 81; Rockefeller, association with, 32, 43, 45, 46; St. Augustine, interest in, 128, 129, 131, 134; salt industry, participation in, 27, 28, 29; Shourds, Alice, courtship of, 90; marriage to, 90, 92; Standard Oil Trust, membership in, 82; will, 250.

273

Index

Hayes, Rutherford B., 77.
Heitlinger, Dr. J. A., 211.
Hepburn Committee, 84.
Hewitt and Tuttle, 35.
Hinckley, John Arthur, 79, 127.
Hoge, Peyton H., married Flagler and Mary Lily Kenan, 193, 194.
Holland, George, 246.
Hollandale, established, 157.
Homeseeker, 241.
Homestead, 211, 216, 218, 220.
Hopewell, New York, birthplace of Flagler, 5.
House investigating committee, 84.
Hudson River, 2.
Hunter's Point, New York, 57.
Huron County, 15.
Hurricanes during Extension construction, 220, 221.
Hussey, McBride and Company, oil refinery in Cleveland, 43.
Hyer, Captain E. M., early merchant of West Palm Beach, 144.

I

Imperial Oil Company, subsidiary of Standard Oil Company, 72.
Indian River, 99, 138.
Industry, in Sandusky, 10.
Ingraham, James E., 154, 156, 167; assistant of Flagler, 143; early life of, 240; Model Land Company, president of, 241.
Inland waterway, 157.
Internal Revenue Act, 20.
Investigation of South Improvement Company, 67; Standard Oil Company, 74, 75.

J

Jackson, Dr. J. M., Jr., 211.
Jacksonville, Florida, 77; description of, 93; Flagler's visit, 103; sports center, 158.
Jacksonville, St. Augustine and Halifax Railroad, 104, 137; extension of, 111.
Jacksonville, St. Augustine and Indian River Railroad, 138.

Jacksonville, Tampa and Key West Railroad, 229.
Jacob, Leonard, 79.
Jennings, O. B., stockholder in Standard Oil Company, 57, 58.
Jennings, Governor W. S., signs divorce law, 186.
Jones, J. J., 47.
Jones, Pembroke, 192.
Juno, county seat of Dade, 144.

K

Kansas-Nebraska Act, passed, 23.
Kenan family, 191,
Kenan, Mary Lily, 191, 192, 201; engaged to Flagler, 191; married to Flagler, 193.
Kenan, Dr. Owen, Flagler's physician, 248.
Kenan, William R., Jr., early life of, 230; joins Flagler System, 231.
Kentucky, petroleum found in, 36.
Key Largo, 215.
Key West, future of, 226; population of, in 1895, 204; reasons for building Extension to, 205, 206.
Key West Extension, 202 ff.; bridge on, 216; celebration of, 224, 225; cost of, 222; labor problems, 209–211; time of construction, 214.
Key West highway, 227.
Kier, Samuel, owned salt wells, 37.
Kirkside, description of, 124.
Knights Key, 216.
Krome, William J., engineer on construction project, 214.

L

Lake Okeechobee, 235, 236.
Lake Shore Railroad, 30, 50, 51, 61.
Lake Shore and Michigan Southern Railroad, 49.
Lamond, J. F., alderman of West Palm Beach, 144.
Land grants, 239, 240.
Land titles, clearing of, 110.
Latham, Hiram, 21.
Lawn Beach, 80.
Leesburg, Ohio, 80.

276

Index

finery possibilities in, 38; Western Reserve in, 1.

Oil City, 37, 40, 55.

Oil Creek, 37, 40.

Oil Industry, center of, 40.

Ojus, established, 157.

Oliver, L. C., early merchant of Miami, 160.

Oliver, Robert Shaw, 223.

Ormond, Flagler bought hotel at, 135.

Otis, Brownell and Company, 31.

Owego, New York, 34.

P

Palatka, 98, 108, 132.

Palm Beach, Florida, 139, 140, 141.

Panama Canal, reason for building Extension, 206.

Panic of 1873, 43.

Parrott, James R., lieutenant of Flagler, 209, 228 ff.

Payne, Henry B., politician, 47.

Payne, O. H., 60, 82, 88.

Pearl Street, branch office of Standard Oil Company, 57; Flagler maintained office on, 81; offices of Rockefeller, Andrews, and Flagler, 45.

Pennsylvania, 37; center of oil activity, 55; petroleum found in, 36.

Pennsylvania Railroad, completed connections to Chicago, 62; hauled oil to Pittsburgh and Philadelphia, 62; served as outlet from oil regions, 49; South Improvement Company, contract with, 64.

Pennsylvania Rock Oil Company, 39.

Pensacola Journal, 255.

Perrine Grant Land Company, 240.

Peterson, Dr. Frederick, 174.

Petroleum industry, early history of, 36–42; growth of, 55.

Petroleum Producers Union, organized to fight South Improvement Company, 65, 66.

Philadelphia, gave promise as a refining town, 55; Ida Alice Flagler born in, 90.

Pineapples in Florida, 238.

Pioneer Oil Works, oil refinery, 43.

Pipe lines, 49; coming of, 42.

Pithole, Pennsylvania, 41.

Pittsburgh, gave promise as a refining town, 55.

Pittsburgh Plan, 68, 69.

Plant, Henry B., railroad developer, 101; Florida developer, 234.

Platt, Tom, 34.

Pleasant Valley, 3, 4.

Pleasantville, New York, Choate's Sanitarium in, 175.

Political activity of Flagler, 254, 255, 256.

Ponce de Leon Hotel, building of, 115, 116; description of, 118–121; excavation begun, 114; opening of, 117; plans for, 109.

Porter, Captain O. S., early settler of Palm Beach, 140.

Potter, George W., alderman of West Palm Beach, 144.

Pratt, Charles, 82, 88.

Pratt, Charles, and Company, subsidiary of Standard Oil Company, 71, 72.

Presbyterian Church, 4; in Miami, 164; in St. Augustine, 127, 128.

Price, Joseph D., 135.

Putnam House, 132.

R

Railroad across Lake Worth, 149.

Railroads, 49, 50, 51, 65.

Rate fixing, practice of, 72.

Rebates, 61.

Reese, T. T., 252.

Regulation of trains on Extension, 222, 223.

Reilley, John B., 160; first mayor of Miami, 161.

Republic, Ohio, 1, 6, 7, 11, 14, 15.

Republican Party, Flagler's membership in, 23.

Richford, New York, John D. Rockefeller born in, 33.

Rockefeller and Andrews, 42, 43, 44.

Rockefeller, Andrews and Flagler,

277

Index

incorporated, 56; partnership, 45, 48.

Rockefeller, Eliza, 33, 34.

Rockefeller, John D., 21, 24, 31, 32, 33, 34, 35, 43, 44, 47; Andrews, Samuel, backed, 42; commission merchant in Cleveland, 19; Flagler, early acquaintance with, 43; oil, first connection with, 42; oil invested heavily in, 42; Standard Oil Company, largest stock holder in, 57; Standard Oil Company, president of, 57; Standard Oil Trust, member of, 82.

Rockefeller, John D., Jr., 88.

Rockefeller, William Avery, Jr., 44, 45, 48, 57, 82.

Root, Elihu, 206.

Rowley, Sims W., 243.

Royal Palm Hotel, description and location of, 163; work begun on, 162.

Royal Poinciana Hotel, 142, 145, 146, 147, 148.

Royal Victoria Hotel, 233.

Russell House in Key West, 222.

S

Saginaw, Michigan, Flagler's departure from, 28; Flagler moved to, 27; salt discovered in, 26; salt producing companies formed in, 28.

St. Augustine, 94, 104–115, 118, 123–131.

St. James Hotel, 94, 103.

St. Johns River, 93, 98.

Salem, New York, 11.

Salt industry, 26–30.

Salter, J. C., personal secretary, 246.

Sandusky, 9, 10.

Sandusky Bay, 10.

Sandusky County, 15.

San Marco Hotel, in St. Augustine, 104, 116.

San Mateo, 131, 133, 243.

Saratoga, New York, 70.

Satan's Toe, Flagler estate, 79.

Scheiffer, Ida, 246.

Scott, Thomas, 51.

Seavey, Osborn D., 104.

Secret purchases of Standard Oil Company, 71.

Seminole Indian War, 100, 150.

Senate Finance Committee, 20.

Seneca Indians, 37.

Sewell, G. E., early merchant of Miami, 160.

Sewell, John, 160, 162.

Sexton Building, offices in, 43.

Shelton, Dr. George C., 171, 172.

Sherman, Senator John, 20.

Shourds, Charles F., 184.

Shourds, Ida Alice, married to Flagler, 90.

Silliman, Benjamin, Jr., Yale chemist, 39.

Sims, Eli, first city clerk of West Palm Beach, 144.

Smith, Franklin W., built Casa Monica Hotel, 105.

Smith, Ruth Deyo, Isaac Flagler married, 4.

Social life, in Palm Beach, 147; in St. Augustine, 125, 126; at Whitehall, 199–200.

Sonce and Fleming Company, subsidiary of Standard Oil Company, 72.

South Improvement Company, dealings with railroads, 64; explanation of, 63; failure of, 66; movement against, 65, 66; organization of, 62.

Spanish Main, 208.

Spelman, Laura, 34.

Spelman, Lucy, 34.

Spencer, V. O., first postmaster of Lake Worth, 140.

Sports at Palm Beach, 147.

Standard Alliance, 73.

Standard Oil Company, 33, 60, 61, 72; dissolved, 89; incorporated, 56; increased stock, 71.

Standard Oil Trust, 81, 82, 86, 88.

Starr, Dr. Allan, 174.

Steamboat era in Florida, 98.

Stewart, Alexander T., department store mogul, 76.

Stockholders, of Standard Oil Com-

278

Index

Worth, General William J., Lake Worth named for, 139.

York, Barney, 16, 25, 27, 28.

Y

Yellow fever epidemic in Miami, 167.

Z

Zopf, George, alderman of West Palm Beach, 144.

St Augustine Settlement p 96
Delray 2d? + anti
jealousy 25?

DATE DUE			
MAR 2 5 1999			
GAYLORD			PRINTED IN U.S.A.